SADHUS

GOING BEYOND THE DREADLOCKS

Reprint 2015

Published by
FiNGERPRINT!
An imprint of Prakash Books India Pvt. Ltd.

113/A, Darya Ganj, New Delhi-110 002,
Tel: (011) 2324 7062 – 65, Fax: (011) 2324 6975
Email: info@prakashbooks.com/sales@prakashbooks.com

facebook www.facebook.com/fingerprintpublishing
twitter www.twitter.com/FingerprintP, www.fingerprintpublishing.com

ISBN: 978 81 7234 334 7

Processed & printed in India by HT Media Ltd., Noida

SADHUS

GOING BEYOND THE DREADLOCKS

Patrick Levy

FiNGERPRINT!

Contents

Foreword

Whilst interviewing people for this book, several people asked me before agreeing to co-operate whether I would use their real names in my book. I assured these people I would not reveal their names. Therefore the names of people and places in this book are at times true, at times fictitious and any coincidences are purely by chance.

The Hindi and Sanskrit words have been transliterated with agreement in the plural. One will find them in italics or with the sign "*" which refers to the glossary. However, commonly used words that have been adopted in the English language, such as maya, karma, yoga, ashram, Upanishad, baba, atman, brahmin, etc., will not be italicized.

Prologue

It is told that Tupala was a great king who was devoted to his subjects, generous towards the brahmins*, gentle with children, respectful of wise men and wisdom and who followed the rules of good governance.

On one hunting night, leaving his retinue far behind, he ventured far and deep into the forest and lost his way.

At dawn, he arrived in front of a hut where an untouchable was cleaning out the carcass of a bull. As he was surprised to find himself there, the King was about to ask where he was and in which province and hamlet he had arrived, when he caught sight of a dazzlingly beautiful young girl. She was simple and smiling, the very embodiment of grace. And of course he fell in love with her.

At the speed of an arrow piercing through space, he forgot about the hunting, his kingdom and government. He was treated with familiarity as if he had been long awaited. He married the girl, and with her came the tannery, the livestock and the forest, the adobe house which had to be patched up after rain, the herd of buffaloes that need taking to the pasture in the morning and bringing back at night, the harvests and monsoon seasons, rough clothes and rope beds... He embraced the worship of the forest Gods and joined with the villagers in prayer. He experienced the peace that follows a hard day's work, and suffered the anxieties of waiting for rain.

His wife gave him a son, then a second one, and then a third. He lived through seasons of happiness and years of misfortune. Sickness took away his eldest son, then his father-in-law, whom he replaced as a tanner. Then came a year of scarcity after a year of drought, and another year there was a great flood, which swept away the cattle. During one monsoon, his beloved wife drowned in the lake. Years had passed, and yet more followed.

One evening, exhausted, he fell asleep in the grasslands and dreamed a strange dream that he was a just and good king, governing his kingdom.

7

One hunting night, he lost his way in the forest, arrived in front of a hut, saw a stunningly beautiful girl, forgot his palace and married her, became a tanner after the death of his father-in-law, lost his eldest son to sickness, then his cattle in a flood, and then his wife drowned in a lake...

One day, his Prime Minister appeared there, in his courtyard, and threw himself at his feet.

'Majesty, we have been searching for you unceasingly all this time; we have scoured the entire kingdom, from North to South and even the outer provinces to the smallest hamlets; we have covered and searched this vast jungle without rest! Thank God we have finally found you!'

As the king was returning to his capital, escorted by his guards and his Prime Minister, he woke up, astounded to find himself in his palace bed.

It had been a dream.

It had all been nothing but a dream, but this dream had had the taste, colour, texture and charm of reality. During this sleep, the king felt perfectly awake, exactly as he was now.

At this moment who was he? A king in his palace, the tanner in the dream or the sleeping tanner now dreaming that he is a king? Or perhaps even someone else, sleeping somewhere in a distant universe about which he had forgotten everything, and who was dreaming that he was dreaming that he was dreaming... And what of the small house in the forest, and the untouchable, his wonderful wife, the buffalo herd, the rough bed, and his sons, the sickness and the drowning? Were these last years merely a few hours in one night? And is life just a moment of dreaming in eternity? Are we but characters in the dream of a sleeping man? When can one know what is true? When does one wake up? Is truth just a word to be found in the humdrum of confusion or is it the continual and indivisible flow of thoughts and dreams?

In the morning, he left his palace in a palanquin carried by four strong brahmins. One of them, uncaring and unconcerned, carried it so roughly, bumping here and stumbling there, that the king could bear no more of it and leapt out to scold him:

"Who are you? And why are you so clumsy?"

"My King, I am tall and fat and rather ugly and I am a brahmin, but tell me, who am I really? And you, who are you? What can you be called? Are you your body? Are you your birth? And why are you a king? Where does this palanquin come from, do you know? Which kind of wood is it made of? Was the tree already a palanquin in the forest? And was the cotton flower already this robe that you are wearing? The air is everywhere, and yet when one blows a little of it in a flute, as it passes through the holes, it produces a 'la', a 'so' or a 're' and finally a melody. In just the same way, there is neither a 'me' nor a 'you', but only one existence in the endless flow of life."

Having heard this, the king felt the power of truth in his heart, beating faster and harder, and was instantaneously freed from birth and the belief in an existence.

The instant of a flash of lightning is all it takes to awaken to truth. Then, all we have to do is go there, where there is neither identity nor the possibility of losing it, neither existing nor the memory of existence, neither birth nor the fatality of death, as if one is endlessly awakening from having passed out and incessantly asking oneself: *where am I*?

Inspired by Vasista Ramayana et Bhagavatham

Part One

First Day

*I*t was still dark over the Ganges. Behind us a bulb hanging from a wire, shed a yellowish glow over the temple gates and three intertwined dogs lying together. A small crescent of the moon descended slowly in the sky and lapping wavelets expired on the bank. Sitting beside Ananda Baba, just slightly behind him, I contemplated my first night as a wandering renunciant. I had been cold, rolled up in my grey, thick threaded cotton blanket under the banyan tree in the temple courtyard. But a female buffalo had come to lie down near me. This deity from the realm of grasses and daisies ensured that I had a beautiful night, next to the heat of her huge, tranquil body and soothed by her deep sighs. A true nativity.

We are sadhus*[1], homeless begging monks, mystical wanderers, renunciants, philosophers, followers of non-action, worshippers of Shiva, hashish smokers, miracle-workers, holy men. Swami* Anand Vishvatma Saraswati Baba is my guru*, my guide. He calls me Prassad – the Offering.

He is forty years old, has the slender body of a man who skips meals, light brown skin that is slightly wrinkled around the eyes and a narrow nose. His broad mouth is set in a permanent grin on his long and thin face. He often laughs. Three large horizontal lines of ash run across his forehead and a thin vermilion stroke rises between his eyes. He wears the colour of fire; a *lungi** and a cloth around the chest, and a turban from which, a high coil of dreadlocks emerges.

The Sadhu order has a history that dates back more than five thousand years. They are direct descendants, from masters to disciples, of the *rishis**, the original seers whose stories are told in the most ancient legends and the

1 '*': Refer to the glossary

first books. They declare themselves to be Brahma's* first born, who emerged from his creative breath. They conceived the Gods and told their myths. The ancient hymns of the Rig Veda*, which they authored, sing their praises: *'They carry the sky and the earth, ride the wind, and know the connection of being and non-being...'* They gave teachings to the Gods, were advisers to the Princes and cursed those who, they decided, were going to die. Alexander the Great called them *gymnosophists*. Buddha practised terrible mortifications with five of them before leaving their practices to start the Middle Way. Sankaracharya* classified their thought into schools.

We had left Varanasi by bus, the day before, at dawn. Around noon we got off in a flat chequerboard landscape of brown and green parcels of land. At the end of a dirt road, flanked with fallow paddy fields and small fields of young dense wheat, we arrived at a rather large village, on the banks of the Ganges. It had flat roofed, whitewashed, one or two storey square houses packed together, with gates opening on courtyards inhabited by four or five buffalo cows. The paved streets seemed golden scattered with pieces of straw; and dung patches with imprints of the little hands that had flattened them were hardening in the sun around the base of the walls.

Delighted to see newcomers, the local children followed us noisily, laughing and joking. Then the teenagers brushed them aside and took their place. One head of family greeted us with *Hari Om!** and another followed. *'Chai* Baba*?'* asked a woman in a red sari. A young girl was already bringing over cups of slightly sweetened lukewarm milk. *'Dudh, Babaji?'* she offered, bowing gracefully.

We arrived on the *ghats**, the paved slopes to the river. Ananda Baba joined his hands and bowed whilst praising the river *'Ganga* Ma!'* I followed his example. We sat on our folded blankets under the shade of a young banyan tree that stood between the temple and the river.

Some of our young escorts assailed me with questions of no real interest: *how much, where and when?* Ananda Baba explained to them that I was a Westerner and had come from France to take the saffron coloured robe and follow the path of renunciants, but that I had only been *samnyasin** since this morning. He pointed out that I was wearing a kurta and white pyjamas*, the colour for novices, and informed them that I speak Hindi. As they continued with such questioning, my guru taught me a magic formula, in front of them:

'Agar aap in prashno ko rokna chahte ho to kaho: Sadhu ka koi bhoot kaal nahin. To put an end to these questions, say: a sadhu has no past.'

It was the response he had used to curb my curiosity a few days earlier.

'But *kaal* also means tomorrow,' I observed.

'A sadhu does not have a future either,' he asserted and burst out laughing.

This made us all laugh.

'Namah Shivayah! * *Shanti, shanti, shanti…'* added my guru with solemnity. Holy words, which summon mindfulness. And everything became calm.

Down the steps, three boats gently creaked at their moorings. The Ganges glittered in the sun as it flowed before us, unhurried and majestic. In the distance, a fisherman was casting a net from his boat. On the other side of the river, edged by a border of foliage, a vast band of sand extended to the sky. In this flat, empty landscape, time itself seemed to have been forever indolent.

Our young friends also had a taste of passivity in our company, and then went off to do other things.

Ananda Baba slipped his hand into his bag, withdrew his *chillum** and then began to prepare a mixture of hashish and tobacco… *'Caw, Caw.'* A raven perched on a nearby street lamp and cawed. Ananda Baba looked at it before answering the greeting with gravity: *'Caw, Caw, Caw,'* he croaked in a convincing voice. *'Ram, Ram!'* the fisherman greeted us from far away. *'Namah Shivayah! I salute Shiva,'* shouted back my guru. Two *pujari** brahmins, with oiled black hair coiled in a bun and cast threads running across their bare chests, came forward to receive our blessings. *'Om Narayan!* * *Namah Shivayah!'* Ananda Baba held out a white cotton strip in front of him. The two priests sat down. *'Where do you come from, Babaji? Where are you going?'* They also inquired about me; Ananda Baba told them that I was a Frenchman, and that I had come to follow the path of renunciation, etc. Then my guru told them:

'The king, who believes he lacks something, suffers the pangs of poverty just like a beggar. In the same way, the man who believes he is his body, is dominated by birth, sickness and death. But if he frees himself from this belief, he finds joy. Under the influence of maya*, that which is perfect thinks it is not.'

In Hindu philosophy, maya, often translated as illusion or ignorance, is the name of the projection power of the mind, which transforms that which is perceived into the belief that that which is perceived is real. Thus, a fundamental and parallel mistake is created: the belief that we exist as a separate entity. Ananda Baba would often talk to me about it.

'That which is in the sun is also in the man, says an Upanishad*,' agreed one of our hosts.

'Babaji is a *jivan-mukta**, a realised being,' both attesting and questioning the other.

'How could the only Being, the unique Self, be divided into two and say that he has not realised his other half?' answered my master with a smile.

'*Hare* Hare!*' applauded our guests whilst bowing.

'*Chillum, Panditji*?*' suggested my guru.

'*Nahi, nahi.*'

They placed a twenty rupee* note on his blanket and one of five on mine, and then left.

Ananda Baba, having prepared the *chillum*, rummaged through his turban and pulled out a box of matches which he handed to me, then raised the conical pipe in front of him and pronounced high, loud and long, like a hymn, an invocation, a blessing, a thanksgiving, a proclamation and a vow all at the same time: '*Aaallaaak!*' which in this ritual was the only prayer.

'What is *Allak**, Babaji[2]?'

'The 'imperceptible', the formless, the supreme jewel!' he exclaimed. 'The wish to receive the *darshan*[3]*, the vision of being. The aspiration to be aware of oneself and conscious of everything here and now. Everything is *darshan*, the supreme sight.'

One remains silent whilst the *chillum* is passed around and even for a while afterwards. One welcomes this moment of transition when, under the effects of cannabis, the brain alters, tears its veil of habits and sees through the illusion.

We crossed through the veil, tore the illusion apart, savoured the vision, remained mindful and dwelt in the presence…

A child brought two cups of chai. '*Hare Hare Mahadev!* God is powerful since he looks after us so well.'

---

2 *Babaji*: Both a respectful and affectionate way of addressing a sadhu or a saint.

3 *Darshan*: To see, to have seen, to consider oneself blessed through being present, to experience inspiration through meeting, seeing differently, seeing differently having seen… someone, a sage or a saint, an idol, a view, a light, the sweetness of a moment, and to feel a particular kind of exaltation. A *darshan* is a moment to find oneself facing the Real. It is the presence without any influence of the past (which no longer exists) or the future (which does not exist.) It is also a point of view, a demonstration and a school of thought. The ultimate *darshan* is the vision, freed of the veil of duality in a non-dual transcendence.

A plump brahmin with thick glasses left the temple and, placing himself directly before the Ganges, called out to Durga in Sanskrit with full lungs. It was at the same time a comic and pathetic scene.

'He's so short-sighted. Durga will have to come up very close. But then again he's shouting so loudly that she might take fright,' I remarked.

Ananda Baba burst out laughing.

'He is calling his mother!' he said. 'Durga is the *shakti** of Shiva, his creative power and so she is the origin of all things.'

The brahmin sat down on a white towel, lit a large thumb sized piece of incense, and holding it between his fingers performed his *puja**. He finished with three *Om**. Before returning, he gave us *ladus,* fried balls of sweetened rice, that he had brought as *prassad** and whose quintessence had been accepted by the divine.

A few minutes later, a man came to speak to us. '*Hari Om! Namah Shivayah!*' He bowed with respect to touch Ananda Baba's feet and then brought his fingers to his eyes. Ananda Baba received the reverence with indifference, as it should be. '*Hari Om!*' He started to bow before me and so I quickly signalled for him not to do so. He was one of the landowners who had greeted us upon our arrival. '*Where do you come from? Where are you going? Do you need anything?*' Ananda Baba told him that I was a foreigner… had taken the saffron robe yesterday… etc. 'He makes him laugh,' he added.

He never used the first person singular or plural. He referred to himself as *this body* or *he*… but *he* could also designate anything and everything else. For him everything was all included in the same unifying impersonal. I have sometimes erased this trait in order to make the reading easier.

The man took our *darshan*, enjoying serenity in our company, and then rose to leave. Ananda Baba offered him a *ladu* and gave one to me too.

A forty year old man then took his place. Hemachandra Vaninath was the owner of a textiles and shawls shop and he wished to smoke a *chillum* with us. My guru requested me to prepare it. Together they conversed about a stanza of Kabir*: '*Ride the mount of silence to find your guru.*'

'What is silence? Can he say?' questioned my guru.

Hemachandra reflected, and then declined humbly. 'The question is too great for me, Babaji.'

'*Bom Bom Bole Bholenath! Allak!*' The *chillum* went around.

Silence.

We shared in communion with our visitor, a conscious moment without speech. The wind shivered in the dust. The fisherman cast his net upon a wave. A dolphin leapt out of the waters and dived back in. A flock of sparrows swooped in a quivering movement across the sky.

'Silence is what he does not hear,' said Ananda Baba. 'Although he does not hear it, silence lets him know something of the unknowable.'

Silence.

Then we heard the loud rattling of a dead banyan leaf falling between the branches just when everything was still!

'There is silence between two thoughts,' Ananda Baba went on, 'and if he is attentive to this, he can also know the unknowable in that way. Guru is everywhere. But silence is a good vehicle for finding him,' he concluded.

Hemachandra put a twenty rupees *guru-dakshina** on Ananda Baba's blanket. My guru blessed him: '*Sarvam khalvidam Brahman...* all this is Brahman*, offered by Brahman and received by Brahman*,' and gave him a *ladu*. Our host then left to attend to his business.

Passers-by greeted us from afar. '*Hari Om! Ram Ram! Namah Shivayah!*' Ananda Baba was cheerful. He seemed to consider the world with a benevolent amusement. It was the springtime and the days were pleasantly warm.

The shadow of the temple gradually got longer and covered the *ghat*.

After sunset, we joined a dozen hairy, turbaned sadhus in the columnar hall of a temple dedicated to a glorious four armed Vishnu holding weapons. Laid down here and there, between the plinths of the grey stone columns, the babas' blankets formed alleyways and quarters, transforming the hall into a small inhabited labyrinth. One was studying a Sanskrit treatise, which must have given him material to reflect upon as he was nodding his head. Another was reading *The Times of India* whilst adjusting his glasses every ten seconds. The others formed groups and talked quietly.

'*Ram Ram!*'

'*Hari Om!*'

'*Namah Shivayah!*'

'Where do you come from, Babaji?'

'They were there and now they are here,' answered my guru joyfully. 'Such is the magic of maya. And yet, are they ever anywhere else?'

'My answer is that I come from India,' interrupted a young sadhu.

'Would Babaji like to lay his *asan** here?' suggested a renunciant who looked like Tagore.

'He cannot imagine a single place where he is not,' replied Ananda Baba in the impersonal, gently laughing.

This answer, I noticed thereafter, set him instantly into the category of people who truly deserve respect. It revealed him to be a scholar and a well mannered man, which is a quality appreciated amongst renunciants.

'Your wisdom is like a million suns,' retorted *Tagore*, who was not lacking in style either.

Ananda Baba accepted the place that was offered with a smile. I laid my blanket behind him, and then went around to pay my respects to the babas. *'Where do you come from? Where are you going? Do you need anything?'* 'The unchanging reality manifests itself as freedom,' the reader of treatises told me. *Chillums* passed from hand to hand here and there several times. An abundant meal was served by the temple's brahmins and their employees: *'Rice, Ramji? – Daal*, Ramji? – Vegetables, Ramji? – Curd Ramji? – Chapati*, Ramji?'* Everyone ate by themselves in their own little space.

They called each others *'Maharaj!* Guruji! Panditji!'* The youngest was about fourteen, the oldest seventy. They came from every social background and were from various states of the sub-continent and, despite meeting just two hours earlier, they seemed as if they had known each other for ages, so simple and attentive they were. They formed quite a disparate gathering yet not in a gloomy precariousness, but on the contrary, in a holy nonchalance but with some aloofness.

I laid down my blanket under the stars in the courtyard on a beaten-earth floor. Before falling asleep, I knew myself to be *the son of the Earth and the Sky* for the first time in my life.

Ananda Baba awoke me well before dawn; we took a bath in the dark, smooth and cold Ganges. We meditated on the *ghats*, facing towards the East. 'Observe the glimmer that precedes daylight slowly entering the dark of the sky; rise with it,' said my guru. 'Don't miss the first ray of light. It is a *darshan* of illumination.' I missed that moment. My meditation had been nothing more than an inner dialogue.

The sun had risen above the sand strip on the opposite bank with its line of foliage. The sky was still indigo on the horizon but was already azure and almost lavender higher up. In the dull tinges of dawn and its humid silence.

The boatmen awoke one another calling *'Rajar! Krishna! Gopal! Chitraksh!'*

Ananda Baba rose. We took our bags and blankets on our shoulders and with *komandalu**4 in hand, we left.

I had feared this transition from being sheltered to homelessness. In the end, the shock was not too bad. What frightens us is often more threatening in thought than in reality. Ananda Baba says that he could never be in need of anything as he affirms that the world is the reflection of his consciousness. As for me, I have neither this confidence, nor the aloofness of my peers.

'Where do you come from? Where are you heading? What's the purpose of your stay amongst us?' inquired the head of the village we were passing through.

He was playing cards with his friends on a wooden bed in front of the gate of his house.

'There is only one mother for all. From her they are born, by her they are fed, from her they come and go,' Ananda Baba said.

The villagers hurriedly rustled up food for their hospitality. The fathers gave orders to the elder sons, who conveyed them to the juniors, who passed them on to the sisters, who carried them out. Pretty young girls brought chai, biscuits, bananas, vegetable biryani accompanied by *puri* (fried wafers).

Seeing them touch the dust of my feet to their eyes seemed to me an undeserved honour and moved me deeply, although this ancestral manner of expressing respect was not really addressed to my person but to the holiness of which I was for the moment an instrument and agent.

Hindu holy books are full of recommendations on seeking the company of saints. Sadhus (the word means *a good man* or a *saint*) walk the streets, sit by the temples, camp under sacred trees, dwell in ashrams* and *akhara** that are found everywhere. They are noticeable, available and approachable. They are called *Baba* meaning Father. One goes to the temple to pray to a God and one calls on a sadhu to associate with God, to attend a living example of holiness, request advice, ask for an opinion, to ponder on what lies further than beyond, converse about the *Invisible Whole* or the nothings of daily life, smoke a *chillum* or receive a blessing. To do nothing in good company. Take the *darshan*: see and feel blessed to have seen, to be there and enter awareness.

If the ambiance is pleasant, the advice judicious, the *darshan* uplifting

---

4 *Komandalu*: A copper or steel recipient used by ascetics to transport water.

and there is an air of holiness, the *baba* becomes a one day guru for someone. And it is a blessing.

Hindus love to love. Adoration is the attitude by which the ego takes pleasure in diminishing. When admiring with the heart, one receives as much love as is offered. Adoration contains nirvana. It is not a question of believing, it is more about blessing.

India is on the brink of modernity. The oxcart and the tractor, water at the well and microwave ovens, clay cups and plastic bags, oil lamps, private generators and nuclear plants, blacksmiths and the world's leading manufacturer of steel, rickshaws* and cable TV, snake charmers and electronic component plants, corruption and *samnyasa* (renunciation) all coexist here. Twenty million beggars and five hundred thousand newly qualified engineers a year, of whom a great number went to pray in a temple or received a blessing from a sadhu before taking their exams. Apparently renunciants represent half a percent of the male population.

A World of Words

We would stay from one night up to three or four weeks in a holy city, a large temple, a *dharamsala** or an *akhara*. *Dharamsalas* are hostels of varying degrees of comfort, established for pilgrims and wandering monks, which are financed by wealthy businessmen. A baba ashram or an *akhara* is a kind of monastery, maintained by sedentary sadhus, that accommodates wandering renunciants and to which *grihastha**, householders and benefactors, pay a visit at various times of the day. There, they smoke *chillum*, discuss various matters and take decisions whilst peacefully waiting for the rice or wheat to grow. In some areas, each village has three or four baba ashrams. In towns, they are often coupled with a temple, whose income is used to maintain a dwelling place for sadhus. Large *akharas*, founded from the 10th to the 12th century, consist of several branches with a register of tens of thousands of babas. In such places we could get a room or just a small space under a shed or a tree or in a chapel, where we could lay our *asan* – at times with over fifty others.

'Ram Giri, do you have some space in your room?'

'There are only two of us.'

This is how things were arranged.

When a renunciant is not wandering, his day is spent in casual idleness. He takes his bath, washes his clothes, accomplishes a ritual of varying length, chants some murmured devotional songs, recites *mantra**, does reading from an Upanishad etc. He chatters, gossips, receives people, reads the newspaper, smokes *chillums* and drinks chai. I listened and I read. I carried two small books in my bag, the *Avadhuta Gita** and the *Astavakra Samhita*. I had also found a second-hand copy of Andre Malraux's *Anti-memoirs* in a book store.

The *arati** *puja*, a short collective ceremony, brought a *circle* of sadhus together at sunset. Conversations and devotional songs alternated during the evenings. '*Shiva Om Shiva Kalpataru... Jay Ma...*' Each one withdrew, in his own time, to retire under his blankets with his bag as a pillow.

Our benefactors, the coolies, bank managers, salesmen and the professionally unemployed all came to huddle around our sacred pipes and our *darshan*. We were a refuge for the lonely, the misfits and the immoderate cannabis smokers; we were a blessed sight for pious people and were seen by them as idols in the flesh. We philosophised with scholars. We taught, advised, blessed… We beautified the days of those who mingled with us.

We also camped in the open air, on the river banks, beneath a rock or under a tree. We shared a baba's remote *kutir**. We washed in rivers or under pumps. We slept on a farmer's veranda who invited us to bless his home. He gorged us with milk that had just come directly from the buffalo's udder. Happy are the people who make a desire out of kindness. For nothing gives as much happiness as helping others.

In all the cities and many villages, some places are always inhabited by babas, even though they may not be the same ones from one day to the next. They can be large trees, or the side of a temple, or a *ghat*. At times we would convene in such places with a circle of sadhus around the *dhooni** – the holy hearth. Those who have settled there, take in wanderers who are passing by. They have possessions like kitchen utensils, a scooter, a transistor radio. A few plastic sheets make a roof and a stone idol makes a temple.

With a blanket, a *lungi*, a piece of string and a stick; given a small space along a wall, one can arrange a splendid haven. Under this tent, protected from the sun and attention of passers-by, I peacefully contemplated the world, and protected from the dew, I slept well at night.

There were many times that we could have found more comfortable accommodation, but my guru decided differently. In this way we would constantly experience a whole range of very different lifestyles.

When we settled in streets, I had to go and receive our meals at places where food was handed out. Rumours spread *'After the morning puja, the temple of Shiva will offer rice and vegetables. There is an offering of puri at Mankarmahini Temple.'* Ananda Baba refused to go. A disciple does not leave his master fasting, so I waited squatting with around fifty other sadhus.

Sometimes, the meal had to be paid for by one and a half hours of praising *Ram-Sita Sita-Ram* with conviction. Prayers for food. A scandal! If we had no money, I preferred to skip meals. But when we did have some, we dined in restaurants.

Indian poverty is terrifying. Cycle-rickshaws and coolies work like beasts of burden for the price of their food. Families live in the streets. Children dressed in rags hold out their hands. But we are not poor. We own whatever we have in the bags we are carrying. Yet we receive a lot of offerings, so a carefree life is possible. A sufficient number of benefactors and institutions provide for our needs; over a long period we do not miss anything essential. So in poverty, we are princes. 'You are bound to act,' says Krishna addressing Man in the *Bhagavad Gita*. But the sadhu replies, 'No, I am not anymore. I will not do anything.' If the essence of Man is action, then not to act is to be freed from the human condition. *Akarma** is *tapas**, our discipline.

Thus, it is not aimed at compassion and altruism – to work for the benefit of others in the name of God or that of a higher principle. We follow the way of *samnyasa*. 'Renunciation does not mean "I" refuse objects,' taught Ananda Baba, 'because this *I* does not exist. *Vairagya* is a metaphysical rejection signifying the dissolution of *me* and *my* and of maya, the world.'

Some householders do not wish to have any contact with us and ignore us. They think we are lazy, dishonest and drug addicts and they assume we take advantage of credulous people. This is not always untrue. For others, we are holy men. They greet us with the names of Gods and touch our feet with respect. They come towards us to contemplate holiness, benevolence, and at times wisdom and to approach the bliss of which our way of being is a manifestation. They offer us money, clothing, food, according to their means, and thus sow merits on the beneficial side of their karmic scale. To be useful to us is to assist God. Through us, the divine One looks at them kind-heartedly. They consider us to be the ear of the Gods. They believe we have insight, penetration and psychic powers… of that I doubt, of course. I am not a saint but we represent saintliness. We personify the self-restraint of non-action and chastity.

One gives us offerings, not alms.

And we do not thank, we bless.

The use of cannabis is a *tapas*, an ascetic discipline and a gateway to the sacred. The chillum-baba finds in it a connection with God, a more intense surge of devotion, a vision of the world less numbed by conditioning and his own habits, or an access to the fourth state of consciousness, which is that of the witness.[1] It is a means to an end. Would it be more *authentic* to attain this

---

1 The fourth state of consciousness: waking, dreaming, deep sleep and *Turiya*, the fourth state of consciousness which transcends the other three.

through abstaining? Babas do not attempt to make judgements or hold an opinion concerning the purity of their practice. They have given up judging and classifying altogether. For them purity is being authentic. And Reality is what they live in the now of consciousness. Going beyond conventions, taking short cuts and casual intrepidness are the marks of this spiritual path, which is also an adventure.

Shiva is a sombre, nocturnal God and even lunar in some of his representations. He is the Destroyer and is known as *Kapalamalin*, the skull holder, with eyes of fire and a cobra coiled around his neck. He dwells in cremation grounds with vultures and jackals in the company of reckless ascetics. In the *Puranas**, he is described as being surrounded by a court of gnomes, demons and phantoms. In him, I saw God as a benevolent anarchist and had chosen him for *Ishwar**, my chosen figure of the divine. But he is also a solitary hermit when, as Yogiraj, he meditates for ten thousand years on Mount Kailash. He is the bearer of the manifest aspect of reality and watches over the world. By his stillness, he triumphs over maya and establishes the victory of consciousness over body and senses. We inhale his spiritual seed through the *chillum*, the symbol of his *lingam**, the cosmic phallus which represents both creative and destructive energy, or in other words the universe or that which is known.

Cannabis does not produce hallucinations in the way that the mind creates objects and situations within itself, as for example during dreams. On the contrary, it reveals things as they are, stripping our apprehension of reality from its usual utilitarian, materialistic or ordinary representations. This is why it is thought of as a *tapas*. It transforms the hypnosis of the world. Through this process, the awareness that sees this hypnosis remains alert. And in this awakening, what we consider to be real is shaken. Our habits and things we take for granted are hypnoses whilst surprise is divine.

Baudelaire spoke of it as an initiation to a new reality, which makes it possible to gain insight into the shape of things beyond their presence. It produces an effect of displacement, which unmasks the identification that we have either of ourselves, or with the constructs of a reality that allows the mundane to dominate. It stimulates astonishment: the function which awakens the mind. It also makes you laugh.

But it is not easy to function in this modified, amplified, changing and hypersensitive state of awareness created by the consumption of *charas** and *ganja** – hashish and grass. I often let *chillums* pass by. During certain holy days, the babas smoke about fifteen of them before sunrise, and strong ones at that! Even at a quarter of this dosage, cannabis is not a dabbler's game and my advice would be not to try it. It is a sacrifice, a fire in which reality is consumed, and a means through which consciousness is investigated. The point is not merely to give in to the somnolence that THC* can produce but to become aware of the forces of maya at work in one's own mind, of observing it while still harmoniously involved in the stream of events. Giving up awareness would be a failure; yielding to somnolence, out of the question. Surrendering to intoxication, losing one's discernment and neglecting good manners or the order of precedence would be a fault.

Ananda Baba was not a constant consumer of it. He was already in a blissful flow of harmony and shrewd awareness without this stimulant. Yet he would not refuse a *chillum* and offered many.

Since religious consumption of cannabis is lawful, sadhus are allowed to carry it on their person. We acquired it at government stores as well as less official sources. In some areas, one can find, beside the village wine shop, a discrete *bhang** outlet, which is generally a large wooden cupboard covered with an awning. On the racks, one finds *ganja* (cannabis flowers) carefully tied up in newspaper packages of two kilos, one kilo, five hundred grams, two hundred and fifty grams, and even smaller and at very low prices. There are also *bhang* balls kept in iceboxes that cost five rupees. Just one of these balls of fresh, chopped and fermented hemp produces more of an effect than a whole day of smoking the bad quality *charas* one often finds in India.

But in other areas, there are no such shops. So through creating economic relationships our *tapas* is a service to society. Our devotees and our benefactors, and even some officers of the police and army, spent a while in our company and sometimes shared *chillums* with us. Now and again they requested to take a small quantity of it home.

In the evening, when we were alone, before a *dhooni* under the stars, or in a room by the light of a candle in a jar, Ananda Baba spoke to me. He taught me the philosophy of his school and lineage.

'The universe is only one being,' he said. 'It is called Brahman, the Immutable One. There is nothing one can say about it, but to give at least an indication, one says that it is *Sat** (being–existence–reality), *Cit** (consciousness–knowledge) and *Ananda** (bliss).'

His teachings formed a metaphysics based on consciousness. It contained many strange Sanskrit words, which I could not completely remove and put into translation because they often have several meanings. Including them makes heavier reading but it enables the opportunity of considering the topic on several levels, which, of course, are merely articulations of the imperial *One-without-a-Second*, aware of its eternal and unchanging oneness.

'*Atman-Brahman* (the Changeless One, Being without distinctions, the most inner being shared by everything...), with maya, (the first modification of Brahman, the first 'other', the energy which gets movement moving, the cosmic illusion in which the world of names and forms is produced) creates *jiva** (vitality, life, the individual, a man with 'me' in his thoughts) and *Ishwar* (God).

'*Jiva* and *Ishwar* together build the universe. *Ishwar* is the objective aspect, *jiva* the subjective aspect.'

I found this a rather clever philosophy, which finds a solution to the problem of the existence of God by ranking him among the illusions in the role of the sentient world and of Creator of this world.

'*Ishwar* transforms the power of maya by assigning objects their determinants. He creates differences in non-uniformity. He organizes the universe, nature, the outside world, the physical body. All that appears, appears in the duality of which maya is the cause – the other.

'When he dreams, *jiva* (man, me) is like God: He creates other men, animals, mountains and even Gods! During *jiva*'s waking state, Maya creates *Ishwar*, (Gods, nature, a universe of names, forms and feelings) and *jiva* (man and life.) But actually, only *cit* – awareness – really exists. See that.'

Thus spoke Ananda Baba.

He was not concerned with the physical or biological reality. He spoke about consciousness, its states, its shapes, its majesty, its rituals, and of the meaning of its modifications. He spoke of its Oneness. And this way of describing reality was also a means of freeing oneself from it.

'For some people, the world is a story: it was created by a being who was never born, was never conceived but had children and *avatars**[2] and a whole story ensued. Oneness has no story. For those, like you, whose intellect can concentrate and understand and for whom Brahman as consciousness is only covered by a veil of ignorance, *sankya* (the method of intellectual inquiry) and

---

2 *Avatar*: The descent of the divine. An incarnation of God in a living being – human or animal. Gandhi has recently been added to the list of Vishnu Avatar which includes a fish, a tortoise, Rama, Krishna and sometimes Buddha.

vichara (discrimination) are effective. By investigation and discrimination, one can understand and attain the One-without-a-Second.'

As we were walking through a village, a sadhu on a motorbike caught up with us to offer his guru's hospitality. We arrived, with three of us on the motorbike, in front of a vast rectangular storage place covered and enclosed on three sides by corrugated sheets. About fifty men had gathered there hosted by a baba sitting on a large *takhat** surrounded by a dozen of his *shishyas**.

'Ballaknath Baba,' whispered the envoy.

His stomach formed a paunch above the *gomcha**, which was no longer white, that he wore around the hips. The remainder of his body was rather thin but his face had a dilapidated look, with a boil on the nose, a falling mouth, a white and unkempt beard, and dreadlocks falling on his shoulders.

'How can a mountain and a precipice be compared? One goes towards the sky and the other into the depths!' said Ananda Baba bowing to the guru's feet and laughing at his own insignificance. Ballaknath Baba stopped him and bowed as well saying: 'But one is the condition of the other.' He invited him to sit beside him. I sat down in the assembly. The conversation began again; the *chillum* was passed from hand to hand. 'Where are you from? Where are you going? Do you need something?'

In addition to this shelter, this *akhara* included a kitchen, a few rooms, and to its left, a five-storey temple which was under construction. A small white Maruti-Suzuki was parked to one side.

Ananda Baba and Ballaknath Baba were chatting away. I heard: 'Neither passion nor detachment…', 'Wheat and white radishes…', 'A reality that nothing can disturb…'

A young man gingerly stepped over people and made his way to come and sit beside me. Bhagwat Sharma was preparing for a Master's in English Modern Literature. He told me that Ballaknath Baba was born in this village and had left it at the age of nine to become a sadhu.

'He returned forty years later, in 1997. People believe in him,' Bhagwat explained simply. 'He recommends living modestly. He preaches love, fraternity, peace, assistance, reconciliation between people and communities. He started a tradition: the day after the new moon of February, our village offers a meal to all the local villages. He says that the merit of our actions will make Kawali a holy place and a pilgrimage like Varanasi.'

A little higher than the others on his *takhat*, Ballaknath Baba was also listening to what was being said here and there whilst alimenting the *chillums*. He tore the end off a thick piece of hashish that was as long as a finger and gave it to a man on his right. The man prepared a *chillum* with a shaft as large as a water glass. Then his cell-phone rang and he answered.

He did not play the role of a guru. He was a village saint living with his flock, creating a social life, shaping an awareness and an atmosphere whilst promoting harmony. On his left hanging in a frame was the portrait of a bearded, grey haired, stern looking old man.

'It's his guru! He could become invisible and heal people,' Bhagwat Sharma informed me.

'Could he order rain and sunshine too?' I retorted looking at him sideways.

'The villagers are simple, but their thoughts are elevated,' answered Bhagwat gracefully. 'They try to be aware that what affects one, affects the other, just as much here as everywhere else.'

Arrivals and departures followed one after another in the assembly. Villagers passed by and stayed a while. They paid homage to Ballaknath Baba, then to Ananda Baba, then to each *shishya* baba, bringing the fingers which had touched the knees of holiness to their eyes. Finally, sitting down in the assembly, they requested news. Before leaving, some left a banknote or two. One of the *shishya* led a woman in front of the *lingam* erected in the courtyard, and there, he stroked her gently on the head with a peacock feathered object, pronouncing a *mantra*.

'He preaches the ideal and not the idol,' said Bhagwat Sharma. 'Whatever you do, do it for humanity, not for yourself.'

A group of children, aged between four and fifteen, suddenly arrived in a deafening tumult to look at me closely. Apparently, they had not often seen a white man. They asked me, all at the same time and in different ways, to look at them, see them, know them. They wanted me to give them the *darshan*: my awareness through looking at them. I looked into each of their eyes for a few moments, trying to be present, without missing anyone.

At nightfall, a light bulb hanging on wire above the assembly was suddenly lit. So the light was blessed '*Om Namah Shivayah!*' A man brought an aluminium bowl in which four large dung cakes were lit. The *takhat* and its turbaned guests, and the puffs of *chillums* surrounding them now seemed to float on the clouds of smoke the dung was producing. It was like an image, in the world of mortals, of the Gods in their celestial palaces of the kind one sees on temple frescoes.

The cook served us dinner and another man led us to a room with a pile of mattresses.

The following day, Bhagwat Sharma, and a group of five young men claiming to take me for a visit to the village, took me to the room of one of them to offer me hot milk and to talk.

Several posters of Yuvraj Singh, the famous cricket player, covered the walls of the small room which opened on to a shed where a red Yamaha was parked. On the side adjacent to the road, the shutters remained closed. We all sat on a large *takhat* covered with a thin mattress and they allocated the rolled up quilt to make a bolster for me.

'Why are you a sadhu?' 'Do you believe in *moksha**?'

'Baba-life moksha hai. For me, liberation comes from being a sadhu.'

I pulled the *Astavakra Samhita* out of my bag and read:

> Everything that exists is in being.
> This is what is known
> When one has become nobody
> And owns nothing. [15 6]

'Atchaaa!*' they all admired.

'But do you know that?' asked Bhagwat Sharma.

'I think about it and then I forget,' I admitted. 'I am a novice.'

My host prepared a kind of a *chillum*, introducing hashish into a decapitated *bidi**. 'The elders do not hang out with the young ones,' he said to justify that they did not smoke at the *akhara*.

'So everyone smokes here?'

They answered laughing:

'Yes.'

'Not every one.'

'Men only.'

'Some play cards.'

'Wheat grows by itself.'

So if this village had two thousand inhabitants, half being women; less two hundred and fifty children under sixteen; less two hundred men who play cards, that left five hundred and fifty men who smoked cannabis regularly. A quarter of the population, I figured.

'What about women?'

'Sometimes they take *bhang.*'

'And is it the same in every village?'

'I don't know if it is like this everywhere, but in Haryana, Punjab, Madhya Pradesh, yes and probably in the Hindu areas of Uttar Pradesh and Bihar.'

A population of about two hundred million.

We spoke about genetically modified rice and about Monsanto's latest trick. 'As far as the law is concerned their seeds are not sterile, but if one sows the rice harvested the year before, many grains do not germinate,' said one. 'We cannot afford to lose twenty percent of the harvest,' explained another. The father of one of the boys had bought an American buffalo. There was no shortage of water. Harvests had been abundant for many years.

They guided me through the village with its paved lanes, cubic houses, open gates and the omnipresent dung cakes stuck onto the walls. We passed by a wedding hall, a woodwork shop, a *pariah** quarter of adobe and plastic sheet houses and a settling tank planted with water lilies. In a shelter was the tomb of a late baba and his framed portrait was adorned with garlands – his *samadhi**. 'We venerate them as holy saints after their death,' whispered Bhagwat Sharma, 'but we honour them simply as saints during their life.' And in front of the temple we saw 'The *pujari* is an employee, a servant of worship; Ballaknath Baba is a saint.' The hairdresser's was a little *akhara* of playful banter and laughter. I did not manage to follow the conversations or grasp their play on words. Everyone was joyful.

It was there that Rohtash Sharma, the Maths teacher, wishing to tell me a secret, took me away. He led me to his fields where he told me he thought babas were crooks and liars and that he attended the *akhara*. But one day, Ballaknath Baba gave him twenty thousand rupees making it clear, 'Don't speak to me about this as long as I don't speak to you about it.'

'I was poor then. Twenty thousand rupees is a very large sum for somebody who hasn't even a thousand. Then, I became lucky and I earned more than one hundred thousand rupees a year.'

'*Atchaaa!*' I exclaimed in amazement. So it turned out that the village saints also secretly strive for the material well-being of their people! This was something previously unknown to me.

Ganesh Sharma lifted a long white radish out of earth, washed it and offered it to me. He then told me his secret. One evening, he went to the *akhara*. 'I was with three other men,' he specified… 'Ballaknath Baba was feeding a little fire with kindling. He was angry. 'Go home!' he shouted with a sullen look and then locked himself up in his room. But we remained in front of his door and, a little later, although he had not come out, we saw him coming back from the road.'

So the previous guru could become invisible and heal and this one could pass through walls without being noticed.

'Why is this a secret?'

'Because if I had spoken about it no one would have believed me.'

There had been four witnesses to this marvel, but I did not believe it either. Why would Ballaknath Baba be invisible leaving and visible returning? Nobody walks through walls without being noticed.

When I found Ananda Baba again, he was somewhere in the fields. Here and there brick shelters housed powerful motor pumps which were adjoined to concrete tanks. We sat down on a rope bed found in one of them. The edges of the plots had been dug out to create an ingenious irrigation system, making it possible to flood precise areas of the land.

The chlorophyll and peppered thyme scent of the young wheat perfumed the air which was filled with the calling of distant birds, and the nearby buzzing of flies. The vitality of the thick green wheat struck one's eyes.

'How did it all begin according to you, Babaji, or in your mythology?'

'Tat sristva tad evanupravistat, says Taittiriya Upanishad, 'having projected the universe, he entered it.' This is why he is *Visvam,* everything,' explained Ananda Baba.

'Who is this "he"?'

The ears of grains were listening motionless. An almost full moon appeared in the red and blue sky.

'In Prasna Upanishad it is said that Brahma, the Creator, eager to procreate, accomplished austerities in the form of meditations. It is then that he created the first pair, *Rayim* and *Prana,* matter and energy, then moon and sun, food and the eater. It began with two.'

'And who created the Creator?'

'The Atman (Oneself) was alone. His first words were 'I am', but he did not find any pleasure of this. He did not know any other. This is why he wished to be two. The second was the object of desire which then took on multiple forms.'

'And who created this Atman that could not bear loneliness?'

The sun leant on the horizon to listen… 'All this is Brahman. And you are him. It is you, Prassadji, *he,* the Creator, and the creator of the Creator. You project a universe, then you enter it and you distinguish moon from sun, food and the eater, desire and the object of desire.'

'To recognize in each and every thing a manifestation of oneself must make one become very kind, Babaji.'

He laughed uproariously. A tractor passed putt-putting by. A boy crossed the fields on his motorbike to go and start up a pump. An ox-cart glided silently on the horizon. Then the sun disappeared and the dark night covered everything.

'And you Guruji, what do you say about it? How did it all begin?'

'Ignorance is beginningless because ignorance created time,' he said. 'Before there was the projection of a world, Brahman (the One without second) existed alone. Through maya (differentiation), it became *Ishwar* (Gods) and the world itself and it entered it as *jiva*, (me, a person in a subject-object relation). And *jiva* worshipped the Gods.

'But *Jiva* had the desire to inquire into its own nature. The *rishis* discovered that when, through research and meditation, maya was conceived of, recognized and understood, only Atman remained (Oneself, consciousness without differentiation).

'To this consciousness residing in its own nature, they gave the name *moksha*, liberation. They called the other consciousnesses, servitude, *samsara** (succession of births) and maya (illusion, misapprehension). Servitude is produced by a lack of awareness which therefore disappears with awareness. In consciousness, the subject is just another object. *So'am, I am That**.

'Atman is at the same time consciousness of the ego, the mind, the senses and their objects, and consciousness which witnesses all of them together.

'Mental action consists of two types of successive modifications: the internal and external. The internal modifications take the form of '*I*'. The external modifications take the form of '*That*' and reveal external objects. The external objects are known by the five senses and the mental mind.

'The consciousness which reveals the perceiver, perception and perceived (the external object) at the same time is called the Witness or Witness consciousness (*turiya*).

'The objects are outside the body; the ego is inside. But the distinction between inside and outside applies only to the body, not to the Witness, nor to the Atman.'

Ananda Baba described and guided me in this chaos of strange concepts in which the same word can define a function of the brain, a state of consciousness, a type of consciousness or an experience. He based his explanation on the three states of consciousnesses that we generally know about (the waking state, dreaming and deep sleep) and revealed a fourth: the witness of all three, that transcends them, is always aware, immutable, ever present and covered only by the veil of appearances.

'During dreams, consciousness is not distinct from its object. It is the dream. Just like a dream, this world is an appearance on the unchanging, immutable Brahman. During deep sleep, consciousness is not aware of its state (of being asleep). During the waking state, perceptions change, thoughts come and go, but a consciousness perceives them and this is always the same. In the same way, Brahman remains unchanging although maya projects a world. Reality is a fraud. The conscious principle is the only reality. *Ethadh Athmyam idham sarvam*: All that is the Oneself of This (Brahman). See that.

'Saraswati babas seek and recognize this consciousness, this single witness of all the internal and external creations of the mind.'

'*Atcha!!!*'

What would the *Astavakra Samhita* have to tell me that day?

> See that the forms of things are just things and in
> reality nothing else. Then, in an instant, freed from
> all bonds, you will be in your true nature. [9, 7]

I was there sometimes. But only for an instant.

We took the road again two days later.

Encounters

*O*ur wanderings led us from one hamlet to another, along a pathway knitting through small plots, tiny farms and minute temples... We took the *darshan* of a bronze Shiva with the body of Apollo meditating on Mount Kailash. *Om Mahayogi!* And that of a stone *avatar* holding a bow in his hand. *Om Shri* Ram!* And a golden Vishnu with four arms. *Hari Om Narayan!* We prostrated before stone steles, sculpted deities with human faces and the bodies of snakes placed at the foot of trees. *Om Nagaraja!* We bowed before a saint. *Om Maharaj Guru!*

> There is but one woven thread from one end of a
> fabric to the other, in the same way only acknowledge
> Oneself in the entire universe. [Jnaneshvari*]

Women, with feet in the water, bent over, picked rice shoots from the paddy fields, their colourful saris pulled up to the knees. *Hari Ram Ram!* Naked children played in the dust of the tracks. Skinny men in loincloths roamed barefooted. A big white car drove hooting through a hamlet of three or four low mud walled houses with thatched roofs planted with marrows. Sitting on its back seat was a bloated faced babu* wearing sunglasses. A big cloud of dust was left behind as a souvenir. Three hens, a goat, a cow, a small outdoor kitchen and a vegetable garden with a few lines of flowers... Amulets of limes and chilli hung at door lintels. Mothers were digging the earth, peeling vegetables, wiping bottoms, blowing on embers, milking buffaloes, and sometimes giving me a little smile as they tied up their hair. *Om Namah Shakti! Hari Om, Mata!* Little girls, already busy with mothers' duties, walked the last little brother on their hip, drew water, cut grass, fed cows, sifted through the lentils, collected fresh dung, branches, twigs... just like it had been in the times of *Krishna. Hari Krishna!*

> Unconcerned with his own dignity, he does not distinguish
> between what has value and has none,
> including everything in one, he enjoys bowing
> before all things. [Jnaneshvari]

And each day, we made new encounters.

We settled on a small platform under a quay, just above the bed of Godavari at Nizamabad.

Soon, other sadhus joined us and there were a dozen of us packed into a space of ten square meters. Three bricks made a hearth, two dung cakes a fire. We elected Ananda Baba Guru of this temporary ashram and gave him the title of Jagatguru Maharaj (king and guru of the universe). He received reverence and the *chillum* first.

Lay people arrived at around six. Those who were motivated prepared *chillums*. And then there were about twenty of us on the platform.

One of the babas used the backs of his neighbours as tables to write the name of Ram hundreds of times in the criss-cross pages of notebooks. A temple gave him 20 rupees for each filled note book.

To celebrate *arati* (twilight), Mahendra Baba blew into his *chillum* as one would blow into a conch to produce a strong and full harrowing sound like the cry of peacocks. He again gave two long blows and then a series of short ones, and finally a long one. In four breaths. *Om Sankara Shivay Sambu Mahadeva*. He repeated this *mantra* several times and then the ritual dissipated. In the evenings, Samir Baba played his flute and others sang *Hari Krishna, Hari Krishna!* In the mornings, Ramdasji Baba read the Ramayana aloud for two hours on the quay because those who hear this entire epic during their life span are promised deliverance from the cycle of birth. He offered passers-by the merit of hearing parts of it.

'*Hare Hare Guruji*,' exclaimed a baba as he arrived. He hustled through the crowd and fell at the feet of Ananda Baba, prostrating before him.

'*Hare Hare* Niranjan Baba!' my guru responded.

'I was a robber before meeting Guruji!' he explained. 'The last time I broke into a house, I got caught. The owners were out, but they returned. I gave myself up without a fight. They called their neighbours and beat me, tied me up and were taking me to the police station when Guruji, who was staying under a tree, saw us and called my guards.

'"Come here," he ordered. "Why did you beat this man?"

'"He is a burglar, Babaji; we caught him in the act," they answered.

'"A man is called a father by his son and a son by his father," said Guruji, "husband by his wife, brother by his brother, a liar, generous, courageous... and still he is the same man. The one you call a burglar is certainly not only that."

'He made us sit around him and added:

'"God should not be imaginary. He should be seen on every face. *Bhagwan** (the one you name God) hides himself as a robber, don't you know?"

'And he told us this story:

'"A brahmin made an offering of *gulab jamun* to Vishnu every evening in his temple. But in the morning, the sweet balls in syrup were missing and he was surprised. Who took the *gulab jamun* every night? he wondered. One evening, he decided to watch and see who came. During the night, a man slipped into his temple and he grabbed him. Why are you hiding, Vishnuji? You are only taking what is yours! he told him.

'"*Bhagwan* is the only being," then said Guruji. "He is the sin and the sinner, the burglar and his victim. How would he punish anyone without punishing himself!"

'My guards were a little appeased by now.

'"Why do you steal?" Guruji asked me.

'"Isn't everything *Bhagwan's*?" I said, hoping to get off the hook.

'"Indeed, everything is created by God and belongs to him," Guruji approved. "But when you say it, you repeat what you have heard; you don't know it. If you knew, you would have already given away all your belongings because whatever you own also belongs to others! Only when you renounce the objects of this world, can you say that nothing belongs to you, and that everything belongs to God." Guruji spoke to me like this. From then I took the saffron dress and I became his *shishya* (disciple). I walked in his blessed *darshan* a whole year! He taught me everything.'

'Each leaf falling from the tree makes its own way to the ground,' concluded Ananda Baba. 'The saints did not arrive ready-made.'

'Valmiki was the greatest thief of all times,' added an elder. 'One day, Shiva appeared to him and said: Valmiki, if you are such a great thief, why don't you steal me?'

'And he did exactly that,' commented Ananda Baba. 'Valmiki gave up his stealing, became an ascetic and wrote the Ramayana.'

'There are so many ways to find God,' exclaimed a sadhu.

'Do you know the path of the mad man? He howls God's name morning to evening...' said Mahendra Baba.

'He would do better to meditate alone in the forest,' cracked another.

Samir Baba, the flute payer, added:

'There is also the path of tears. *Bhagwan* does not resist the devotee who cries.'

'And joy!' reminded Ananda Baba. '*Bhagwan* does not resist the one who laughs at his world.'

'My guru said, 'When one purifies his heart repeating the Name of God, *Bhagwan* finds his place in it and dwells there,' said the scribe who had filled the notebooks with the name *Ram*.

'He who sees the *darshan* of being in all faces, where would he seek *Bhagwan*?' asked Niranjan Baba, the reformed thief. 'This world is the body of *Bhagwan*.'

'And there is the path of those who do not know there are paths...' I added to the anthology.

'And what about those fearful people who go to the temple mornings and evenings, without even looking at us, what path are they taking?' asked a baba, before taking a puff from the *chillum*.

One of our *grihastha* invited me to sing a song of my country. I chose the Song for the Auvergnat by Brassens, which I translated transforming it slightly: 'This is your song, *grihastha*, who one day gave three *chapatis*, to this baba who was hungry...'

'When I beg, I sing from the *Veda*,' said Mukunda Baba: 'No, Gods did not make hunger the only kind of death; other deaths await those with full bellies. The wealth of the giver is never exhausted whereas no one will pity a miser.'

That made us all laugh.

Every day was a feast. Our benefactor ordered chai and sat at our feet.

Among us, Arjun Yogi Baba was an enthusiast of *kriya yoga* and praised its pledge: to live eternally in our body. It is a secret yoga but secret means that one can acquire it with several years of practice under Arjun's direction or his guru's direction.

'It is not true,' I disputed. 'Nobody is eternal. That doesn't exist.'

'Krishna taught it to Arjuna; Patanjali mentioned it in his Yoga Sutra,' assured Arjun Baba.

'Hoping to live forever is the path of maximum greed, not that of *samnyasa* (renunciation)! Think about it,' I told him.

'Why should I be interested in your *kriya yoga*?' asked Jayram Baba. 'What do you do in this yoga?'

'Withdraw from external phenomena; fix your gaze internally at a point situated halfway between the eyebrows; neutralize the two flows of *prana* and *apana* (which run inside the nostrils and the lungs); control the mind and the senses; banish desire, fear and anger...' recited Arjun Yogi.

I have always found yoga to be complicated and demanding.

'To wish for an everlasting future is like an inverted kind of suicide; it's the same refusal of the here and now,' I insisted. 'And it's useless, you still die anyway. Don't push this idea away, but prepare yourself.'

As usual, Ananda Baba burst out laughing.

'Everyone ends up as carrion or smoke!' said Jayram Baba, determined it should not be another way.

'Either way they both stink!' joked another.

'As a burglar, Niranjan Baba was useless,' someone realised suddenly.

A roadside tent made of plastic sheets, bamboo canes and pieces of string was the *akhara* of Pinaka Baba. A shoot of *tulsi** planted in an opened up oil can and four pebbles made up a little devotional stop. Pinaka Baba paid homage to them every morning and evening with orange powder and fresh marigold. That day, four sedentary sadhus received four passing sadhus.

I was talking to Shakti Puri, a Naga* Baba. He was seventeen and belonged to the Juna akhara of Lucknow. His father was a clothes' salesman. He had three brothers. As a child, instead of going to school, he spent his time with sadhus. He had taken to renunciant-life at the tender age of nine.

'And you travel alone?'

'I move like water in a river,' he answered proudly. 'But not alone, with *Bhagwan*!'

He had walked all around India and was afraid of nothing —but as if impressed by his own daring.

'What did you learn at the Juna akhara? What did they teach?'

'Devotion to the guru, sword fighting, *mantra*, *tapasya**, how to accomplish miracles... I practised the *panch dhooni tapasya*.' This mortification consists of sitting in the midday sun surrounded by four dung fires.

'What miracle have you accomplished?'

'With twelve other babas, we stopped a train through concentration alone.'

'You succeeded?'

'Yes.'

I grimaced sceptically, but he affirmed:

'The engine exploded! It is still over there now, in the same place. You can see it in front of our *akhara*, in Lucknow.'

Shakti Puri and I were both sadhus, but neither for the same reasons nor with the same affinities: he belonged to a world of wizards and magicians and I, to a lineage of wandering philosophers. One does not enter the wandering life as one subscribes to a dogma. And one lives it as one wishes, but…

'Nobody stops a train with his thoughts,' I asserted.

Ananda Baba then mocked me:

'Try to find in yourself the source of this belief!'

'It is not a belief, Babaji, it is an inference,' I argued. 'The phenomenon is so rare that nobody has ever seen it, like a white crow, a pink elephant and the real Father Christmas. One can draw the conclusion that it does not occur.'

'Do you know many people who are determined to explode an engine using their psychic forces alone?' he asked me.

'No. In fact I don't know anyone like that,' I acknowledged.

'Then it's not so surprising that you never came across this phenomenon,' he reasoned. 'The source of this belief is the limits which this consciousness places itself within.'

'Can you stop a train with your thoughts, Babaji?'

'It is not with thoughts that one stops a train, it is with energy. Everybody can stop the world!

'Take this jar full of water. Look in it. Water occupies all the space within the jar, therefore the space in the jar is contained in the water.'

'Yes.'

'Now, look at the surface of the water, the reflection of the moon and the stars. That outer space is also contained in the water. The water in the jar and space in the sky are both contained in the space limited by the jar. It is only a play of illusion. In the same way, Oneself is in the body and in everything.

'This is a *darshan*, the direct knowledge of Brahman as Oneself (Atman). The space delimited by the jar is hidden by the water which it contains and by the sky which it reflects, in just the same way as the unchanging reality is hidden by vitality. See that.'

Thus spoke Ananda Baba.

And the unchanging reality was there. And everything stopped. For a moment.

In the *Avadhuta Gita*:

> Brahman alone is pure consciousness.
> In truth there is no jar, and no jar-space,
> no embodied soul, nor nature. [I 32]

In the afternoon, five youngsters came to show us the snake they had just slaughtered. Coiled around a stick, its head crushed, the poor animal was still moving. They were proud of their exploit. One of them told us that his father would be happy to welcome us at his home. Ananda Baba replied that our *dhooni* was here. They stayed. A pup approached and one of the young guys hit it.

'Why did you hurt it?' I asked calmly.

'It does not feel anything,' he answered with alarming naivety.

'It has feeling just like you and me!' I exclaimed. 'Its body is made of muscles and nerves, just like yours.'

But he did not believe me. I then kept quiet as my guru was about to speak:

'Only a demon strikes without reason,' he said.

That, he understood.

The bitch found its pup and led it to the heap of rubbish. The youngsters went away.

A little later, my guru made me sit in front of him and said:

'One can see the Atman in the interval between two *vrittis* (mental modifications), or when they are absent as in deep sleep. Also, on the cusp of the three states of consciousness (the moment between sleep and waking up; when falling asleep; and between dreaming and deep sleep). Also at the time of the sun reaching its zenith and at the passing from night to day and day to night.'

I sought the cusp, the interval and the passing and found the moment of limitlessness, the threshold beyond which there are no more thoughts. And in this outside, this silent awareness aware of itself, was the background to everything, the unchanging, the immutable One.

It is like learning to ride a bicycle; one should not seek balance but let it find itself.

I gradually understood that, through examining the means that consciousness takes to reveal a reality, or to make it disappear, Ananda Baba was creating a *darshan* made of words, an ontological point of view, a

Weltanschauung, a way of seeing the world which when told provokes a state of consciousness which liberates one from it.

'The presence or the absence of something is knowledge. It cannot be anything else but knowledge, whether there is or is not anything behind this knowledge.'

Thus Ananda Baba spoke.

But how can one accept an abstraction like this?

'*Maharaj-ji*, who was your guru?' This question would arise regularly in conversations with babas or benefactors.

One enters baba-life through a door. This door is a guru. Later, one is free to diverge. These lineages of renunciants and mystical walkers, their knowledge and their practice thus continue and evolve.

Ananda Baba answered that he was ignorant and had never understood anything, but the name of his Master, Vishvatma Satguru Baba, disciple of Maharishi Dayanand Saraswati, who were both admired as saints in the oral tradition of the babas, earned him respect. However there was no monument, no ashram and no book which bore witness to their existence. Their intelligence and their wisdom had disappeared with them. Only a few tales were left and it was now Ananda Baba who embodied their lineage, although he declared himself as being unworthy of it (as is proper in such traditions). When sadhus who knew him, met him, they greeted him with *Hare Hare Maharaj Guru!* and bowed before him.

Maharishi Dayanand Saraswati, the guru of his guru, was known to have written on his flag, at the time of a Kumbh Mela* at Haridwar (a great annual pilgrimage): 'REFUTATION OF BLIND FAITH — HERE.' He fought idol worship quoting Basava[1]: '*What can they give, these Gods who live on charity?* God is One. I am one as well.' Some say that he had survived a poisoned *paan** offered by a brahmin.

About Vishvatma Satguru Baba, his guru, Ananda Baba told that one day, a British officer brought him a prisoner accused of theft, allowing him to decide his fate. Vishvatma Baba gave him his freedom, explaining: "I came to liberate people from their bonds, not put them in chains. If cruel people do not

---

1 Basava: Basaveshwara ou Basavanna (1134–1196) philosopher and reformer, he fought the caste system and brahmins' orthodoxy.

give up their cruelty, why should we lose our own good practices?" He once broke the sword of a man who attacked him and said: "I am a *samnyasin*, I shall never do anything that would not be for your good. Go! May God give you some wisdom."

I found my ancestors inspiring. My kind-hearted anarchist tendencies cherished these unorthodox wise men. I liked the lineage destiny had led me to.

Ananda Baba was Shivaist and belonged to one of the schools of thought listed in the assembly of the Ten Names of the Renunciants (*Dasnami Sampradayas*) by Sankaracharya, in the 8th century: the Saraswati lineage.

Saraswati is Brahma's consort, the feminine aspect of the Creator God. Her name means life-giving-fluids. Goddess of music, learning, poetry and arts, when she is portrayed with four arms, she holds a book and a *veena**. When she is seen as a river, she is the emblem of fertility, purification. As goddess of speech, she indicates the way to wisdom, spiritual knowledge (*vidhya**), and beyond knowledge – enlightenment.

The Saraswati school does not prioritise devotion. It favours knowledge. It declares: 'knowledge more than action (karma*) destroys ignorance'. It pledges: 'learning and studying the principles of *advaita** makes it possible to have indirect knowledge of the One-without-a-Second and to understand. However, this indirect knowledge can be instantly transformed into direct knowledge. Until then, 'reasoning drives out the traces of darkness and confusion, reflection illuminates, and meditation is the direct realization of Brahman as the achievement of consciousness in its own form.' The Rig Veda, the Upanishads, the *Vedanta** and treaties of the Masters of *advaita* (non-duality) model their *darshan*, their point of view, the philosophy which they embody.

But Ananda Baba was also a Shivaist. Somebody who plays with fire, honours *chillum*, dwells in forests and who enjoyed being alive and aware. I imagined that he must have been a well-read man or a researcher or a teacher who had given up a life of books, and perhaps a family, to wander in knowledge itself… rather than reading about it.

'At eighteen, I didn't have any skill,' Paagal Baba told me. 'That's why I became a sadhu.'

He had a full and solid body, was forty years old with short hair, without a beard or moustache. He said that he had spent his childhood moving from one city to another due to his father's profession as a switchboard specialist. Of this descent, he had kept the wandering life he had inherited, it seemed to suggest. He appeared to be completely normal, so I asked him:

'Why are you called Paagal, the Mad one?'

He looked at me for a moment as if trying to guess if I was worthy of something like an answer, then he began:

'Ten men cross over a river. On the other side, they count each other but there are only nine. Yet each one forgets about counting himself and worries about the missing tenth man. They lament. A priest passes by and tells them that the tenth is alive, in paradise. And they believe him and give him money. Suddenly, the one who considers himself to be the most intelligent amongst them discovers that they were never ten. 'We were only nine on the other side. Nobody is missing!' And they rejoice. A sadhu passes by and tells them: 'There are ten of you! The tenth is oneself! What is known is known unto him.' But they believed they were nine and now they are ten and looking for a stranger amongst them… In this mad world which denies its madness, there is a pleasure in being mad that only a madman knows,' concluded this sadhu who was perfectly sound in mind. Only the colour of his kurta set him apart from an ordinary middle-class citizen.

Later, he offered a piece of *charas* for the *chillum*.

'O Lord! O God! You are so generous!' proclaimed a baba to thank him.

'God? I shit on God,' retorted Paagal Baba, without reserve.

'Dogs will even bark at the sun,' answered the laudatory baba after a moment of reflection.

'I see dark clouds on your face,' retorted Paagal Baba. Then addressing me: 'Those who look at me imagine that I act. Why should I care about their imagination? I am free!'

It was true. He was free.

A Western baba was beaming away on the steps of a shop in Rishikesh. He had a kind of natural grin that revealed an inner calm. I greeted him with a *pranam** from a distance and continued walking behind Ananda Baba. Then I saw him again, seated on a stone bench, in front of Lakshman Jhula Bridge.

'You flew here!' I exclaimed sitting next to him.

He was tall and thin with a long wavy blondish beard, a grey turban and a sleeveless shirt of the same colour on an orange *gomcha* which rather short for his long legs with blond hair folded under him. He had a handsome face which was almost Christ-like but joyful. His blue eyes expressed a kind of continuous rapture on his pleasant face. He placed a finger to his lips. He was a *muni** and did not speak. But he showed me his 'Baba' ID Card. He was from Zurich, Switzerland, and was thirty-eight years old.

'Which language do you not speak?' I asked him, 'French, German, Italian, English, Hindi…???'

He nodded to approve.

'It must be relaxing not to speak,' I went on in English.

He agreed. But, as he did not say anything, I said for him: 'In this talkative world, I imagine there must be a pleasure to be a *muni* that only a *muni* knows…' For a moment I contemplated taking the vow of silence… I thought of myself being speechless. To give up using words. What a break! Not to have to assert my existence, nor to have to draw a 'me' out of oneself anymore. If I don't speak – who am I? Tranquility. But the Gods did not choose tranquility. And this thought drove out the previous one, and the world continued to be restless within me.

Duma Giri Baba was a Naga baba and he spoke. He consented to wrapping a terry towel around his thick and flabby waist, but at night time, he would only wear the ashes he threw on his body.

He had erected a *mandir** of sorts at the foot of large *pipal** along the *ghats* at Haridwar, bordered by a few piled whitewashed bricks and scarves embroidered with mirror sequins, a small marble Shiva statue, a Durga riding a lion, a jubilant four-armed Ganesha on a lotus, and a black-stone *lingam* with a small conch and a trident. Passing pilgrims set down their offerings. It was a profitable outfit. Duma Giri also owned a large plastic sheet tent, set up opposite the *mandir* on a concreted platform, and next to it an open air kitchen where two cooks were constantly busy preparing chai in front of a wood fire.

He was built like a wardrobe, with fair skin, four rings on each hand, a high chignon of grey dreadlocks and a beard plaited into a cylinder shape. Sitting on a white plastic camping chair in front of the tent, he invited sadhus for a rest and a chai, and challenged passers-by with his thundering voice: *Whose body is this?* He spoke to street sweepers as though an important man and an important man as a commoner: *Do you know that you could have been this street sweeper rather than a babu? Come and have chai to think about it!* He would call sadhus to witness: *They repeat like parrots 'Bhagwan Bhagwan only one being' but who really knows it?* He had fun. He liked to hassle and provoke: *What body? What freedom? There is nothing.* He was at the same time buoyant and impressive, casual and unpredictable but also benevolent in his flippancy. There were a few of us enjoying his hospitality under the generous shelter. *Chillums* were handed around and two large steamy teapots did the rounds, continuously pouring chai.

Duma Giri had caught a well-groomed young man with neatly combed short hair, a patient and considerate smile, wearing jeans, a bold striped shirt and smart shoes.

'What is truth, Babaji?' he asked him with the required humility when one addresses a saint.

Behind the ashes-mask covering his face, Duma's eye movement betrayed a thinking man. But he did not say anything.

The young man handed him a banknote and said:

'Here is the *guru-dakshina*. Now will you answer me, Guruji?'

Duma Giri accepted the teaching wages.

'This is for chai!' shot the showman for his audience. 'Now what can I say? The truth! He wants the truth. And what will he do with it? A dead cat does not hurt a rat. This is the truth!'

This of course made everyone laugh. But the young man was waiting. Duma had to say something... He scratched his belly and then turned to his questioner and said: 'One plus one equals one. This is all there is to know as true.'

As the young man was about to leave and take this mathematical mystery cum metaphysical revelation with him, Duma Giri seized his eyebrows and pulled them vigorously; on releasing them, he slammed the boy's head with the flat of his hand and finally he struck a great blow with his fist on his back, then raised him up and smiled at him. His host was punch-drunk, but smiling as well. Ananda Baba was also laughing.

'It's a striking truth and an energetic teaching,' said my guru, bursting with laughter.

'Do you think he understood something?' I asked doubtfully.

'One plus one equals one is a powerful *mantra* and he made sure that this boy never forgets it.'

Gathered around a *dhooni* in Rishikesh, Swami Chidananda told me that he had been an executive for Johnson & Johnson and then for Prestige Pressure Cookers. After his wife died, he entrusted his twenty-four year old daughter to one of her uncles, gave away his three apartments and a portfolio of shares to his five sisters and left. 'In possessions, there is happiness but also sorrow,' he explained. 'I had a great deal and I was unhappy. Now I don't have anything and I am fine. No tension.'

'We run after money believing that when we have enough, it will free us,' I approved, 'and when we finally discover this is not true, we are afraid of not having enough to remain captive under the same conditions.'

Ananda Baba scratched at his chignon and then burst out laughing.

'You haggle over words! What is that about?' asked my guru.

'My life story, Guruji.'

As we were warming up under the sun on the *ghats* after our bath, a young man wearing glasses and jeans stopped a moment to stare at us and then drew near.

'*Om Namah Shivayah…*' he said to us bowing in respect.

'*Jay Shiva,*' answered Ananda Baba.

'Did you take your food today, Sadhuji? May I know what you eat?'

'You want to be *Bhagwan* for them, Babuji?' answered Ananda Baba. 'They will take whatever is in front of them.'

He left and quickly returned with two full plastic bags steaming with rice and *daal*.

Om Namah Shivayah!

Later, this friend of humanity also offered his hospitality.

'If *Bhagwan* sends you, let it be,' consented my guru.

Moses was thirty years old. He told us that a few days after his birth, he had been abandoned at the gate of a temple. He was wearing a small amulet tied around his tiny waist, which designated him as a *dalit**. No caste family could have adopted him without losing status. A sadhu took care of him and, a few months later, put him into the care of a Christian family. Thus, Moses considered himself Christian by adoptive faith, Hindu by birth and a wanderer from the very beginning. However he did not take to roaming the roads, as he would rather offer hospitality to the babas. He kept one room in his house for himself and offered the other three to passing sadhus or to those he would invite.

'I chant Krishna to remember that I am God, but I keep forgetting and I become very small,' he said that night.

'It's not so serious,' Ananda Baba told him, 'because you remember to remember, and thus he is with you, he was with you and he will be with you because he exists in you.'

During the evening, he would at times close his eyelids. A luminous smile would then shape his lips and his face became smooth like a teenager. He was a blessed sight to behold and I wished that every man on earth could resemble him.

What Did You See

Along with *moksha* – the liberation from the cycle of life and death, and maya – the delusion that makes one perceive objects and thoughts as real, karma is the third foundation of *sanatana dharma**, the Hindu religions. 'Each action produces consequences, which influence the becoming of the one who creates it, either immediately or later, in this life or in future lives.' That is what a swami, who had never left the well-beaten philosophical paths, stated to me, one day in Varanasi.

Nothing is ever lost according to this theory which applies to all aspects of the physical, metaphysical and moral universe the empirical experience of cause and effect. It therefore postulates an immanent, absolute and heartless, justice. Karma concocts a pitiless universe; this cosmic apothecary judges one's acts, calculates one's merits, weighs up the misdeeds, grants advancement or condemns one to be born again with a contingent of misfortunes as a donkey, a monkey, a pauper or an ill-fated person.

Karma measures happiness and delivers sufferings, justifying it with forgotten former unkindnesses. Karma is all-knowing and will return your deeds to you. Rotten shame! The poor are guilty. An accident carries out a sentence. Destiny holds an invoice. The victim pays his debts. Karma builds a mechanical universe with moral parts, transforms life into expiation, and denounces in the afflicted a sinner who deserves it. It is a merciless order, if there were not many Gods to love and philosophy treatises teaching one to free oneself from it.

Although love of life is deeply rooted in his heart, a Hindu fears that death will not enable him to truly die. He presumes he will return to this world and he grieves over it. He believes himself unwillingly almost immortal and craves disappearance into the ocean of bliss. But karma – the bonds which the past extends towards the future will prevent this. He will start over again several times. Millions of times.

There are quicker ways or even instantaneous means of freeing oneself from all of this, through realization, a sudden and definitive grounding in knowledge, understanding, awakening – freedom, the exit from maya – the delusion of considering objects and thoughts as being true or real, and consequently this theory as well. Maintaining one's mind in this paradox is a state of realization.

I did not believe in liberation from the cycle of births; I did not have enough conviction in this bondage. I postulated everyone to be innocent of whatever had preceded him and free to enjoy life and the pleasures of being alive. As for the question of a personality who, in the form of a soul or energy, would transmigrate from one life to another, I did not like myself enough to believe I had to live with myself for infinity and did not hate myself so much as to feel condemned by this. But I understood that I was nevertheless a prisoner of myself, were it only of the person I was yesterday. I called this 'gravity'. And I wished, as much as possible, to lighten it.

'*Sanatana dharma* is the Law of balance,' Ananda Baba taught me one day. 'This Law expounds the means by which one reaches the state of *advaita* (not-two), which is not something to reach but to contemplate. And karma at the same time designates action, cause and effect. From the *not-two* point of view, there is no difference between them. Actions, which are in accordance with *sanatana dharma,* do not produce imbalance or effects. They are non-acts. Those which produce an imbalance generate effects, karma, continuity, life.'

'On whom do they produce effects?' I asked.

'On the one who believes himself different from the *not-two*. Ego, mind, *jiva* (the person, me with a me in my mind),' clarified Ananda Baba.

'And how can one free oneself from it?'

'By being constantly aware that consciousness and nature are not-two: *Sarvam khalvidam Brahman*. Everything is him. The One being. If the act has no author, there can be no former acts.'

In order to find freedom, liberation, balance or lightness, immediately, and not later, sadhus practise methods, which are passed down from master to disciple. These are the *tapasyas*. Ananda Baba wanted me to meditate two hours before sunrise. 'Observe what happens when you do not act... Place your attention on your thoughts but do not identify with your thoughts and you will find yourself at rest.'

Rest. What a promise!

I never paid so much attention to looking within. Gradually, in each sudden burst of activity as well as in each observed thought, which I had as much difficulty identifying with as not, I examined how I thought, breathed, digested, reacted, wished, fantasized… I sometimes imagined myself as a meditating sadhu having reached perfect contentment and then for a moment I was perfectly satisfied. Until another thought came along and replaced that one!

I am not naturally introspective. Nostalgia does not come easily and I am not unstable in soul. I doubt I have a soul. I am content with little and adapt easily, provided there is intelligence at work and good manners. If some nice qualities like benevolence, mercy and love also drop in even at a low dose, I am fulfilled.

'I'm watching my thoughts unravel. I'm observing the nooks and shadows of my mind,' I told my guru one day. 'So?'

'Don't judge or blame yourself, don't lie to yourself,' recommended Ananda Baba. 'If there is no punishment, there is no lie. There is no longer a *me* when there is no *my*.'

This exercise was a complete absolution. What I think is not me, what I've done is not mine. Thank you, Babaji.

At times ghosts appeared at the crossroads of my meditation, a painful world of memories, old wounds that never healed, from the past yet still alive, elusive but stinging, which immediately bleed when evoked, humiliations, regrets, blunders… The kind of things that leave a trail of discontent in the mind, a bitter taste, a hopeless regret, an irrevocable shame, a dent in ones' own image. These old emotions, which haunted my more or less conscious memory went and dissolved in the benevolent insignificance of the Impersonal.

To concentrate, I repeated sentences that my guru sometimes proclaimed and which gave me a way of reading the world. Another *tapasya* to use. I also endlessly read and re-read the *Astavakra Samhita* and the *Avadhuta Gita*.

> Know Oneself (Atman) as a witness of all,
> As consciousness itself. [*Astavakra Samhita*]

My work as a monk was to attune my consciousness to these injunctions: searching the single, unmoved, intimate and evanescent Self.

> It is neither visible nor invisible,
> neither luminous nor dark, neither small nor large
> because it does not have any form.

So that's what I was trying to seek, as if it were a charade, a koan, a mystery: a way of being attentive. A *darshan*, here in its meaning as a *point of view,* for those who are interested in paths that thoughts can take to eventually transcend themselves.

Trucks screamed by before narrowly missing us. *Know that which has a form as unreal and that which does not as permanent,* says the *Astavakra*. What does not have a form? It was the koan of the day. A divine joke.

The one who, having transcended existence and non existence,
Is satisfied and freed from desire, and wise,
Although in the eyes of the world he may appear to act,
He does not do anything. [*Astavakra Samhita* 18 19]

Non-action does not mean lingering in passivity or to let things occur in a forced submissiveness; it is an act of attention, a quality of awakening, which produces insightfulness and, when necessary, appropriate and unselfish acts.

We had spread our *asan* under a *pipal*, whose branches extended like a giant umbrella covering the entire village square with a low and fresh ceiling.

Farmers had come throughout the day to greet us and seek blessings. At a time when normally no-one would come, a young woman appeared, prostrated at the feet of Ananda Baba, and sat down in front of him.

'Guruji, I cannot believe in God any more,' she said with shame and in despair. Tears drenched her high-pitched voice. 'Can you help me find God?' she begged with very much deference.

Ananda Baba considered her with kindness and then questioned:

'Which God would you like to meet?'

'Hari or Shiv or anyone you want,' she replied desperately.

'That takes time, but not much time,' said my guru. 'Come back tomorrow, I'll give you something.'

The following day, Ananda Baba bought a five rupee string of red plastic pearls from a hawker who passed by. In the evening, he offered it to the young woman with a recommendation.

'Do you know what *Shivo' am* means?'

'No, Babaji.'

'It means, *I am Shiva.* I am the supreme God. I will give you a *mantra* that you will repeat. Come closer.' And then, he whispered in her ear: '*Mayatmakam sarvamidamasti. Shiva iha sarvamasti. Shivo' hamasmi.* All this is of the nature of a mirage, Shiva is everything. I am Shiva.

'Repeat it often. Make a friend of it. And wear this necklace during the day. At night, take it off and leave it under your pillow. In the morning, put it on again. Pursue your search of God, don't give up. One day this necklace will give you an invaluable indication.'

Ananda Baba made her repeat the *mantra*, and then laid his two hands on her head to bless her saying: 'You will see God inside yourself.' The young woman went away.

I never failed to try to understand my guru's wisdom made up of kindness, lucidity, perspicacity and clairvoyance. I sat down at his feet, if possible lower than him and questioned him.

'How can this necklace help her find God, Babaji?'

Ananda Baba smiled at me:

'One morning, she will not find her necklace under her pillow. She will look for it everywhere, and still under the bed and in the kitchen and she will believe she has lost it, until she will discover it hanging round her neck because the day before she will have forgotten to take it off. She will remember that this necklace was to give her an invaluable indication. She will repeat her *mantra*: *All this is of the nature of a mirage, Shiva is everything, I am Shiva.* The words of Anand will come back to her memory: 'You'll see God inside yourself!' And, maybe, she will understand that, just as she believed that she had lost the necklace she was wearing and was looking for it everywhere else, God was and is always in her.'

'I am God, all things and the illusion of all things,' I paraphrased.

'Saying it, you free yourself of it.'

'*Atchaa!* Babaji,' I said pulling the lobes of my ears in humility.

What does the *Avadhut** say?

> The God who makes everything, he is me, no doubt.[1]

Although Ananda Baba had a *hairy, above it all, sleeping under the trees* style, he was a refined man. He was a scholar in his subject – a luminous presence, often tranquil, available, he greeted whoever came with a joyful and wise serenity. He did not try to dominate situations; he initiated streams, planted

---

1 *Avadhuta Gita* translated by Swami Chetanananda, Advaita Ashrama, Calcutta, June 2005.

seeds, freed vitality here and there, in consciousness and thus pursued in the contemporary world an ancient ministry. A sadhu's duty is to awaken.

'Non-action means not expecting anything... If you hope for something, you create the one who hopes, and you have already started making action,' explained Ananda Baba. 'Without expectation, without any thought of success or failure, without desire of reward, who acts? The act is accomplished. *Bass!**'

Ananda Baba adapted his answers to the situation. To some, he gave a *mantra* and a necklace. To others, he reminded them to love or offered advice. To me, he taught a philosophy of discrimination and its methods. Sometimes, in the evenings, he would elaborate for me one of the mental paths, which lead awareness to itself, to an intuition of itself. He would construct a reasoning using the states of consciousness that we currently know and end it with a question about something indeterminable and a challenge for the mind to jump into an abyss: 'neither real, nor unreal, nor both, nor either of them.' If we were in a group, he would invite me to sit in front of him and spoke in a low voice.

'A snake appears on a rope like something on emptiness. It is the transfiguration of emptiness. It's difficult to understand but this comprehension makes it possible to be freed from *samsara*, i.e. to be *Ajanma* (without the waking state), and *ajagat* (without universe).

'The ignorance of the Self in the dream state stops naturally when we wake up. How can one awaken from the hypnosis of the waking state?

'Just as during sleep, a power inherent in *jivas* (individuals, individual vitalities) generates dreams in the same way the power of maya, inherent in Brahman, projects, maintains and destroys the universe. The laws of the world of dreams are different from those of the waking state. But if the power of dream is so great, why should the power of maya be weaker? Space, the elements, universes, animate and inanimate phenomena are this maya, these appearances produced by consciousness within consciousness.

'But the third eye, the one which looks within, destroys illusions and realises Brahman, the unchanging Oneness.

'This is a *darshan* (immediate knowledge) of Brahman: Fire, flames, sparks, embers, ashes... are various conditions of the same thing. Likewise the waking state, sleep, dream, and *samadhi* are various states of consciousness of the same consciousness. Beyond plurality, beyond somethings and nothings is an immutable transcendent.

'See that.'

———— ❧ ————

We rested two days in a small, somewhat abandoned temple on a river bank. Ananda Baba honoured the stone divinity with fresh water, flowers and sandalwood oil which he carried in a tiny bottle in one of the pockets of his bag.

During my meditations, my thoughts roamed about; they elaborated, worked out, inquired, stretched, multiplied, distracted, twisted, turned and returned… before I realized that they had done all this without my consent or even my liking. But I had been making a distinction between a 'me' and 'my thoughts.'

I practised the *dharana* meditation: concentrating attention on only one sense organ, a method Ananda Baba had taught me in Varanasi. It was the most natural and effective method for me. My thoughts would focus easily on what I see, what is seen, the vision, seeing – That. It was the same for hearing. *I belong to the object of my vision*, said Merleau-Ponty. 'Uniting the seer and the seen opens the door to Brahman consciousness. In the same way, unite the hearer and the heard…' said Ananda Baba. '*So' ham* (I am *That*[2]).'

When we arrived in front of the Azamgarh railway station, my guru decided to take the first train due to leave. Without a ticket. Not that he was suddenly in a hurry, it just took him sometimes. We changed district, scenery and story. He would never explain. I tried to rationalize the world, to uncover its mysteries; Ananda Baba read them, dwelt in them. Half an hour later, he decided to get off the train.

Indarapur was an ordinary town with colourful crowds around the station, its shops abounding in goods, its dirty and broken streets, sleepy temples, roaming cows, skinny and mangy dogs which awaited darkness to take control of the city.

A coolie approached us to tell us that a great soul lived nearby, on Dohri ghat road. We went to his *kutir*.

———

2 *That,* in italics and uppercase, *Tat* in Sanskrit: Consciousness in a state of identity with whatever appears without a "me", an "I" to whom it is appearing.

Krishnanand Baba, the *mahatma**, lived in a house comprised of two rooms linked by an open space where there was a *dhooni*. This is where he was to be found most of the time, on his *asan* made of jute sacks, and surrounded by bowls, *chillum* and rags. There were a few coins, some notes, a small lump of *charas* on the offerings plate and two small bowls containing the white and orange powders of Hanuman's *tilak**. A wooden bed stood in a corner. Around the doors and windows were the bright orange auspicious imprints of a large hand: the mark of the monkey God, a symbol of fidelity.

Ananda Baba bowed before the ascetic.

His white hair was crowned with a bun of brown dreadlocks. He wore a long and full grey beard, a *lungi* on his shoulders and a *gomcha* around his hips. His bulging joints accentuated his skinny limbs.

The ascetic turned towards me and looked at me. A gaze from the heart without pretence, that was neither cheerful nor severe. A quiet gaze that had been present in the now for a long time. One that pierces personality without reading it, that gently nullifies it; showing ego that, all things considered, what it thinks it is, is nothing but a puerile idea because it is the only one that believes in it. In such *darshans* nothing remains; just the reflection of Being.

Krishnanand was a *muni*; he had taken a vow of silence. We spent several days in his ashram without pronouncing a word, each of us in his own universe. What a rest it is to keep silent!

The fire fed by two large branches, which Krishnanand brought closer or drew apart, alternately produced an abundance of smoke or intense heat. Ones' gaze had to pierce this fog, the flames and a round pavilion with five marble columns, to detect a horizon of sun-kissed hills deformed by the torrid air. Behind the pavilion, a broad staircase led down to an underground temple dedicated to Hanuman. Below on the left, a great number of tombs bore witness to the fact that sadhus had lived here for many a century.

Devotees passed by during the day, sat down and plunged into a moment of shared peace and then left. Krishnanand Baba placed the *tilak* of Hanuman on their foreheads.

We left to find at the entry of a village, a small stele of an eight-armed Durga astride a lion, in bas-relief under a large banyan. There, we honoured the divine and smoked a *chillum* or two.

'What did you see?' asked my guru.

This was, at times, his manner of teaching when I began my wanderings.

'He is a *muni*. He did not say anything,' I lamented, a little disappointed by silence and distressed by its ungraspable nature.

'In a *darshan*, there is nothing to understand. You have to see!'

'I saw an old man, rather pleasant, calm but not talkative at all! He was luminous. His gaze was like... an ocean, at the same time empty yet alive.'

'Amazing for Prassad to say such a thing!' exclaimed my guru.

'That's true! But Babaji, I would say that your eyes are always sparkling and I prefer bubbles.'

'Not preferring but seeing,' he insisted.

'What would you say you saw, Babaji?'

'An empty and alive ocean,' he answered, sparkling.

'Why would one renounce speaking?' I wondered.

'To cease haggling with words,' he said laughingly.

'Tukaram said: Words are the only possessions that I own, the only clothes that keep me warm, the only food that feeds me, the only wealth that I lavish.'

'Yes, but Tukaram is a poet.'

We sat on the steps of a temple closed for the afternoon nap which was devoted to Ayyappa and Ganesha and faced a small green mosque flanked by two short rather symbolic minarets. Villagers were chatting peacefully on two stone benches set against a house front, smoking *bidis* as large as cigars. Pot-bellied Hindu land owners sat on one, short and skinny Muslim day-labourers on the other.

We greeted and blessed them. Close by, two goats licked, tore and then ate the posters of movies playing at the neighbouring town's cinema. The title had already disappeared, the baddie was still grimacing but with one lick the bloody dagger he was holding was confiscated.

'To be everything is to not be,' I told Ananda Baba when the excitement caused by our arrival had abated.

'And thinking about not being would still mean being a little, would it not? Prassadji... Consider that you were never born.'

'If, during dreams, the mind does what it wants of the world, in the waking state objects compel their recognition. They offer a certain challenge. This world exists in resisting my will. And I live in it. There is a temple behind us and a mosque in front, and people next to us. I feel that I owe some loyalty to materiality. And to myself,' I argued.

'A child becomes a man who grows old and dies, objects wear and break, in what is all this so different from forms and objects created by the mind in imagination or dream?' Ananda Baba answered. 'During dreams, one sees the world inside oneself like something different from him and very real. What is the difference with objects perceived during the waking state? Both are momentary. The swiftness of the transience is perceived differently. But consciousness is the same and it remains unaffected. The reality of an object is not different from the reality of consciousness.

'You don't believe in God, but you don't want to believe you are the Creator!

'When you look at a painting, you don't believe that the mountain or the horse is there. And if you did believe it, this ignorance would affect neither the landscape, nor the horse or the canvass. It would affect the mind only. In a movie, one does not believe that the characters projected on the screen really exist. One identifies with them temporarily, as in a story or a dream, but one still remains to be oneself.'

'You strip things of all their meaning, Babaji.'

'To consider the transmigration of consciousness and the oscillations of pleasures and sorrows which go with it as a reality, carrying meaning and affecting it is called nescience – confusion.'

'This answer is awfully dogmatic,' I protested.

'*Atcha*,' he agreed, before starting again differently.

'When you look at your image in a mirror, although you identify with the image, you do not take the image to be yourself. In the same way, Brahman is that in which 'I' is the reflection. The mind thus lightened, contemplates Brahman through what existence presents itself with, and performs like an actor in a role.'

Actor! I sometimes tried to play being me! This dis-identification produced an effect of unreality, of weightlessness, quite simply of play.

> He does not feel any desire for the world's dissolution
> nor aversion for its maintenance. He has eternity before
> him and is happy to keep quiet. [*Astavakra Samhita* 17 7]

Paddy fields, hills, forests, mountains, roads, tracks, villages, cities... we travelled through a very real world.

'This world that you call illusion, how does it become so real, Babaji?'

'It is through *cit* (consciousness) that maya manifests itself. With differentiation and *manas** (the mind) maya holds onto *cit*, Brahman's consciousness (the evident unchanging immutable). This is the teaching of *The Pancadasi** and Shri Sankaracharya.'

'And how does the illusion disappear?'

'Ego does not cease to be and the world does not evaporate. They are perceived through the knowledge of their illusory nature. Maya arises on *cit* as does discrimination. *Aham Brahmanosmi* (I am Brahman).'

'But if I say "I am Brahman", I am inevitably telling a lie, because "I" must disappear for this assertion to be true. But then who would say it?'

'Very good!' appreciated my guru. 'This is why one must differentiate between immutable and illusion to say *Aham Brahmanosmi*.'

I have acquired *The Pancadasi*, a manual on non-duality and a masterpiece of analysis concerning the non-reality of the worlds, written in the 14th century by Swami Vidyaranya, a distant disciple of Sankaracharya, but Ananda Baba explained this much better and I gradually entered into his way of thinking.

Nothingness

Red carpets of chillies drying under the sun. Branches of fresh cannabis on market stalls, between carrots and cauliflowers. Tractors parked under sheds. Far away, on the river bank, a small temple with columns, lonely but leaning on itself in the emerald nestling of its liquid reflection. One night, in a tree, thousands of fireflies lit up and then faded in unison, enacting the creation of the universe to an audience of stars. Massive black buffaloes silhouetted against the setting sun. The hips of girls swayed amply carrying water jugs on their heads. O, what a magnificent *darshan*!

> As the branch bearing fruits leans naturally to the ground,
> he bows before all the creatures. [Jnaneshvari]

We went North, then East, then South, according to the circumstances and inspirations, which were beyond my comprehension. We set off again in the morning, walked or took a train and then stopped between noon and midnight, obeying whatever happened, as Ananda Baba would say. We also travelled by bus, rickshaw, buffalo cart and lorry. The goal of the path is the path itself, endless movement, which was not supposed to lead us somewhere but elsewhere. Towards oneself? I do not know.

'If there is no goal, there is neither any concern about attaining something.' Ananda Baba used to say. It is in this nowhere liberation is found, in other words that one discovers oneself to already be free.

A few days of walking on dusty roads and being jostled by trucks and buses hooting their shrill horns. At these times survival took precedence over serenity and we had to keep looking behind us so as to jump out of the way in time. We walked during the day and at night I dreamt of walking. Who is the dreamer? And then suddenly, periods spent idly in a lonesome temple or forest. Long and sweet days spent at the edge of a water tank or on a river bank, inhaling perfumes of the sun, contemplating the hues and shades. *Allak!* Long and sweet days in *akhara* and ashram, lingering on *chillum* and chai, from one group to another of my brother and father renunciants. *Hari Om, Gurubhai*! Namah Shivayah, Guruji! Jay Ram! Bom Bom Bole Bholenath!*

In the silence of the evenings, we were satiated looking at the dotted lights of the universe or the dance of flames and then the quivering of embers; simple and welcoming women proud to receive us for a night in their beaten ground courtyard; the sighs of buffaloes; the acrid taste of the *bidi* our host would give us to share in the well deserved rest!

The household awoke at dawn. The children went to school in white shirts and khaki shorts. The grandmother would sit at her weaving loom. The mother started cooking. The father was already in the fields.

Now and again there would be a party! A *bhandara** with hundreds of sadhus gathered for a meal offered by a benefactor, a rich baba or a temple. During these, we found hundreds of ways to embody the virtues of those who are devoted to the divine: intrepidity, modesty, firmness, mortification, piety, softness, benevolence, happiness… And in this gathering of free men, renouncers of possessions as well as of standards, each one expressed, in his own way, a victory.

What do the crows say when they gather by the hundreds before the great black of the night? *Om Namah Shivayah*.

And the *chillum* that a sadhu prepared, so strong I felt I was falling to the ground. *Bom Shankar!* The Big-bang took place in my skull. My thoughts spun and I was conscious and frightened of their relativity.

And the appeasing coolness of the moon.

Domestic quarrels by random neighbours thundered through the night. *Ek bichchu kate tera ling! – Bhagwan kare tumhari jeebh kat jaye!* – 'May a scorpion sting your penis!' 'May God cut your tongue!' And stops at chai-shops in the shade of palm roofs where the burning hot tea revived us! The sound systems howled the undulating and high pitched voice of the latest Bollywood singers. Widows in white saris. Smallpox pits on hollow cheeks.

> The universe exists only through ignorance.
> Only you truly exist. [*Astavakra Samhita* 15,16]

But who am I who only exists truly? This naked child, eyes underlined with kohl, playing in the dust with dried snot under his nose? This boy doing his homework under a street light? This old flabby breasted woman with the skin of her chest as wrinkled as her face, who forgot to readjust her sari?

The scent of the hot earth beaten by our steps; that of chopped straw mixed with water to feed buffaloes. The bitter-sweet sweat of my skin heated under the sun. The humid coolness of the temples. Ah, the taste of the *Glucose* biscuit soaked in a glass of chai!

A few days holiday were spent on the Pushkar ghats in front of the holy lake and its jewel case of white temples; three weeks at Bang Handi temple, an *akhara* in Delhi; one month under a tree in Haridwar.

I learned to sleep on my back, to cut my nails with a knife, to brush my teeth with a stick, to eat with my right hand only, to wash without soap, to launder my clothes striking them on a stone, to blow my nose without a handkerchief, to urinate squatting and defecate in public. I learned to live without a mirror and to greet whatever situation presented itself.

Our expectations shape what we take for what we find unpleasant and our rigidity amplifies this. By taking the flow of events as a spouse one endures a great deal. However, bathing in cold water is the first time every time. The apprehension may lessen but the shock is always the same. It is a powerful surprise that is indeed like a rebirth every time. *Om Namah Shivayah.*

What does the *Astavakra* say today?

> Be it a beggar or a king, owning much or nothing, in crowds
> or alone in a forest, there is no difference for a detached man;
> his inner nature is empty of thought. [*Astavakra Samhita* 18 11]

'What could you want for in this consciousness that includes everything?' Ananda Baba used to say. The offerings of our benefactors, the clemency of the climate and the network of ashrams, *akharas* and *dharamsalas* allowed us to be free of worries, focused, our minds simply present in the passing day.

And the days went by.

We had come to a crossroad between a very minor road and two mud tracks flanked with a chai-shop on each side. Here a flow of rickshaws loaded heavily with passengers, regional buses and tractors pulling tows overflowing with mountains of hay or sugar-cane passed by.

'If I am an illusion, who sees through this illusion, Babaji?' I asked my guru.

'Nobody! The illusion disappears the moment it is recognized.'

Preceded by two drummers, a family procession crossed the road and headed for the nearest village. One man was holding a big reddish-brown rooster in his arms, another carried two aluminium buckets filled with vegetables; a goat jogged along between them. A dozen women wearing their most attractive saris, made up and adorned with jewellery followed behind. The women were escorting the wife-to-be, whose face was veiled by a curtain of jasmine flowers.

'Doesn't rice burn your fingers when you eat it without a spoon? And don't these drums make the insides of your ears vibrate?'

'Maya manifests itself as a creation in consciousness; we experience this in dreams. We experience the absence of maya in deep sleep. How could its existence be denied? You can doubt and deny everything except the doubting consciousness. That consciousness which is always there, is Brahman; whether fingers are getting burnt or not.

'This is a *darshan* (direct knowledge) of Brahman: he who perceives this world is as deceptive as the world he perceives. When you fix your consciousness on this principle of double illusion, you find the consciousness upon which this game plays itself out. See that,' said Ananda Baba.

This was a sort of yoga.

'That which is without name and form is the underlying knowledge of everything. Looking in this way the mind is silenced,' he said on another occasion.

These words produced, in their clarity, a kind of mental blankness, and it was exactly what Ananda Baba had sought to make me perceive: the empty background of consciousness, Brahman. Being with a capital 'B', beyond any suffering.

That worked instantly. The release effect caused by the disappearance of names immediately placed my conceptual mind in the here and now, in a state of suspended awareness.

I could conceive this world as a mental image, and I no longer had to protest so much. Awareness became energy without matter.

> Flames and fire are one,
> The lotus petals are united to the flower,
> And the fruit and the branch are the tree itself,
> In the same way, everything in the universe is Self. [Jnaneshvari]

Hundreds of ashrams stretch along the roadsides of Uttar Pradesh and Haryana. They can be two small houses in a courtyard or a compound as large as a village with temples, a palace for a living God, reception halls, guest-houses for laymen, and sadhus' quarters, kitchens, dining halls, printing houses… These havens of peace are financed by the disciples and benefactors of gurus with varying degrees of renown. One goes to them to receive spiritual teachings, worship an *avatar*, to do a retreat, practise a *sadhana**, rest the mind, enthral the world or repent. When the founder is gone, his disciples try to continue his work. Then, it becomes an institution managed by arid administrators, and then it decays.

Since the arrival of tourists, there are ashrams for Westerners: the all-in-one spiritual supermarkets, offering those who arrive with preconceived ideas of Hinduism and comfortable asceticism, programmes of yoga and relaxation, meditation, ayurvedic* treatments, health and well-being and spice-free vegetarian meals. Everything is *à la carte* with extras if needed. But the sadhus are not welcome in these places.

We arrived in a large, clean and quiet ashram, at the end of a winding road, four kilometres from the first village, very far from the tourist routes. The rules were clearly posted, and some of the people in charge, obsessed by rules and regulations, strictly imposed their will on the natural tranquillity of the place. Smoking *chillum* was forbidden.

A large white marble Krishna temple, open on three sides, held the central place at Ramrati Ashram. It also included a *mandir* dedicated to the founding guru, a school, a dispensary, a free canteen, a herd of eighty cows, fields, a paddock confining fifty gazelles living with geese, hens, rabbits and peacocks… and in the back, a house with two elephants that were used to ring the bells for the *arati puja*. It was something between a family park and a pious place of pilgrimage.

Several buses ferried in pilgrims all day long.

Small gardens in front of small verandas, brick walls painted the colour of mud and a thatched roof, a narrow door and a window; such was the set up for about fifty of these identical *kutirs* arranged like a district of mobile homes, forming straight, shaded alleys under the trees. They were mostly occupied by old docile civil servants and middle-class men in retirement: wearing short hair and bright new looking orange *dhotis**, cosy, late life renunciants, their *tapasya* was nothing more than boredom.

In comparison, Ananda Baba and I were unpredictable and associating with a more cheery kind of divinity. In the fable, the sadhu is the wolf and the ashramer is the obedient dog. I would have prescribed them a stimulant of a *chillum* or two, had I been credible as a doctor or a guru.

It was too hot to walk anywhere; we spent two days in one of the *kutirs*. As there were no visitors, Ananda Baba told me a Sphinx story and enigmas in the Mahabharata* style:

'Yudhishthira and his four brothers had walked all day long without drinking and they were very thirsty. When they finally rested, Sahadeva, the junior of the Pandavas, went in search of water. He discovered a lake. When he bent to drink, a *Yaksha** appeared:

'"If you drink before you answer my questions, you will die," threatened the spirit of the lake.

'He did not wait, and died.

'The three following brothers went searching for him and suffered the same fate. Yudhishthira, the eldest who was known for his wisdom, on seeing that his brothers had not returned, went to explore the surroundings where he found the lake, his four lifeless brothers and the *Yaksha*.

'"Your brothers died because they refused to answer my questions," said the spirit.

'"Ask your questions," consented Yudhishthira.

'The *Yaksha* asked more than one hundred questions, including:

'"Which is the most valuable possession?"

'"Knowledge," answered Yudhishthira.

'"What is true knowledge?"

'"Consciousness, which has consciousness for an object."

'"What leads to this knowledge?"

'"Immobility!"

'It is from the point of view of stillness that one understands motion,' commented my guru. 'Sit down. Observe the impulse to move in yourself, but don't move. This impulse is related to the source of life. Stillness gives you its knowledge. Go beyond, you will discover consciousness that has consciousness for an object.'

I went to sit down in the *mandir*. I was alone. The stone floor refreshed my feet, my buttocks and my brains. A white marble guru stared at me looking at him. I reflected. What does it mean *consciousness which has consciousness for an object?* I observed my thoughts from the point of view of stillness, as Ananda Baba had suggested. Every thought which generated an impulse of motion was inhibited by the decision to remain seated. This decision made me become a spectator of myself, a witness of what I believed I was the author of. Thoughts appeared – from the futile to the sublime, not necessarily in that order. Through watching them closely not for what they said or meant, but as ideas, as unqualified creations, I realized that my consciousness had my thoughts for objects. But which consciousness was aware of that? This question made my consciousness become its own object and aware of itself. But as soon as I became aware of that, the thought, the object of thought, the thinker and consciousness once again assumed their distinct role and their usual dynamics, with me at the centre. I was not to know that I had reached what I was seeking. Maintaining awareness in that state of surrendering to nothing, of non-being, is difficult.

At around four o'clock in the afternoon, we stopped at a temple, whose gate opened onto a shaded and deserted courtyard. The *pujari*, dressed in a red gown, walked out of a small side house. We did *pranam*, *namashkaar**, *Ram Ram* and *Namah Shivayah*.

'Who is your *Ishwar*?' asked Ananda Baba.

'Adipara-shakti, the Mother goddess. She is a Dravidian goddess that our Guru rediscovered after having been forgotten for over a thousand years,' the priest explained. 'She is older than the Gods. She created Shiva, Vishnu and Brahma.'

'Atcha!' said my guru.

'When one speaks about Gods, youth is not a positive attribute,' I grumbled in English.

Ananda Baba broke into a laugh.

'God is old, by definition, since he was there even before the beginning,' I carried on. 'Eternal! That goes back so far!'

The *pujari* guided us to the temple. A new, square concrete building with yellow painted walls embellished with pink and blue ornaments. Inside, the stone idol was so worn that she was impossible to make out and inevitably beautiful just for being what it was. We prostrated before this dilapidated symbol of the great womb.

'She performs miracles,' assured the *pujari*. And as if to confirm this, he added: 'On full moon we offer a meal to the poor.'

Outside, five children played at performing a *puja*. Four *neem* leaves on a metal plate containing a little sand mimicked *prassad*. A broken brick for an idol. A little girl offered imaginary curls of smoke holding a piece of straw whilst chanting gibberish Sanskrit verses. The others prostrated before holiness imitating humility.

We spent ten days in this temple that was almost always empty.

'Stillness is delicious, Babaji,' I said after meditation. 'There is a moment when I feel I could remain there, satisfied for eternity. It feels as if there is no more *later* or *elsewhere* to desire. But this moment does not last very long and I already long for the infinite patience that I just saw and which fled from me.'

Ananda Baba grinned.

'Who said that eternity had to be long?'

I consulted *Astavakra* and read aloud:

> When liberation from bonds does not involve expectations,
> *Moksha* is not even the object of a thought. [XIV 3]

Ananda Baba commented:

'*Moksha* is like finding something again. You suddenly remembered you had lost it.

'In *The Pancadasi*, Swami Vidyaranya shows the way of nothingness as a *darshan* of consciousness (*cit*) of *SatCitAnanda** Brahman. See that:

'The first modification of the One-without-a-Second is *Prakriti**. *Prakriti* is this '*second*', the first effect of differentiation. It is the second moment which creates movement. It is emptiness before space. Emptiness without space,' insisted my guru as if he wanted to empty it even more. 'When one takes the idea of space away from emptiness, what remains?'

'Nothing,' I asserted with confidence.

'That which is represented by the concept *nothing* is thus revealed to consciousness (*cit*). Existence (*Sat*) should therefore be allotted to it. Producing no misery, it is also bliss (*Ananda*). Consequently there remains not *nothing* but *SatCitAnanda* (Being and existence, consciousness, and bliss). The common element to everything represented by names and forms is *SatCitAnanda*.

'This is a direct knowledge of *SatCitAnanda* Brahman. Your mind, thinking of emptiness which cannot contain anything (without space) is emptied of anything else, and thus reveals nothingness to itself, and makes the reflection of consciousness in its immutable nature occur.

'While you seek this emptiness without space, your consciousness observes nothingness, sees the existence of nothing and thus can observe itself in it. And this is beyond suffering.'

'*Atchaa!*'

'Who had lost nothing and who found it?' asked my guru.

'You, I assure you, Babaji, with your virtuosity in revealing Being everywhere, even in the nothingness of emptiness without space.'

I bowed deeply before him.

As we were leaving, the priest gave us some sweets. He had put on a comfortable kurta-pyjama and was watching a Bollywood drama on television.

In a single file, on a red dirt track, women carrying on their heads large flat round baskets overflowing with vegetables. Buses and lorries drive over rice husks spread out over the road beating it. Buffaloes rest in the shade of mountains of hay. A few hens peck at the ground, a goat skips along the narrow pathway. The smell of fried garlic and curry wafts out of an open door.

From a hill's summit, the waves of land disappear into the azure distance.

A shanty-town runs alongside a canal with black, putrid, waters. Frothy white clouds rot in this stagnating sky obscured by swarms of flies and mosquitoes. Plastic bags, aluminium packaging, shards and rubbish lay strewn on the lanes with sewage streams running across them, lingering odours of old urine and incense wafting from a neighbouring temple. A sound system installed on a rickshaw screams out propaganda from a political party. Indifferent to the false promises, the squatted day-labourers and their tool bags await the arrival of employers at the corner of a street.

A hundred thousand footsteps away, back in Jalalpur, some people told us that turning left in front of the brickyard, on the road to Faizabad, following the small trail behind a large rock, we would find the *kutir* of a *samnyasin*, perched on a banyan tree.

As we did not have anything to offer, on the way Ananda Baba picked up some dried leaves which he pinned together with small twigs so that they formed a little basket, in this he placed a pink and grey stone the size of a chestnut and a flower from the ditch which he chose carefully and upon which he whispered one of his *mantras*. Finally he refreshed this still life with a spray of water from his *komandalu*. It was a beautiful offering.

Three small white clouds turned the sky into paradise.

'Keep silence within you when you take a *darshan*,' Ananda Baba reminded me. 'Don't think. Let it be. Offer your gaze.'

A bamboo pole topped with an orange triangular flag signalled the final approach of this *kutir* which had been built in a tree. *Om Namah Shivayah! Namah Shivayah!* Ananda Baba shouted to announce our arrival to the saint who was still not visible. We climbed a pile of unstable bricks, hoisted ourselves onto one branch, then onto another and arrived in front of a young man in his twenties, sitting on his heels, with a straight back, wearing nothing but a *gomcha*. His gaze was fixed. Unmoving.

A mat of rice straw covered with a blanket marked out the limits of this ascetic's *asan*. In front of him, a floor of unstable planks were covered with jute bags. Consisting of wooden beams, cardboard, scraps of black tarpaulin, used rice bags and pieces of string, were walls through which the daylight pierced in several places.

We sat down to his left in front of the opening.

A vertical wrinkle between his eyes gave him a stern and resolute glare. His determination seemed unwavering. For me, he was as mysterious as the world's beginning, or its end, or the essence of time. His chignon standing twenty centimetres high established that he had been a renunciant for a long time – since he was a child.

As a model of the superhuman the Greeks came up with the athlete; the Americans created a flying superhero dispensing justice and the Indians chose the ascetic. If stillness was an Olympic discipline, they would win all the medals, I thought.

Silence!

Seeing without thinking. Without thoughts, I thought, there is nothing to see. Without reference points nothing is seen. This man is an emblem of absolute refusal, an Adonis representation of the dedicated enemy of Creation. The very embodiment of immobility. How could I explain that to Babaji? Whatever I see comes from my own representations. How could I see differently!

Silence.

The hot breeze was embellished with tiny rustlings, buzzing sounds and the indistinct breaths that punctuate the vibrations of life.

I offered my gaze.

Interspersed feelings arise. But even feelings become thoughts. Feelings of eternity. Feelings of an immanent harmony. The feeling that I was freed from myself... This boy irritated me. He was too gloriously detached, too indifferent, too beautiful, too perfect, too inaccessible in his discipline… This athlete did not move a lash. It lasted three hours. He finally rose and went down. We followed him to the firm ground where he prepared chai. Drinking it and without ever looking at us, he told us that his guru had ordered him to practise this *tapas* for a year. He had meditated more than twelve hours a day for ten months.

'What did you find from this practice?' I asked him.

'I cannot say,' he only answered.

'Why?' I insisted.

'It is not something to understand.'

'Sure, but nevertheless I want to understand,' I said stubbornly. 'Try to say something about it, I beg you.'

He remained quiet for a moment and then added:

'Because there is nothing to find.'

That, I knew since my first trip to India. Ganges, one day, had said it to me in another way: *nothing is to be done, nothing has to be done, there is nothing one has to do.* But between knowing that there is nothing to do and actually weaning oneself from the impulse to act, takes more than an intellectual understanding.

'Did you know that before beginning this *tapas* or did you discover it here?' I questioned.

'It is in patience,' answered the wise young man. 'You must give power to patience,' he explained.

Back to the road. And then in front of two glasses of chai, a teaching on *darshan*: 'What did you see?'

'He did not appreciate your offering even though it was very nice,' I said in a mood for blasphemy.

'He makes Anand laugh,' said Ananda Baba, laughing suddenly. But then seriously: 'He did not look at you for one instant. It was a blessing for him to allow you to observe him. He was teaching you about concentration.'

'So that is how you interpret this… composure?'

'Would you have been able to stand his gaze for a long time?' asked my guru.

'What a strange question! But surely not, indeed,' I said after thinking about it. 'I would have been ashamed of myself. I find him heroic.'

'What did you find heroic?'

'I find it heroic to attack life with such resolve. I imagine, I fantasize about perfection in immobility, power in gentleness, purity in anonymity.'

'What are you ashamed of?' Ananda Baba asked.

'My agitation,' I replied.

Babaji grinned.

'You see, he taught you concentration.'

I asked him: 'For you, has he reached the ultimate?'

'The ultimate of what?'

'Of anything.'

'He has reached a state of great control over himself.'

'Is motionlessness an aim of life?'

'The supreme power is in the unchangeable. Actionlessness and surrender are means of knowing it. Even the Gods do not have control over it!'

'You know, Babaji, I'll never have such exaltation undergoing voluntary paralysis like that.'

'Stop haggling with words. Find the source of speech in yourself,' my guru advised.

It was his way of making me shut up. I then burst out laughing and so did he.

Where is the source of speech? Who talks when I talk? And who thinks when I think? Faced with this question, either one articulates concepts or one simply observes oneself thinking. By doing this one finds that everything arises from thinking; thoughts build and animate everything and place this 'I' in the centre. But 'I' is just a thought as well and only exists in agitation; it is not the source.

In this investigation, I saw that the source was not somebody but a soft and pleasant feeling without cause. I saw that an underlying continuum of joy or happiness accompanies life from beginning to end whatever the circumstances, even the darkest. From the twists and turns of the *self-other* distinction arises either acceptance or refusal, happiness or irritation, and pleasure or pain… The source of everything was a minute imperturbable joy.

'Babaji, you sometimes say that Brahman is everything, then nothing, only one but also the multitude, that the world is illusory although it is also real, existing as Brahman…'

'They are suggestions for meditation: seeing the world like this then like that, thus seeing it several ways to understand that none of them is true and that they are all true. The Union of opposites is where truth is. If it thinks it is this body, the mind is this body. If it thinks it is Brahman, it is Brahman. But when it is quiet, the mind returns to its cause.'

'Talk to me about bliss, Babaji.'

'Light puts an end to darkness; knowledge puts an end to ignorance. The attachment of the mind to the object is cause of bondage, freedom from attachment leads to liberation in the same way as fire dies out when there is no more fuel for it. The one whose awareness does not know restlessness and sorrow dwells in bliss. This is the teaching of the *rishis*.'

I Met Him in Varanasi

*A*little further down the road we stayed in a small village *akhara* where Kaushal Baba and his two *shishya* lived. The paved yard was swept and hosed every day. It was surrounded by a wall on three sides, and opened out onto a pond colonized by frogs and water lilies. Scattered here and there, vault-like chapels with brick walls covered with mud were devoted to Hanuman, Ganesha, a *Shivling** and to the *samadhis* of the *mahatmas* who had lived and died here. At the centre of the courtyard were four square rooms arranged in a cross formation. To the left was the mud clad hearth of the *dhooni;* fire tongs and a trident were driven into the thick bed of ash, standing to attention. In a corner of the garden, marigolds mixed with carnations and cannabis plants. In the distance was a tiled bathroom and an old Maruti-Suzuki stood in front of the gate.

Kaushal Baba had been the head of this baba ashram since 1996. He was fortyfive years old and from Rajasthan. His features were angular, he had rabbit-like incisors which protruded forwards and his expression revealed a kind of faithfulness to sorrow, but he had studied at a Sanskrit school in Rishikesh. This was an austere baba, thrifty, orderly and gloomy, more like a *pujari* – dedicated to worship – than a sadhu – freed from forms and habits. At dawn, he performed a never ending *puja*, which took him to the front of each vault. His disciples prostrated at his feet and performed their *omkar** whilst blowing in a little whistle. Villagers passed by. No *chillum* did the rounds here.

Just like any other morning, wrapped in my blanket, I was meditating behind Ananda Baba. The pond was still as black as the sky and almost silent except for the occasional bubbling sound. In the distance, dogs barked sporadically. A rooster crowed. I was staring at my guru's upright back, high nape of neck and wet dreadlocks in a bun. This was a man who could remain motionless for a long time. But what did I know about him? Almost nothing. He answered any personal question with 'A sadhu has no past.' Final and non-negotiable.

A few months earlier I had noticed his arrival one afternoon on the *ghats* of Varanasi. Blanket and bag on shoulder, he had put down his *komandalu*, joined his hands and lengthily grinned at the Ganges. He then slowly descended the steps and took his bath. Untied, his dreadlocks fell to his calves. Later, when he was drying off in the sun on one of the promontories which stretch along the *ghats*, I went to him, bowing, hands joined:

'Namashkaar. Kya Babaji mujhe unke paas aane ki agya dete hein? – May I approach Babaji?'

'Namashkaar. Where from?' he acquiesced with a wide smile.

He asked me the *ten standard questions*: where are you from? What is your job? Are you married? What is the purpose of your coming to India?

'I am unmarried, French, Cartesian, and I believe in Darwin,' I replied the way Indians do when saying they are atheist. 'And I came to India to talk to you, since we are talking to each other.'

'What does all this mean?' I asked him, halting his questioning whilst embracing the river, the sky and the whole universe with my wide open eyes, 'Can you tell me?'

He agreed to change the subject.

'One cannot give meaning to the infinite. Because the infinite has no limits. What you seek is not a direction like an arrow, it is a point.'

He chewed English with a thick doughy accent, typical of well-read Indian men. And he smiled abundantly.

'A point… of view?' I asked.

'A *darshan.*'

'A vision,' I translated. 'Do you accept the world as real?'

'Uske liye nitya kya hai?'

And him, what does he take as real? I understood. 'What does he believe in? What has he seen?' he added in English.

He had a beaming gaze, as though above it all.

'I tend to believe in me, but you will obviously think of me as pretentious,' I answered.

He burst out laughing.

'He makes Anand laugh,' he said seeming to beg for pardon, then added *'main, mujhe,* "I", "Me", what is it?'

'Biochemistry, biophysics, a psycho-chemical process, intelligent matter.'

'Splendid! But when a frustration arises, you see that you've been living in illusion, don't you? Who is this "I" who is speaking? Where is this intelligence?'

'Nowhere. It is this body itself, an organism which even manages to create pleasure with its thoughts. It's incredible,' I replied.

'Do you think you control your life that much?'

A glare of light sparkled in his eyes.

I direct it but do not control it completely. There are surprises! I could have answered, but I felt like agreeing to be led where he wanted to take me.

'I don't know.'

'"I" or "me" is a mental construction. The mental faculty creates a limit made of identifications (with the body and the environment) in the infinite which does not have any.'

'However, this me is born and will die…'

'Birth and death are only an idea which takes the shape of a body, then leaves it. This idea is a character in the dream of Brahman whose universe is the play. If the idea is transcended, being alone remains.'

There were voices around us, the indistinct words of the passers-by, the protests of a child being vigorously washed by his mother. And the lapping of the waves arriving on the bank, the strokes of oars of boatmen on the river… And also a deep silence when I looked at Ananda Baba.

'Do you believe infinite to be apart from you or in you?' he asked me.

'I am certainly a part of it,' was my bet.

'Then why do you want to conceive of yourself differently?'

'You are suggesting that I think of myself much smaller than I believe myself to be and also as large as every conceivable thing. To embrace in the same state of consciousness, the almost nothing and the boundless whole because smaller than the whole, for you, is nothing. Nothing is real, you would say but maya makes you powerless in acting upon the world and against injustice. Taking the world to be real makes it possible to tame it a little – to invent the internal combustion engine, the tractor, the aeroplane, chemistry, medicine and the telephone…'

'Don't stop there. Enquire even deeper until you uncover the mysteries of your own nature,' he interrupted.

'What about my nature?'

'When you dream, you talk with people; the words you have uttered were not pronounced in sounds, and yet they have been said. Who spoke and who answered?'

'Me!' I claimed with imperial confidence, 'Of course. We are not dreaming. We are both sitting on this pavement but we do not look at the same things. You don't know what I will ask you or answer.'

'More than "Me",' added Ananda Baba, imitating me. His bun swayed. 'Dreams give you a convincing experience of the confusion between the world of ideas and the world of objects. You play all the roles there. You are all the characters – even those who want to hurt you. You are the landscapes, the objects, the light and even the spirit of this reality. But you do not know what you will say or do one minute later. You never even think about this. And yet you are evidently the author of it. When is it an illusion? When does it become real?'

'The question is: for whom?'

'You already said: Me!'

I burst out laughing.

He enjoyed talking and I enjoyed talking to him.

'Even though there are no external material objects in dreams, a man is nevertheless ruled by pleasures and sorrows. Neither pleasure nor sorrow is felt when the mind is temporarily suspended during deep sleep, fainting and *samadhi*. Therefore, the outside world can disappear. So we have to conclude that the outside world is a transitory state of consciousness.'

'Ok,' I agreed without saying it.

Two sadhus put down their *asan* a few steps away. A young American sat down and passed a *chillum* around. Then two young Varanasi locals came, asked the *ten standard questions* and then tried to draw my interest towards buying silk. One of the sadhus asked me:

'Which God do you like?'

'I don't believe in Gods,' I told him honestly. 'One just has to look around with a little clarity to have some certainty that there is no reason to trust in God. The world is full of misery. Although God is supposed to do everything, he cannot do better and for many it's quite far from enough.'

'Atchaaa!' Ananda Baba exclaimed laughing. *'Atcha!'* He continued, thoughtfully this time. 'God is *sakhara* nirakhara**, with form and without form.'

'What is a God without form?'

The two silk salesmen then started bothering the American who promptly left.

'The God that is not to be believed in,' Ananda Baba answered laughing even more. 'The One-without-a-Second cannot have a form since he is all forms.

So he is with and without form. Is it by looking up a river that you find the water from the source? No. You must descend the river to find the source everywhere in the ocean. God is not found in an inaccessible elsewhere. He is here, he is *That*,' he concluded widening his eyes to embrace the universe in them. 'He is whatever happens, whatever turns up. Anand sees its Presence.'

Thus spoke Ananda Baba.

The sun was now low behind us. He got up and I offered to show him a pleasant place to stay. It was at Ranamahal ghat where six chapels devoted to *lingam* as tall as a man border the stairs that ascend the wall of the river bank. They opened laterally. A black phallus shaped stone, half a meter high seemed to shoot out of the ground. Five years earlier, during my first stay in Varanasi, I had lived in one of these urban caves for a few weeks.

Ananda Baba laid down his *asan* and I sat on the cold concrete slab.

'When you dream,' he went on, 'you are the dreamed character who is awake and who believes he exists in a world. But are you not also the man who sleeps and dreams, lying on his bed, unconscious of his body and of the bed. When you do not sleep, you believe yourself to be a man, with a degree, somebody's son, of Western origin, etc. But now, are you the awake man who believes he is not dreaming or a character of dream? How do you know? Or then, are you the *mukti*, an awakened one, who knows that he is dreaming? What you believe real is always a mental construction, whether you dream it or not.'

For a few moments I tried to convince myself that I was dreaming. But I could not.

'An awakened one who knows that he is dreaming, isn't he dreaming that he knows he is dreaming?' I said, trying to catch him out at his own game.

'You can go back like this *ad infinitum*, Prassadji,' he answered, calling me Prassad for the first time. 'Being and non-being are the same whole. You are yourself this Whole. What could possibly exist outside of consciousness.'

It grew dark. I put down a one hundred rupee bill in front of the *lingam* before leaving.

I had come back to Varanasi after having stayed there previously for six months. I will speak about this later. Meanwhile I had learned Hindi with an illegal immigrant and, this time, I had left my work and given up my apartment to come and live with sadhus. I was looking for the one who would guide me, whom I would choose as my guru. I had imagined he would be someone like…

this Ananda Baba – pleasant and intelligent.

I met him again the following day on the river bank. An aroma of incense wafted by us. Two triangular sail broad barges charged with logs and sand were slowly descending the stream. A squatted man was vigorously lathering soap on his head. Others washed their clothes.

'Five years ago, here, I found peace,' I said.

'Do not bind yourself to this peace. *That* changes all the time,' he warned me. '*Bhagwan* (God) will surprise you.'

'*Bhagwan!* I doubt it.'

'*Tat*, That,' he corrected me, laughing and coughing.

He dug about in his bun and withdrew a pack of *bidi*, and then he probed his turban to pull out a match-box. He lit the little cigarette in the palm of his hand, and then inhaled through his closed fist.

'Take whatever arises,' he added. 'Why should *that* be only peace or love? Or always the same? Peace is the first step. But it can be the last obstacle if you don't let it go.'

The feeling of peace that I had previously experienced here and had now come back for belonged to a dream which had suddenly been shattered. In its broken fragments, I then saw for a moment *the awakened who knows that he is dreaming*. And I smiled at him.

'This peace had told me: *Nothing has to be done; there is nothing one has to do,*' I added.

'If there is no goal, then there is also no concern about realising something. Only the realised exists,' he approved.

During the following days I spent increasingly more time with him on the *ghats*.

'And in my dream, one of the characters would tell me that I do not exist. He would tell me that I am dreaming…' I said, pursuing our first conversation.

Ananda Baba was looking at the glistening river. He answered with his cosmic smile:

'Doesn't one dream thousands of dreams in a life? And yet all these dreams are only one life. In the same way, all the lives are only one dream.'

'Hmmm. So you don't see any difference between being awake and dreaming?'

Ananda Baba laughed his silvery laughter.

'You're the one who does not see any difference. It is when you wake up that you know you were dreaming.'

'Waking up is knowing that I'm not dreaming!'

'To wake up is to know that you were dreaming the moment before. Waking up is, when you awake in the morning, perceiving the not-yet-determined pure Being, then the not-yet-determined pure Being being invaded by "I" and then being "I". Being is not "I". "I" reveals being.'

A little later, he suggested:

'First, limit your world to that which you perceive. In other words, pull yourself away from speculations and establish yourself in the here and now.'

'And then?'

'Then you will be able to examine this reality. How is it? What does it tell you? What is your relationship with it? What emotions, what feelings does it produce? Examine all this. Examine the reality of this.'

'What am I supposed to find?'

'You want answers? Babaji does not give any answers. Be the witness. It does not require any effort.'

'It is difficult to place consciousness in this position in which it stands back, but it is even more difficult to maintain it there. Passivity is an effort.'

'No. You should know that is not,' he affirmed with authority.

We remained quiet.

Life was pleasant in his company.

I had my copy of the *Astavakra Gita*. As we took a chai near Dassawamedh ghat, I flicked through and read:

> The true bliss of this supreme idleness is reserved to those for
> whom blinking the eyes becomes exhausting — not for others.

Would I dare postulate to this ambition?

'Are you a baba for the lifestyle or for *moksha*, Babaji?' I asked him, provokingly.

He smiled.

'Liberation is also a lifestyle.'

An engineer student came to him to receive his blessing and we talked. He had a *tilak* on the forehead and wore a large red and green bold stripped polo shirt that puffed up his already ample waist.

'American?'

'No. French.'

He was curious about the West but his understanding of geography was minimal.

'Do they give visas?'

'Educated Indians want to leave their country rather than change it,' I answered because I was asked ten times a day. 'Corruption is endemic, justice is flexible and equal opportunity is unknown here,' I said, 'and nobody seems to care.'

His reply was incredibly egocentric and politically indifferent:

'I have an education; I have a good karma!'

'Karma!' I exclaimed. 'The theory that justifies injustice as being a boomerang returning to its author makes it possible to exonerate everything which is unjust! I believe each man is innocent of what preceded him.'

'Karma is what, in you, is resisting change,' interrupted Ananda Baba bursting out in a merry and benevolent laughter.

'Hmmm,' I said, touched, without knowing exactly where.

'To conceive oneself as different is to conceive oneself in a form, and to identify with it, and so to become a habit. This form, that you call "I", is also named mist of ignorance, *avidhya**. It is on this mist which is like a screen, that karma is played out.

'Consider it from a higher perspective. No life is better or worse than another. What was there before there was a before? Who was born? Who lived? Rebirth of whom? There is no who. *That* occurs. *That* is. Maya (the projection of a world on the immutable Brahman) creates *Jiva* and *Ishwar*, (The "I" awareness and the creator of the physical world, *That*, God).'

The following day, David, a young, recently demobilized Israeli, sat down with us. Slim, tidy, alert and clever, he was tanned and wore short dreadlocks which suited him very well. He asked questions about yoga.

'Agree not to seek anything for a moment,' recommended Ananda Baba. 'Establish yourself in a state of disinterest. Then, direct your attention to your senses and then towards the interior, to the mind impressions caused by the senses. This is *Pratyahara* – gathering. Do it now.'

David straightened up. I did the same and concentrated like this. Ananda Baba let two minutes pass and then said:

'Second phase: *Dharana*, concentrate thought on one point only, only one sense, one object or one thought. That gives you a simple experience of Oneness.'

I concentrated on sounds, the lapping of water, multiple voices overlapping and reverberating against the walls, the cries of budgies bickering in flight, and the remote cawing… to which I was attributing words. And then there were the sounds themselves and… Hearing.

'Third stage: *Dhyana*. Focus your attention on a single point uninterruptedly. Only one precise object.'

I concentrated on the lapping.

'Once that is established,' Ananda Baba continued, 'let go of the method, the aim. Let go of the one who thinks. Give up the object and the subject. This is unity, *samadhi*, the "gathering". You are not in the centre anymore, nor anywhere else in reality. You are reality.'

That…

'Where do you find reality if not in illusion?' I refuted, waking up from this hypnosis.

'You are making progress,' he appreciated.

I was the first one to be surprised on hearing this.

'What is the goal of this *asana**?' asked David.

'There is no goal in this consciousness.'

'What is *moksha*? What does one get freed from in this liberation?' he continued asking.

'If you want something, you do not want the whole. For the whole, you must give up all the "things",' he answered.

'It's a funny kind of logic. Nothing can be left!'

'Very much is left but what disappeared is choosing, and therefore the one who chooses. *Moksha* is a consequence of renunciation. When there is no longer anything opposing change,' he added looking at me.

And then he burst out laughing.

And when he laughed, he embraced everything with a light which also lit me up.

'You must bend to learn,' he added between two silences. 'If you do not bend, if you remain stiff, how can you receive new knowledge or greet whatever is happening?'

I bowed deeply during the moment of calm that followed.

It's him, I thought.

'What did you do before you became a sadhu?'

'A sadhu has no past,' my question was swept away as a matter of principle.

A man with no life story.

In *Avadhuta Gita*:

> How can one speak of illusion concerning oneself?
> And how can one say: I am in the illusion.
> There is neither soul nor form,
> Realize that Brahman only exists,
> Which is neither knowable nor made to be known.

Five or six days passed.

'I would like to stay with you, Babaji,' I declared, deciding it in the Ranamahal ghat *mandir*.

'Anand moves. Anand does not stay anywhere.'

'I will walk with you… I shall be your disciple.'

'Anand does not take disciples. Anand walks alone!' he objected firmly.

'Anand cannot turn down a disciple who comes,' I said, imitating him. 'Opposing changes, refusing whatever arises…'

'He makes Anand laugh,' he said smiling. He added: 'You are young. Later, you'll have the time to retire on the mountain or in the forest. There is no hurry.'

'When I'm old, I'll have neither the strength nor the courage to do it anymore,' I answered. 'And I don't want to withdraw to the forest; I want to walk with you. There is no hurry but I am ready. I want you for a guru, Guruji.'

'Anand has already explained everything. Baba-life is the same life. Go back home. Ganga is going to your head.'

'Please take me seriously.'

He looked at me as if I were a strange problem needing a solution. Once his examination was over, he concluded:

'Do you really want to give up the worldly way of life?'

'The truth is I am not absolutely sure. But I want to try.'

'Do you want to give up your name and your past, and consider your parents dead? Can you rise beyond ideas of good and bad, not only in thought, but in acts, in your body?'

'I don't know.'

'Do you want to?'

'I think so.'

'Do you have the courage to become poor?'

'I don't know; I have never been poor.'

'It is in uncertainty that the magic of the world's play occurs. Renunciation is not the opposite of desire; it is a positive act. You give up running after life because you are life. You know it. Renunciation is giving up "I", "me" and "mine". What can you want in this consciousness which already includes everything?'

The prospect of travelling without money frightened me. I had never been penniless. And believing in magic and miracles presented an insurmountable problem. When poor, one is vulnerable. It's an idea one has to get used to. I don't have the spirit of a hero or the detachment of an ascetic. But if Ananda Baba had survived up to this point, I'll survive with him; I tried to talk myself into building up this confidence. I'll always have parents and friends in Paris ready to save me from an inconceivable danger or to pull me out from the depths of misery. I kept this ultimate confidence within me. Whether I gave it up or not, I held this benevolent elsewhere within me.

'Why do you want to take the saffron robe?'

'Because babas show me that, whatever I will achieve, I shall not reach what I lack and they have without pursuing anything: Peace. Tranquillity, joy. Blissful laziness.'

'So, you want to take baba-life for a lifestyle and not for *moksha*?' he asked mischievously.

'For *ananda*, bliss,' I answered. 'For me you are *Ananda avatar*, the incarnation of bliss, Babaji.'

Completely insensitive towards this flattery, he asked me a hundred questions about my life…

Ananda Baba was motionless. Birds started to announce the arrival of daylight. The rooster crowed once again.

I was for him, that day, what had turned up, I thought.

The following day, he gave me a cotton bag the size of a laptop: 'You will only take what this bag can contain. And two blankets, one to lay down and the other for the body. And a plastic sheet two meters long. And a *komandalu*. No money.'

I had returned to Varanasi to find a man whom I did not know and follow him and was now facing the ultimate decision to do what I had wanted. A last glance at my credit card made me waver in my resolve.

I bought two blankets, a stainless steel *komandalu* and a long quilted sleeveless yellow Nehru jacket. I changed the two hundred dollars I had, paid my hotel and distributed twelve thousand rupees and some clothing to the beggars and the sadhus in the area. It was a feast everywhere on the *ghats*, that night. *Chillums* were handed around. I cut my credit card but kept my passport. I took two kurta-pyjama, my sandals, a sweater, two briefs, a tee-shirt, my pocket knife, a bar of soap, my toothbrush, a pen and a note book, and three small books: the *Astavakra Samhita*, the *Avadhuta Gita* and the *Bhagavad Gita*. Is it possible to live without a towel? My bag was full.

The night was split open. The orange line of dawn now separated the heavens from earth. And the darkness dissipated in a last breath of fresh wind. A red arrow of light pierced the horizon, aiming up towards the sky. Water lilies, still closed, appeared before me, green, white and pink. Behind, I could hear the whistles of the *shishya* babas proclaiming devotion to their gurus. Three long strident blows: Kaushal Baba's conch proclaimed his devotion to the Gods and announced the beginning of his *pujas*. Ananda Baba rose. We went to fetch our bags, took leave of our hosts and set off on foot, then took a collective rickshaw, then…

Part Two

Varanasi, 5 Years Earlier

had just arrived from Delhi. A powerful wave of happiness came over me when I saw the Ganges in Varanasi for the first time. There was a startling contrast between the railway station, with its crowds, its hordes of vendors barking their sales pitch to the traveller dazed by a twenty-hour journey, and the lazy, radiant and almost motionless river. Everything was calm, bathing in tranquillity, pervaded by the magnificent, generous and pleasant sun that reflected a sparkling array on the river's surface. The light of the Ganges splashed my eyes. A slight breeze carried scents of flowers, fresh water and incense. I could breathe with confidence for the first time in ages.

Varanasi is not a large city. The whole place points to the river which runs at its feet, facing the rising sun. The river was low but its width remained substantial. It formed a concave arc, a sort of bay. Over on the opposite shore where the wide, flat, virgin land is free of any buildings, the sky meets the earth unobstructed. Nothing impedes one's gaze but a few barges, which slowly make their way up and down the current.

A wide path paved with yellow stones borders the bank, on the city side. These are the *ghats*. On one side, flights of steps are lapped by the water. On the other, stairways ascend the walls which support the embankment and its palaces, ashrams and hotels. A city lays hiding behind this frontage with its tapestry of lanes, alleys and dead-ends, Hindu quarters, Muslim districts, *chowks**, bazaars and markets in a somber, muffled and damp atmosphere.

I went along upstream as far as Manikarnika ghat. There, a dozen pyres were consuming corpses which were being reduced to various states of ashes. *Ram Naam Satthya Hai!** What are they saying? The name of Ram is truth. Death is the only thing that is true, Lacan also stated. This is one of Varanasi's specialities along with silk, sitars and the Hindu University. To die in Varanasi ensures that one will be received by Shiva in his celestial paradise. You can read it in the *Lonely Planet Travel Guide*. Those who take this promise seriously, come from far away, succumbing to this last hope. Others, who are already dead, are brought here to be cremated. A one-way traffic. Dead end. Five mortal remains awaited. A *domra** was collecting ashes from a pyre to throw them into the river fifty steps downstream where seekers of gold were panning. Next please!

As for the living, other *domras* negotiate with families over the price and height of the pyres. *Coolies* carry huge heavy logs on their bare backs. Around the smallest pyres, where they know they can expect leftovers, dogs lay in wait for the right moment to nab a piece of human flesh – not too well done please! The barbers shave the heads of those in mourning; the locks of hair are swept away by the wind. The smoke of human bodies spread, tossed about by the breeze. Roast aromas upset vegetarians; but the Gods' barbecue arouses the appetites of the non-vegetarians. A dog started barking furiously at me and I cleared off.

I found a hotel in an alley near Dassawamedh ghat, the broadest and least abrupt access from the city to the river at the centre of the bay. It was a corner house which was narrow and tall in height with four storeys, five rooms per floor, a staircase on the blank wall and a square light shaft which opened onto the blue sky. It had a flat roof with a view over the Ganges.

A green double door on the second floor: this was my room. Whitewashed, yellow walls, cement floor, cord bed covered with a thin mattress and a faded floral print sheet. An iron ceiling fan hung above. The hums and sounds of the lane arose through two shutters. A view of the opposite house was afforded through three horizontal bars. No window pane. A ray of dust was levitating between the closed shutter and the window frame. Spartan, clean, cheap and well-situated.

'Where do you want to go, Ludo?' Gregory, my childhood friend, had asked me.

'To India,' I said.

'Why?'

Lying on the bed in my hotel room, my memories were transported back to France. I had spent an evening drinking a 1993 Chateau Soutard with Gregory. In his large studio, stood a bed, a long table with two computers, a black leather sofa and an armchair. Financial newspapers and magazines lay in piles on the floor. A view of Seine could be seen through a bay-window.

'To witness the living past,' I had answered, 'India is the philosopher's ancient Greece, but in the age of cell phones, Internet, jet planes, antibiotics and ATM. I'll try to find contentment with little amongst turbaned Epicuruses, stand in naked Diogenes' sunshine, discuss with Socrates-style gurus… Hindus love millions of Gods, the elements, rivers, trees, time… Apparently you can meet fire-worshippers who are descendants of Zarathoustra, Kali* sectarians – a bloody allegory of time – sacrificing goats, aboriginal animists, idolaters, polytheists, several forms of monotheisms, *avatars*, begging monks, mystical philosophers who are devoted to and teach non-dualism. Every conceivable demonstration of the sacred from time immemorial endures there. This country produces wise men and venerates them, builds them ashrams, which become schools of thought: Ramana Maharshi, Vivekananda*, Ma Ananda Moyi, Nizargadatta Maharaj…'

'India does not exist!' Gregory retorted. 'Indians say it themselves, not me. They don't believe in the reality of things.'

'That is precisely what's disconcerting. How can one not be a materialist?'

He was a junior executive for Bank Lazare. Take-over bids, hedge-funds, acquisitions, mergers, outsourcing; a mercenary of free market economics.

'By being poor!' he replied, definitive in his sensualist realism. 'And ancient Greece, without wine or sex, isn't really up to much. Wisdom is destitution! The renunciant's religion is death! Indians have an amazing tolerance for filth! Their environment is alarming. It's fatalism in the visual realm, and it pervades everything.'

I had noticed that. People who do not believe in reality have undoubtedly less motivation to maintain it. However I did find *chillum* smoking naked Diogenes, turbaned Epicuruses acquiring a following, various Socrates pontificating in orange kurtas, Antiphons that do not get attached to money, fame or love, and plenty of shaggy hairy philosophers and begging monks, a Pantheon of thirty million Gods – more symbolic than helpful – personifying a myth or a legend or designating a state of consciousness, and even crow gurus, masters in one of the world's oldest trades: robbery.

From ludo.onatrip@hotmail.com To gregory.tatelbaum@free.fr

(…)

The Delhi-Varanasi Express had stopped. My coach was suddenly empty. Two men passed in the alley. *Where are we? Allahabad. Varanasi?* Something like *further.* They took a seat on the other side of the aisle. One of them changed places, settled in front of me and, speaking in Hindi, tried to show me something through the window, on the other side of the platform. *There? No, there, look…* I did my best to understand but I could not make out exactly what he wanted me to see. The man became weary, excused himself and left. His companion had already disappeared. Answering a niggling worry which translated itself into thoughts much too slowly, I finally understood and stood up to see that the smallest of my two bags was missing on the top berth.

Never mind; I keep my money, passport and credit card in a belt that I always wear. I lost my *Lonely Planet*, some books, my watch, three bananas and my cell phone…

This morning, I had my breakfast on the roof. Chai and toast on a small coffee table facing the blue Ganges in the distant blue of the sky. Alone. Two crows landed on the balustrade, one on my left, the other on my right. They kept a respectful distance. The one on the right started making little jumps, bowed, swivelled, twisted his neck, hopped on the spot and did a little dance which intrigued this man endowed with intelligence that I am: What was he trying to tell me? Suddenly, on my left, the other flew away with a slow applause of its wings above and below it. In his beak it had… my toast.

This time I swore, but late, once again, that I would be taken in no more…

Too bad Aesop did not mention this trick in his fables. He seriously underestimated the crows.

In the Ganges plain, men live with them and have watched them for thousands of years. This performance must be known to everyone. The thieves on the Delhi-Varanasi Express and even the birds know that it can still deceive a tourist! First gurus and first teaching.

Your friend

Ludo

The following day, I woke up before dawn to take the *darshan* of the rising sun.

The *darshan*! Seeing. Feeling a breath of well-being and positivity just looking, being there, having been there.

The city was still asleep. A few regulars converged towards the river. There, in small baskets made of dried leaves, clay oil lamps glided on the river's current carrying offerings of light. Points of moving flames in the depth of night. A first ray of light pierced the horizon and then withdrew. A faint light then appeared yet was still dull. Finally, the red curve rose in the Earth's bluish fog. Half immersed in the Ganges, a small quiet crowd, hands joined in front of their chests, greeted this glorious reincarnation.

I remained on the bank.

Celebrating the rising sun is not only worship; it is also a way of life. Touched by the first rays of the sun, the skin takes on a reddish hue and radiates in return. One keeps a radiant shine which lasts all day long. Everyone goes on living his own life afterwards. Except for the sadhus who stay longer on the *ghats*. Or arrive there soon after, which was when I could speak to them.

'*Namashkaar Baba*,' I said bowing, hands joined.

The first sadhu I met was old. He was sitting on the yellow stone paving slabs. He raised his face, adjusted his glasses and answered in a shrill voice, smiling: '*Hari Om. Whherrle fllrom?*'

'France, Baba, France!' I answered, sitting down.

He did not have many teeth left but he smiled profusely. An emaciated bun gave him a kind of grey crest. He wore a red quilted sleeveless jacket. His thin and frail legs stuck out of his saffron *lungi*. He eventually told me his name, Chandrahas Baba, that he was seventy-seven and had been roaming about the roads for forty-five years. He was rather proud to have reached this age. He was heading to Badohi, and then doubtlessly to Allahabad.

'And then?'

'*Bhagwan* will tell him.'

'Tell whom? Me?'

'No, him,' he said, pointing to himself.

His chest was hollow under the sternum.

'What are you looking for, Sir?' he asked me.

'Peace,' I improvised.

'*Aaah!*' he greeted. 'And where is your home?'

'In France, France.'

He already knows where I come from, I realized at once. I probably should have answered *I live where my feet lead me* or *where I put my head to sleep…*

or *a world of appearances...* No. It would have been a lie.

'When it will be here,' began again the toothless wise man, pointing his index finger on his bony chest where the heart is, 'you will find what you seek. Live in your heart.'

'What does it mean "to live in my heart?"'

The sun started to pierce the still wet and cold morning air and warmed us up. Two barges glided on the sky-blue river. On the other side, the almost white sand bank formed a nonchalant curve.

'There is nothing outside of the heart.'

'Then, surely I must already live there,' I said, unrepentant arguer.

Chandrahas Baba smiled helplessly.

'He tells you to place your consciousness in your heart and to look at it as the source of everything,' he added staring at me in the eyes.

His gaze was neither severe nor penetrating; on the contrary, it did not go further that his pupils, as if he was embracing the entire universe in a clear, boundless and joyful love. Something like universal forgiveness. A gift.

Then, for a moment, the colour of the world changed; the sky, the Ganges, the stone wall, the passers-by, the sand bank, Chandrahas Baba, my hands... everything became orange.

I took fright and the world returned to its banality.

A few days later, at Dandi ghat, Prajeet Baba, tried on the 'where is your home?' question. I pointed my finger to my heart with a beatific air. He was surprised but resolved:

'The whole universe is the manifestation of your real Self.'

He was wearing a Santa Claus red hat decked with white edges and a pom-pom. Before leaving him, I left a ten rupee bill on his blanket. He picked up a little stone from the ground, touched it to his *mala* and then handed this talisman to me.

Sitaram Maharecht Baba was warming up under the sun after his bath. He wore an ochre cloth around his chest and a torn washed-out pink blanket as a skirt. He was forty-eight years old, squat, dark, with a weather-beaten face. He told me, in his minimal English, that his parents had died when he was eight. He was taken in by a sadhu who brought him to the Akhara of Sadatchunam Katagiri Maharaj, in Parly, Rajasthan, close to the Pakistani border. There he learnt how to repeat *mantra,* was taught some principles and evidently, although he did not say, he picked up the habit of speaking about himself in the impersonal third person singular. As a Shivaist and Naga, he did not wear underwear. 'Because Nagas are free,' he explained.

His *tapasya* was limited to leading a regular life, keeping away from greed, controlling his desires, taking *darshans* from saints and holy places, repeating his *mantra* and seeing everything as a dream.

'He does not believe in tomorrow.'

'However, each day is the tomorrow of its preceding day,' I said, stating the obvious.

'No, every day is today,' he persevered calmly.

'Were you never attracted by the householder's lifestyle?'

'No.'

'Don't you have any desire?'

'No. He is well.'

'Are you happy?'

'Yes,' he answered without hesitation. 'He is satisfied with water, chai and *chillum*. He vowed not to hold out his hand,' he added modestly. 'Who is your preferred God?'

'I believe in none,' I answered honestly.

'God is the supernatural power. The soul seeks his power.'

I came across Sitaram at various times of the day. He did not talk much nor did he have much to say. 'The soul does not dwell in this body all the time; it travels with thoughts... Death is deep sleep.' We remained quiet in front of the Ganges. Pilgrims came to share a moment with him and left him money. He was serene. And wise in his own way, a master of himself. He did not try to model his life on a particular theory. He inhabited a way of life, it seemed to me, living off whatever life brought him, each day at a time. He ate in a temple, slept in a *dharamsala*, smoked *chillum* on the *ghats*. He was a master of nonchalance. All his moments were devoted to gentleness. Lighting a *bidi*, passing the *chillum* or taking his cup to his lips, his movements were always smooth, delicate and elegant.

I met many others sadhus. Some devoted to passivity, some in love with beauty, seeing beauty everywhere, real saints or apprentice saints. Philosophers of minimalism, applying in their lives the truth their intelligence had perceived. Men whose harmonious peace was a visual elixir, a *darshan*.

I also came across simple-minded fellows or at least who appeared to me as such, and also very ordinary men dressed as monks, obsessed by the precariousness of existence or by their own self-esteem – or by the precariousness of their self-esteem – and whose philosophical or spiritual bearing was unnoticeable. They are numerous and I do not mention them. Nor the 'seekers' who complained about everything and always wanted or needed something. To them I would say: 'Everybody needs money, but you, didn't you renounce it?' Or 'I'm not the Bank of India; ask God…' 'Are you a sadhu or a beggar?' I don't talk about the chillum-babas who somewhere along the way had lost renunciation and beatitude and were now only obsessed with their hashish trafficking. *Chillum hai, Babu?* they called out carrying their closed hands and an imaginary *chillum* to their lips to mimic a great aspiration. Those who started out like this inspired me very little. Some played at being gurus but only taught things to believe in: karma, reincarnation and fear of not being fearful enough. I met men who, in retirement, gave up family and pension to obey the ancient prescription to end their life in renunciation and I guessed that they had fled from a life which had become bland. They had been craftsmen, salesmen, farmers, policemen, government employees or bandits… The latter told me that he had had enough of stealing and killing, sowing hardship and fear. He spoke of it shamelessly. He had returned what was left of his loot and had taken up wearing the fire coloured robes.

I had spotted a bookshop on Madanpur road. I read the *Avadhuta Gita* and the *Astavakra Samhita, the Teachings of Ramana Maharshi, Hindu Philosophy*, by Theos Bernard and *Hindu Mythology*, by W.J. Wilkins. This author had made a detailed description of the extremely complex and intricate Hindu Pantheon where one-and-only Gods live alongside other such Gods as well as with God couples and polygamous Gods, triad Gods and a multitude of not-one-and-only Gods. Possessing four, eight or one hundred arms, with human, animal or chimerical figures, in pleasant or terrifying, grotesque or anthropomorphous forms. I liked the Hindu Gods because they are what they should be: the enchanting vehicles of philosophical, spiritual and moral positions, characters one does not have to believe in to love.

Govinda was German, and about thirty years old. He thought of himself as an enquirer of truth and believed India favourable to spiritual life. He had settled in Radha Kund near Mathura three years earlier and had found a guru. He was planning on serving him for the next twenty years, but his master had died suddenly.

'What will you do now?'

'I'll continue to live in Krishna's land and see through his holy eyes... and love.'

He had come on a pilgrimage to Varanasi with his friend, Rama Chandra, a medical doctor, philosopher and renunciant who told me he had only ever practised medicine for free. He offered his time and skill to dispensaries and hospitals of religious foundations like Ramakrishna* Mission or Kripalu Free Hospital. He met his guru while he was studying medicine and wanted to give up the faculty to live at his feet but was ordered to obtain his diploma and marry. He said that he had experienced several times for periods of several weeks, states of unity with total oblivion of his body.

'My guru took care of me like a child. He spoon-fed me, washed my clothes, and led me to the toilets... One day, returning from a trip, he asked me whether I had already visited Ujjain. "Of course," I answered, "I was there with every being and every phenomenon since the beginning of time." I did not know what I was saying.'

'Would you be ready to give up this body this very minute or do you wish to live one minute more?' I asked him.

'I am eternity, this body is me and so is death.'

'What can you say of your experience of unity consciousness?'

'Everything is my consciousness; the guru, Brahma, Vishnu, Shiva, the universe, all is me. "I" is there only.

'During your dreams, you don't know that you are one, and yet, aren't you one, the dreamer? Ultimately, this state of oneness is "I". All comes from me. "I" is there only.

'That we are, is obvious. One does not need to remember oneself. One cannot forget oneself. This "self" is obvious. "I" is there only. "I" is self-evident. "I" is the beginning of creation. "I" is what first comes to consciousness after birth, sleep and in the universe. Everything depends on the senses, – what I see, what I hear, what I feel – except "I". "I" is one with oneness. This "I" who includes everything is all-pervading, omniscient, non-born and proof of itself. You are "I". You are eternity.

'This is the secret knowledge that my guru gave me. Very few people are ready to understand it, although it's very simple. Simple like one. There is no realization to realize, ultimately.

'A *sloka** of Mahahari says:

> All comes from me
> All is in me
> All disappears in me,
> This consciousness is reality.'

'I like this creation just as I like my dreams, most of the time,' I slipped in.

'It is me actually!' he exclaimed. 'This dream, this world, this revelation, it is me in fact. Maya means what is not. (*Ma*, "no, not", and *Ya*, "what is" or "me"). It is not what it is; it is not me. Only "I" exists. When we were children, we were afraid of the robber lurking in the shadows. He is there as long as you believe it. If you don't believe it, he is not there. "I" is there only.'

'And if there is a real robber?'

'Even the "real" robber is not. This robber can be a guest or a friend. There is only "I". Everything is my consciousness alone. "I" is there only.'

Repeated so many times, these four words became hypnotic. But I resisted hypnosis:

'If there is only me, who are you?'

'I am you. You are me. There is only one "I".'

He was very different from Sitaram Baba, much less serene and much more educated, but credible enough, however for me to try to believe in this unique "I" for a moment. '"I" is there only' is a hypothesis which carries its own proof because what I live is only lived by me; this me is the awareness I have of it. I cannot know anything other than my awareness.

This metaphysics which was taught by Plato in *The Republic* and exemplified in *the myth of the cave* is called solipsism: everything is subjective; I only have access to the reality of my mind. This projected me into an existential abyss of loneliness, but gave me no new power over myself. Where was it supposed to lead?

Govinda and Rama Chandra left Varanasi the next day.

I hired a translator through my bookstore's manager. Gurdeep, a dynamic young man, was more fluent on the register of silk and sitar than on the subtleties of states of consciousness, but I managed to speak with sadhus through him and he was helpful. I was interested in their lives before they became sadhus and I wanted to understand their way of seeing the world.

Namdev Baba had taken the saffron robe at the age of sixteen. He was destined to be married, but he felt family-life was not for him and he fled. A group of eight sadhus who walked together recognized him as the reincarnation of their master and took him for their guru. He taught them whatever he found out intuitively. One day, he met Swami Harikhan Hari, gave up his companions and followed him to learn yoga and mental concentration. He also entered the Sankaracharya's monastery at Badarinath and studied philosophy. Then he set out again and practised meditation in a cave for ten years…

'I walk alone now.'

He was a very old, thin, long man with brown skin and fuzzy eyes of misty gentleness. His long dreadlocks afforded him a scarf which made several turns around his neck. At a certain point you could see the moment his hair had turned from brown to grey. They had been grey for quite some time.

'Ask him: "What did you understand? What is there to understand?"' I told Gurdeep.

'Take anything,' he answered, 'remove its name and its form, what remains?'

I did not answer.

'This nothing that every single thing contains, this dumb and awakened state is Brahman. He is this universe: creator and created.'

As I put down a *dakshina* at his feet, he added:

'Just as the good hunter is wary of the animal fallen into his net, the wise man knows that mind is neither obedient nor reliable.'

Later, on the same day, I sat opposite a sadhu whose name I never got to know as he did not speak. This ascetic sat in an impeccable meditating posture with a straight torso, hollow belly, solemn chin and fixed eyes. His dilated gaze lost all active contact with the outside world. Present, but uninvolved. A half-smile slowly appeared on his face. This posture was his teaching. Long after I had left him, he was still completely motionless.

Ramasharvan Swami was about thirty years old and had the stature of a wizard-like visionary with his dreadlocks raining down over on his red kurta, a score of necklaces, amulets and reliquaries hanging down his neck, and dirty nails. He said: 'In the throat of the snake the frog still wishes to eat and tries to bite the snake's flesh. Whatever kind or shape of wood you have, fire will consume it.'

Even in English, I did not understand everything.

A sadhu had his face and body plastered with an ash paste which made him a white mask head to toe. The invisible man! I never saw his face and he did not speak either. Incognito for *tapasya*… Or a bandit on the run?

'*Bataiye Babaji, aapne kya paaya?* Tell me, Babaji, what have you found and what is the easiest way to reach there?' I could now say without assistance.

'This Self, (atman) is here,' Akarma Baba, a naked Naga baba, answered between two coughing fits, his index finger between his eyebrows. 'It shines like a diamond,' he assured, his eyes red from the *chillum,* with a stare like fire.

He showed me his laminated ID card, "Issued in Gangotri, state of Uttarakhand", "Name: Akarma Baba", "Address: Cremation ground."

'Shiva baba!' he added proudly pointing to his chest. *Shiva power is here, full power!* He closed his fists and stretched his arms on his knees. 'Another month, I'll go back to my ashram.'

'*Moksha?*'

'*Ananda!*'

Liberation did not concern him; he had found bliss.

'Are you a sadhu for lifestyle or liberation?'

'You choose nothing.'

Thus I went from one sadhu to another and talked with him if we shared a language or if my translator was available. I smoked *chillum* if he smoked, I took his *darshan*; I questioned his point of view and his presence. Why had he decided to give up everything to wander about? How had this great change finally come about? What had he found? Although they were not supposed to have a past, some were more open than others in talking about it, and sometimes they lit up something in me with a question or a remark.

None of them prided themselves on a having a mission to accomplish. They did not think of themselves as saints or heroes. Society's outsiders yet living alongside it, they sought something like an antidote to life, without seriously wanting to die. Some, practised *tapasya*, others dwelled in blissful laziness.

An Inclusive Logic

I was relaxing on a promontory overhanging the steps of Kedar ghat. A swami came over to me, laid down a large handkerchief and sat there before asking me the *ten standard questions*. With grey hair tied in a bun, a long face, and fair skin, Swami Nripendra must have been between 60 and 70 and wore the intellectuals' white, but worn out, *dhoti* and kurta. To the inevitable '*What is the purrrpose off your trrrip to India?*' I answered as a joke that my goal was to see God face to face.

'To see God is of no interest,' he answered very seriously. 'The goal of a man's life is *moksha*, liberation from the cycle of rebirths. If you give all your money to Swamiji, you will be instantly liberated.'

'All my money!' I exclaimed both amused and scandalized. Money does not weigh so heavily on me.

'But for *moksha*, it's nothing,' he retorted categorically. 'Do you know that you could be reborn thousands and thousands times, and not always in the ease of Western life? All the money in the world is still cheap to obtain liberation.'

'You frighten me, Swamiji. Are you liberated?'

'*Shurrrrre*. Swamiji is a *jivan-mukta* since a long time,' he assured me shamelessly.

'So you don't need money!' I scoffed at him gently.

'*Nooooo*. Swamiji does not need money,' he swore. 'Swamiji only takes your money to help you, not for himself.'

'And if I give my money to a temple or charity, will I still be liberated?' I asked slightly ingenuously.

'*Nooooo*,' he said with disgust. 'Priests are corrupted. They only worry about filling their already inflated paunch. It should be given to Swamiji,' he insisted pointing his forefinger on his rather hollow stomach. 'Swamiji can transform it into *prassad*, an offering which will destroy all your karma. You know what karma is, don't you? Our actions produce consequences…'

'Then, can I give my money to a beggar?' I interrupted.

'A beggar!' he burst out indignantly holding his nose. 'Karma must ripen. Nobody can escape it. Even Gods cannot prevent karma from ripening.'

'In this case, you neither.'

Swamiji nodded gently, realizing that he had said something silly.

'Swamiji can transform it into *prassad*,' he tried one last time.

'You won't escape your karma, which is not to receive my money! Did you ever have a client for this offer?'

'Swamiji liberated several people,' he answered, laughing.

'It is difficult to reach liberation,' I said as a dilettante philosopher.

'As difficult as to spend money…' he grumbled as a professional one.

'Did you take your meal today, Swamiji?' I inquired respectfully.

'Today?' said the swami trying to remember. 'No.'

'I would like to invite you then.'

'Swamiji is vegetarian,' he said.

He chose a restaurant run by brahmins. Food was served on banana leaves laid on sluiced down marble tables. There was no utensil to confront the mountain of steaming rice and sauces.

After this meal, Swami Nripendra told me that, forty years earlier, he had been dispossessed of his land by a dishonest relative who had forged a fake document. Ruined, he could not have married with dignity. Belonging to the caste of brahmins — and the purest caste, he specified — many jobs were prohibited to him. He had worked as a *pujari*, officiating-priest, in a small village temple. From his grimaced expression, I could guess it had not been very profitable. He then came to Varanasi and was living in a small room in the garden of a distant relative. He practised astrology, considered himself a scholar and claimed to know numerous Upanishads and the arguments of the five schools of philosophy, not to mention that he had learned the rites in his youth and could confer initiation…

'Would you like to teach me Hindi, Swamiji?'

'Yes, *offf courrrse!*' he answered beaming at me.

From then on, I took a daily Hindi lesson at about noon in the shade of one of Annapurna ghat's parasols.

I knew some Sanskrit words I had gleaned in books — *karma, dharma, advaita, darshan, moksha…* — and sometimes I found them in conversations with sadhus, but I could not ask for a glass of water, the price of a meal or someone's name. I soon started to grasp the construction of a sentence, recognized nouns, adjectives and pronouns, and was able to ask simple questions: '*Usaka ghar kahaan hai?* His house where is?' The word order is more or less the opposite of French, and there are no articles like in English. Thus one says 'Large red teapot table on is.' The vowel "a" has four pronunciations: "a" so aspirated that one does not hear it, an "a" which is almost "ai", an "a" so totally emphatic as in ass and an "a" doubled making an "aa" sound.

When I had had enough of studying declensions, I asked questions on other subjects.

'Why are Hindu philosophers so set against ego? How can I deny "I"!'

'Ego thinks he is the chief, the master, whereas he is only a function,' explained Swamiji. 'The brain acts in four different ways; it has four functions: *manas*, *buddhi*, *chitta* and *ahamkara.*'

Under the parasol next to ours, a bare-chested brahmin, wearing his ostentatious caste thread, was giving an astrology consultation to a woman, with her head leaning forwards under a green veil.

'The five senses bring information to *manas* (the mind or the mental activity) which, like a sixth sense, selects them, rejects or accepts them, and transforms them into ideas. During dreams, the senses are withdrawn into the domain of the mind which then creates sensory objects within itself.'

'Ok.'

'*Buddhi* carries out the duty of judging, analysing and deciding, and *chitta* is the dynamic memory necessary for mental activities and associations. *Chitta* brings memories or the known to the present moment.'

'*Ahamkara*, – *aham*, me, *kara*, which acts – our feeling of individuality produced by the mind, the intellect and the memory, is a function in the brain; it is not a subject.'

'What am I without me?'

'*Manas* creates the idea "I" in a situation. There is an instrument of knowledge and imagination but no author to this knowledge.'

With Swami Nripendra and the sadhus, the *ghats* of Varanasi were at times like an ancient open-air university. But the lanes of the bazaars offered a very different adventure. Nothing but solicitations. *Hallo, Hallo...* trying to draw my attention to his store: mineral water and postcards. *Sir, sir...* selling saris, *Here my shop...* tried to intercept me whilst pointing out bronze idols while somebody behind me was chanting away with a deep voice *charas, ganja, brown, coke, luds, amphetamine… Hajiii!!* the cycle rickshaw slapped the bench of his mount with his opened hand. *Hun! Hun!* insisted the *pujari* directing his gaze towards his offerings plate. *Baksheesh, baksheesh…* on a roller-board, a legless cripple with baseball cap and sunglasses begged for alms. *Baksheesh, baksheesh…* a one-armed man. *Baksheesh…* a child holding out his hand with a facial expression painted in feigned utter misery… *What's your name? First time in India? Change? Good price, dollar, yen, euro. Here my shop. Excuse-me… What do you want? Wherrrre fllromm? Wherrrre fllromm?*

Longing to go unnoticed, I went to a tailor and ordered two kurta-pyjamas, an outfit made of a long shirt with a Nehru collar and fine white cotton trousers. Then gradually the shopkeepers became resigned and spared this Western tourist who did not go home and never bought anything from them.

From ludo.onatrip@hotmail.com To gregory.tatelbaum@free.fr
(…)
Those who live in the street are folding the plastic sheets they use as a roof. On over a hundred meters children are shitting in the gutters. A young girl leaves a cardboard house, as fresh as dawn in her immaculate school uniform. Women prepare chai between three bricks on camp fires fed with plastic bags under the shade of a gigantic film poster – a smooth faced hero and a scar-faced baddie facing each other and grimacing, with a fearful young girl in the background. Life is hard. And threatening.

Shopkeepers arrange their displays which encroach greatly on to the pavements. The kitchenware retailer sweeps in front of his door and pushes the dust just a little further away. Gathering it seems out of the question.

A sweeper in a red flowered sari puts down her wheelbarrow at the foot of a street light; she holds the *pallu** of her sari with her left hand, seizes her broom of branches with her right hand, searches the heap of refuse with undecided gestures, but does not find anything worth leaning over for any further. The sparrows seem jubilant. The milkman arrives on his motorbike loaded with six milk-churns, stops in front of the chai stall and counts out three measures of fresh milk. Beggars settle side by side and are already testing their tall stories of poverty on the first onlookers. The cycle-rickshaw who spent the night hunched on the bench of his mount, stretches and goes to piss, squatted in the gutter. And he is already assailing the passers-by…

It's six o'clock, Varanasi is waking up.

At the hairdresser's, in restaurants, at the doctor are the omnipresent garish representations of Shiva, Kali, Vishnu, Rama, Krishna, and a few dozen other incredibly kitsch superstar Gods in eighteenth century Maharaja style with silk brocades and pearl necklaces, or in low-relief, 1000 years BCE style with loincloths and bows. These Gods pose, framed and garlanded, beside the portraits of fathers and grandfathers who are also Gods by merit of genitors. At the entrance of a sari store, Ganesha, the elephant-headed God, in white marble, is honoured with a garland of fresh marigolds with rose petals spread around the floor. He is smiling.

Before opening, a restaurant owner brings her employees together to an image of Lakshmi*, the Goddess of wealth, printed on an advertising calendar – courtesy of Jay Shree Tea Industry Ltd. – hanging behind the cash box. Beside her, Krishna plays flute for Radha, sponsored by Sign and Neon Co. After a short ceremony, she lights the stoves with the flame from her sacred lamp.

A small trade economy of minor exchanges and modest services fills the streets. A bucketful of peanuts with a few pieces of newspaper to wrap them in make a livelihood. A bathroom scale, a telephone on a stool or a pile of books and a few posters on the pavement and one has a business. An aluminium trunk chained up to a tree contains industrial chewing tobacco and a few cigarette packets: it's a shop for commerce. A man buys the plastic and jute sacks from rice merchants to resell and thus provides for a family. Chopped tobacco leaves, branches of *neem* used as tooth brushes, some bananas on a cloth – one manages to survive.

In a corner, on flattened cardboard, an itinerant orthodontist practises his art with, for laboratory, a pot of carmine resin, a couple of dental moulds with emaciated smiles, a bucketful of water, and a kerosene stove from which, with a pair of pliers, he pulls out a very pink denture with gleaming white teeth.

In front of the Law Courts, public writers listen to their clients typing on old Remingtons, using carbon paper.

A little touristic interlude.

From your friend
Ludo

I spent my evenings with sadhus gathered in small groups around a fire, beyond Asi ghat, downstream at the end of the bay of Varanasi. Many smoked *chillum*, but not all of them. Most spent the cold season on the plains but lived in the mountains for the remainder of the year.

I would go back during the day. I was fascinated by their peace, their dispassionate nature, their undaunted easy going confidence, their faith.

Their benefactors were regular visitors who passed by, bowed deeply and were invited to be seated on a newspaper or a jute sack... They came, as I did, to glean some of their cheerful serenity, have a taste of their peace, and smoke holy grass. And they left a little money before leaving.

I did not play the role of a quivering devotee, and they did not play the omniscient guru. We watched each other simply being. They liked me. I questioned them on their life before, on their quest or on a philosophical issue. Or I listened to whatever they felt like saying: they would then offer me a *darshan* of words.

I liked to ask them, out of curiosity and touch of irreverence: *Are you in it for the lifestyle or for moksha?* Most of them did not practise extraordinary *tapasya* nor did they make particular efforts of any sort. There, I met other Westerners who took part in this "blissful laziness" as Dyan had said, a young Israeli who was wise in the easy going way of a man who knew how to have a good life with little.

My daily sunrise session put me in a good mood. And at times I tried to live in my heart.

It was a hot night. There were five of us around a camp fire: three hairy babas and a forty-five year old middle-class man who had the air of an early retired man. The small flames were dancing to the rhythm of their own murmuring. A few steps away, the Ganges lapped softly against two rowing boats squeaking at their moorings.

'Real, not different; different, not real,' summarized Monish Baba, preparing a *chillum*.

Then, he handed me his match box, and solemnly upheld the pipe in front of him... In the distance, dogs were barking their territorial *mantra* with determination, cicadas were making their incessant flirtatious shrills, stars and satellites were winking at each other while Chandra Shankar, the benevolent Shiva in the form of a moon crescent leaning on the Earth watched this half naked man on the banks of his holy river, in front of his holy fire, raising a *chillum* in his honour: *Bom, Shankar!*

I struck two matches.

'Give everything whilst smoking this *chillum*,' he said interrupting his gesture. He sucked several times at the pipe through his closed hands before drawing up a long and full puff which filled his lungs right up to his eyes and then enveloped him in an aura.

One needs to have a throat like cast iron to inhale from this torch with such conviction.

Cannabis gave me a state of mindful awareness: a feeling of peacefulness in an attentive wakeful state, comparable to the combined effect of caffeine and nicotine, but longer. At the same time, thoughts became concentrated and enlarged; agile. This simultaneous centrifugal and centripetal effect was increased with a higher dose. Impressions were amplified. And at times in this joyful merry-go-round, doubts, misunderstandings and paranoia also tried to intervene. Candour, humour and self-mockery as well. There were blissful states. Letting-go often came about naturally.

'It is from renouncing everything within you that renouncing appearances happens,' said Monish Baba a little later.

'Renouncing what is within me would be like calling myself a liar and making a principle of it!' I answered.

He burst out laughing. Then approved:

'"I" is a liar no matter what he says. You are right.'

'So then who says that? One cannot say "I am a liar" without lying.'

'"I" is not a liar, it is a lie.'

Between two *chillums*, my companions also discussed the merits of the latest cell phones, complained about rising prices, reminisced about their guru or a Holy city they had visited, told stories of Shiva's prowess in an epic episode or suggested a state of consciousness… *If it is different from you, it is not real.* Or of happiness… *Ganga Ma!* exclaimed this son of a river with gratitude, standing to salute mother Ganges. Or of surrender… *So' am*, I am *That*, or on the contrary… *Neti neti, I am not that*, remembered Akarma Baba, a Naga baba clothed by the wind. As for me, I asked questions:

'If birth is caused by karma, how could the first birth ever occur whereas there was no former action?' I asked one of them one day. 'How did karma begin?'

'Birth is that of non-knowledge; knowledge puts an end to it,' answered this scholar.

'What happens when knowledge is reached?'

'It is a world without birth.'

Sometimes I fantasized living like this. Wandering and begging with one of these philosophers… *to realise the real self or to know what's beyond the beyond, find the exit door, spend one's life sitting, observing Being in all things or the Creator in oneself…* I belonged to those for whom idleness was a taboo and work a value! *Perhaps not forever…* I then re-negotiated with myself. *Renunciation is for depressives*, I would then consider with great lucidity. But I began to catch a glimpse of the virtuous aspect of laziness, as well as its ecological and political dimensions. It's not "working more to be able to consume more" that makes life an exciting adventure; it ruins the world and leads it to its doom, and makes us live outside of life. Working less, much less and taking slowness as an aim allows oneself to return several times a day to the awareness of being alive. My fantasy became a debate that I did not take very seriously. *I will die in three days time!* I always concluded with conviction.

At fourteen, Mahavir Baba went on a pilgrimage to Amarnath, in Kashmir and met his guru. Five months later, he left his family to follow him. He was thirty-one, had a brother who was a doctor and a sister who was a history teacher; his father was a salesman in Assam.

'What does your family think of your way of life?'

'There is no problem. Baba-life is as difficult and meaningful as being a doctor or a professor. I learned a lot.'

'But didn't they try to dissuade you?'

'No. It is not for this body to stay at the same place. This life, this rebirth, is for being a sadhu-baba,' he said pointing at himself. 'I walk. I travel from place to place.'

Veer Devadutt came from Kolkata and lived under a tree near Asi ghat. He wore a white kurta and pyjamas and had short hair. He was a renunciant but did not belong to any lineage.

'My father left my mother for another woman when I was ten,' he told me in very decent English. 'In 1969, I was a depressed teenager. I did not find a meaning to life and I was afraid of death. I could not concentrate; at school, I had bad marks. I could not sleep any more. I prayed to God to grant me sleep. In order to relieve me of my depression and my fear of death, my sister gave me some *bhang lassi**. I took three glasses of this curd drink mixed with fresh cannabis. And then, I saw the God without a face. A light. And I spoke with

God. I then gave up college and I studied music. In 1979, I read *The First and Last Freedom* by Krishnamurti. Before that, I had many questions about God. Afterwards, I knew moments without thoughts. In 1985, silence came but the mind was still working unconsciously. I felt a kind of drought in my head.'

Veer Devadutt was about fifty now. He had been employed as a *bhajan** singer in a temple at Haridwar where *Hari Krishna Hari Krishna* resounds 24 hours a day. 'Two hours singing plus two hours being there, two thousand rupees a month,' was how he summed it up. He had left this job to come to Varanasi and gave Hindi lessons to an American for 50 rupees per hour. He took his meals in a temple and slept in the street, close to the gate. He sent what he earned to his mother who lived with his sick brother and his three children. He said that benefactors provided him with everything he needed.

'Before meditation, you are in a cage. Afterwards, you are free.'

He practised the meditation Krishnamurti taught:

'First, I examine my surroundings thoroughly. Then, I close my eyes. Questions arise within me: What am I doing? What should I do? They are thoughts. They pass. They die. If a desire arises, I look at it. It is a thought. Desires die out rapidly if the mind does not get involved. Remain motionless. No aspiration, no goal. Look. Watch. Observe. No identification. No judgements. Do nothing. Only observe. Contemplate all things without acceptance or denial. Watch the activity of the mind.'

As I was about to leave, he added: 'I am not a saint. I told you my story so that you stop doubting.'

If sitting, looking at Ganges for an hour or two and letting my thoughts wander about at the same slow pace as the river current was pleasant for me, remaining motionless like Veer Devadutt observing his mind for hours seemed impossible. It is not for this body to remain without moving, Mahavir baba had told me. Perhaps not for me either.

———

At Ranamahal ghat, six small *lingam mandirs* line the staircases that ascend the walled bank. They open laterally and all are dedicated to the *lingam*. With a shawl hung up in front of the opening, a sadhu had transformed one of them into a cave, a niche, his hermitage.

One day, I sat before one of the long upright black stone which symbolizes Shiva, the universe, desire, erection, everything and the whole... I did not get time to consider much as someone was already calling me.

'Sir... Sir...'

I did not answer. '*Sir-sir*' he insisted a little, then sat down on the steps and waited. In a start of impatience and frustration, and of hope, he whispered: '*Pray for me.*'

I invited Shiva of which the *lingam* represents power, to take a little more care of his world and to show some particular concern for this man. It was a kind of experiment. A challenge perhaps...

A young man of Indian origin but obviously living in the West passed-by. A fashion-victim travelling the country of his ancestors. Rich for those who can recognize Versace, Prada and Dolce & Gabbana. *Sir-sir* spoke to him in a low voice. The young man answered. His eyes met mine but I expressed nothing. At the end of this conversation, he handed him a banknote and went away. *Sir-sir* waited a little, and then bowed in my direction: *Thank you*. He still hesitated, then descended the steps and disappeared. The sadhu who lived on the other side of the steps graced me with a smile.

In this country, one takes a placid man for a saint, I thought. And he thinks I make miracles! But I had discovered something: *active immobility*, an oxymoron and perhaps an attribute of God, and a marvel. This out-of-the-ordinary nature of passivity transforms it into an act which affects those who witness it. Much later I understood that when one stays still, one observes, and what else is it than one's own consciousness. But those who believe themselves to be observed are also observing themselves. A passive witness reminds everyone to observe their own awareness. But at that time, there was still a very powerful "me" in me who wanted to analyse the incident and include himself in it.

I went to Dassawamedh ghat to take a chai. '*Wherrre flrrom?*' a sadhu asked me who had been waiting for someone to offer him one. I ordered two.

'France, Baba.'

'*Main bhi, France thirty nine–forty six.*'

'Ha! The 39-45 War! And you?'

'Kerala. Agra gone?'

'No. Not Agra.'

He was toothless and difficult to understand. But it was not long before he was saying: 'God is in oneself,' pointing a finger to his heart, then confirmed: 'God is everywhere because he is here.' He added, with his finger on his temple, 'Maya there.'

Maya! A theory which leads us to take reality as a kind of dream, an illusion! A misunderstanding. It does not motivate one to try to change things. I ran to seek Gurdeep, my translator.

'Tell him: Can one seriously try to believe that the world is not real? Aren't you seized by the cold when you get into Ganges to take your bath? Even if you know that maya deceives you, you are cold; the cold water has an undeniable reality. Your body reacts a great deal in its contact.'

'He says: Cold is a sensation. This body feels cold water and reacts. What is real, the cold water or the sensation of cold water?'

'The cold water is real and it causes a real reaction.'

'He says: To whom has it been caused?'

'To this body, to this man, this living sensitivity...'

'He says: He has finished bathing now. He is not cold.'

A man sat down with us.

'Do you really believe that the world is an illusion?' I asked him.

'No. I live like you,' he answered.

At our noon Hindi lesson, I questioned Swami Nripendra on the subject:

'Everything exists in simultaneous states of reality. The world exists and does not exist. It does not exist only as you think it does. It has another way of existing which you cannot see. Maya is the ungraspable multitude of meanings of things.'

I read in the *Avadhuta Gita*:

> There is no distinction between physical forms.
> "I" and "you" and the world have never existed.
> Cause and effect are not distinct,
> How can one conceive pain or pleasure?
> Indivisible bliss is everywhere equal to One.

If A is cause of B, B is not cause of A. This exclusive, binary, Aristotelian logic is comforting and practical. It describes a rather well-ordered world and allows us, among other wonders, to fly airplanes and manufacture potent drugs. My renouncing philosophers and their books subscribe to an inclusive logic: If A is the cause of B, B can also be the cause of A. And neither A nor B cause of anything. From which one may conclude: 'The world exists and does not exist, neither you nor me has ever existed. Cause and effect are not distinct. How can one conceive pain or pleasure?'

This succession of confidently stated questionable assertions, which deny the whole or part of reality (the world, you, me, sorrow, cause and effect, distinction...) and some of the answers the sadhus had given me made my logical mind rebel. They created a resistance within me but also produced an unlocking effect – an awakening to the possibility of another world. A world where everything is possible.

I was having dinner in a small open front restaurant on the broad and clear avenue leading to Dassawamedh ghat. The cook was standing bare-chested in front of two large pots of rice and *daal*, a basin of bread dough covered with a white cloth and his *tandoori* smoking coal vapours. Recently whitewashed walls, a few white marble topped tables, wood benches…

A man of about thirty years old, entered.

'Two *chapatis* and nothing else!' he ordered putting down his bag on a bench. He left and then returned with a bundle of chervil and ordered the cook to wash it.

He was wearing white *lungi* and kurta; he had combed back, oiled hair and small round glasses.

'Go and buy a lump of butter as well,' he ordered again. 'It's my meal.'

He finally ate his chervil and his two *chapatis* covered with butter while I kept observing him.

'What is *bhakti* yoga?' he suddenly asked me when he had finished.

'Devotion to love,' I answered because I had read it somewhere.

He examined me with surprise, then began again:

'What is *jnana** yoga?'

'Awareness of the unity of all things.'

'But so is *bhakti*,' he refuted.

My book had not anticipated this objection. Swami Aditya Anantanshu presented himself as a doctor of Sanskrit and grammarian, former disciple of Osho, and ordered a glass of milk.

'*Bhakti*,' he added, 'is the surrender of personal desires for God's desires. *Jnana*: no more desire. *Bhakti* is a movement of liberation towards the exterior; *jnana*, towards the interior. Sit with your back straight and close the doors of desires.'

'Have you taken your desires for enemies?' I asked him.

'Desires are thoughts.'

He closed his eyes and remained motionless, as if posing in a cosmic inspiration.

'All that appears to *manas*, the mind, is *manas* itself,' he stated. 'There is no other reality. If *manas* is established in peace and simplicity, the Self appears as *sat*, being–existence–reality, *cit*, consciousness–awareness, and *ananda*, bliss.'

'What do you mean by mind?'

'It is perception, cognition, will, imagination, judgement, reason, comprehension, memory, etc.

'Let's take a moment to digress. Since life has acquired intellectual means, it questions whether there is a reality and what that would be. With Plato, philosophy opposed a reality which is distinct from the mind with a reality apprehended according to our representations. The myth of the cave illustrates that we only perceive a fragment of reality. Reality is an idea. Protagoras thought that men can only know their perception of things and not the things themselves.

'Kant favoured *the thing-in-itself*: there cannot be phenomena without anything appearing; but the *thing-in-itself* is unknowable, beyond any sense knowledge. What understanding lets us glimpse of the *thing-in-itself* is the relationship it has with the sentient world. Schopenhauer compared the *thing-in-itself* to *will*: every thing in this world is an expression of *will* according to the principle of reason. Berkeley believed that consciousness cannot conceive what it is not, nor think what it is radically opposed to or exterior to: 'All things are the object of a thought and are therefore within the mind.' That is what the Indian Patanjali (between 250 BC and 400 AD) also said: 'What appears to the mind and disappears in the mind is none other than the mind itself.' 'There is a correlation between consciousness and the world which appears,' thought Merleau-Ponty. 'Is there an *appeared-in-itself* distinct from who this *appeared* appears to? Or is there an *appeared-in-itself* and what appears to me?' wondered Bergson. However, one cannot experience an *appeared-in-itself* because who would this appear to? answered his critics. 'What is known is not anything other than knowledge,' added Narayana Guru to this concert in the 19th century. 'Even accepting that the known has a reality, without knowledge, it would not be. There is not anything anywhere apart from knowledge. Me is what is known as knowledge. And everything that is, is included in knowledge just like during dreams.'

'One can look at the problem a little differently and from three points of view.

1. The outside world has no real existence. There is only me. This position is called solipsism: everything is subjective; I only have access to the reality of my thoughts.

2. The opposing view is that the outside world exists. There is myself and other. This is the position held by dualists for Indians and empiricists for the Greeks.

3. Between them, there is neither me nor an outside world. "I", the ego (*aham*), does not exist. There is no other either. This is the non-dualist position. The One, transcendent and immanent Oneness principle only exists. Everything else is its illusion.'

Swami Anantanshu explained…

'What exists at the beginning, in the middle and at the end is considered real. Everything else is not…'

Slowly and enjoying it, but in one gulp, he drank up his glass of milk. Then burped.

'There are four kinds of objects in the universe,' he began again. 'The first have only a name: the son of a barren woman, the horns of a hare. The second have a name and a form but exist only at the beginning: the mirage of an oasis, a rope which one takes to be a snake which disappears when it is more closely examined. The third have a name and a form but can only be found in the middle: a pot is clay at the beginning, and when it is broken, it does not exist any more. A cloth is made of woven threads. At the beginning, it is threads; in the end, it becomes threads again. The thread is made of twisted cotton fibre. And when the fabric is burnt, even the cotton does not exist any more. What does not exist at the beginning and in the end does not hold a real existence in the middle either.

'The fourth object is Brahman or the Self. It is without form, eternal, and exists without modification at the beginning, the middle and in the end. It is indivisible, free, non-dual, infinite, all-pervading, etc. Brahman is the only reality. It is Being in each of our four states of consciousness: the waking state, dreaming, deep sleep and *samadhi* (unified, non-dual consciousness).'

'Brahman, this fourth object, is perhaps like the first type which only has a name!' I refuted.

'No. It is different. Something cannot appear from nothing. It is what is not nothing without being something.'

'Let us suppose,' I consented. 'Does *Avidhya*, ignorance, have a real existence since nothing has?'

'*Avidhya* is non-knowledge of the underlying eternal reality. Like maya, it is neither real nor non-real. It is a quality, an attribute of Being. It is without a beginning, but it has a middle because we experience it and it has an end: it disappears with knowledge of the eternal self.'

'How can something be without a beginning?'

'Anything that roots its existence in a cause exists only in the middle. It does not have a beginning because before it was something else. The cause of a pot is infinite: clay, water, the potter, his mother and father, his work, the oven, fuel, etc. There is a pot when clay is baked in that form. But only then.'

If things do not exist, where can we stand up? I did not see the point. I wanted to resist this vision of the world which denies the world... I took the problem differently.

'How could Brahman, which is infinite, indivisible and free, become a limited and ignorant being like me?' I started again.

'It never became you other than in the illusion of the dualistic separation of subject and object.'

'Swamiji, you are not answering!' I objected. 'How did this separation occur?'

'It appears with the assertion "me" or "I am this body". The seed of this body is the mind. It is the mind which creates the illusion that you have a body in the sphere of non-knowledge. The world as well as the limited individual are an overprinting of maya on Brahman, just like the snake which arises as mental appearance on the rope. Only *sat*, Being, the eternal and unchanged One, can be taken as real in this universe.[1]'

'But for the illusion of a snake to be possible, there must be a rope, a real rope,' I insisted.

'The real rope exists only in the middle, like a pot. Brahman is the essence or the background of the sense activities, of the world of names, forms and opposites, of the realm of ideas and concepts. It is *he* to whom that occurs.'

'It is precisely to me that it occurs. And it is because this "me" exists that it happens to him.'

'You said it yourself, me is him. This single Being is like the screen in a cinema. The screen alone is stable; the movie is a projection of images on the only stable thing: the screen.'

'Without film and light, there is no movie,' I objected.

'You do not see them, you forget them.'

'I also forget the screen.'

---

1 Being and real have the same word in Sanskrit: sat.

'But you look at it all the time, without seeing it.'

'Without the movie, the screen is of no interest!' I still opposed.

'The interest is the subjective aspect of the movie. Concentrate on what is stable, the screen. What is this screen in yourself that makes it possible to grasp sensations?'

'And if I mistake a snake for a rope, pick it up and get bitten and die...'

'You die, so what! You are only a thought. Your thoughts die all the time!'

Of course! And this modesty imposed to my vanity did put things into perspective and appeased me.

Later, in *The Teaching of Ramana Maharshi* I read: 'The world and the mind appear together and disappear together.' So what does remain when they disappear? I wondered.

We cannot separate a subject from a universe, nor the observer from the observed, observed quantum physics, nor really know the phenomenon we are trying to study because observing them alters them. The observer influences and modifies the object he perceives, and it is probable he also makes it up! Our apprehension of reality is immediately polluted by thoughts, judgements, and a whole backlog of knowledge, mental systems and classifications with the purpose of recognizing more than knowing. And reality becomes invisible, warns the Hindu philosopher.

I went to the cybercafe to learn some more by surfing the web. I found: http://www.sanatansociety.org/hindu_gods_and_goddesses/shiva.htm. This article made me understand that Shiva is not always the same Shiva. The inclusive logic was everywhere, on Earth as in the Heavens.

Shiva, 'the benevolent', can have up to 1008 names: Bhairava, the dreadful; Kapalamalin, carrier of skulls; Triambaka, the one with three eyes... He is also called Mahakala – Time which destroys everything. He is both kind and terrible. He personifies perfect knowledge, the interior fire which burns ascetics, death, life and regeneration.

He is worshipped from North to South India, although one does not give him the same aspect nor the same rank in the metaphysical hierarchy.

In the North and for sadhus, Shiva is given the figure of a meditating ascetic, a third eye opened between the eyebrows. He is then known as Yogiraj, the perfect yogi, motionless ten thousand years on Mount Kailash.

He is also shown half male half female, merging with Vishnu. Or surrounded by his wife Parvati and his two sons Ganesha and Ayyappa dressed like Maharajas. Or associated with Shakti, his consort, which is none other than himself as a power to manifest a reality. One sees him everywhere in the form of the lingam, an erected phallus which symbolizes nameless, formless creative energy beyond time, transformation, birth and death.

In some Puranas, he is creator of Vishnu and Brahma.

As part of the Brahma-Vishnu-Shiva trimurti*, he is destruction following creation and maintenance. In Varanasi, in his role of Lord of the universe, Vishvanah is a personal divinity somewhat similar to the God of Jews, Christians and Muslims, unique, omnipotent and omniscient Creator, master of Justice, but he differs in that his creation is not external to him. By play – his leela* – he creates forms, phenomena, events and even individuals who believe themselves different from him. Everything is him. Shiva is absolutely transcendent and yet also all-pervading. The doctrine of non-dualism (advaita) makes it possible to unite what is conflicting.

In the South of the sub-continent, Shiva is worshiped as Nataraja*, 'the Lord of dance' because his steps are cosmic.

Kashmiri Shivaism and philosophers regard him as a name for the impersonal Absolute, synonymous with nirguna Brahman, without attributes, formless, beyond being and non-being, symbol of non-dualism and of Turiya, the fourth state of consciousness transcending the three others (waking state, sleeping and dreaming).

As I was at the cybercafe, I sent a mail to Gregory…

From ludo.onatrip@hotmail.com To gregory.tatelbaum@free.fr

(…)

I have left my room and moved into a small *mandir*! The one in which I once asked Shiva to take care of a beggar. There are three of them partially opened on each side of the stairs going up the wall at Ranamahal ghat. A sadhu occupies one of them. I chose the residence opposite and, like him, I have hung a shawl to close the side opening of this urban cave. I bought a quilt and laid it down in the depth, behind the *lingam*. This dark and fresh stone den is an unusual but very pleasant room. It is only ten steps away from the Ganges and is rent free.

Rujul Baba, my neighbour, is an extremely discrete, very gentle short man. He seldom speaks and never answers direct questions. He is about forty, has a beard, moustache and long hair and performs a particular *tapas* I do not really understand the meaning of. There is a repetition of a ceremony a great number of times, a kind of penance or redemption to please a God, exonerate an error, erase a sin or remove a bad habit. This sort of thing... He puts an enthusiastic zeal in it, sure that later he will be free of this. And he will then resume his aimless roaming.

For now he only moves to go take his bath. I buy food and dry cow dung for fuel, Rujul Baba cooks for two. For shower and toilets, I have made arrangements with the Ellena's lodge, just up the steps.

Before dawn, the muezzin of Gyanvapi *masjid** invites the devotees to hurry to instil the day with praises to the glory of its Creator. Then, the smaller mosques compete with decibels. In a round. A little later I attend the rising of the sun on the river. The first neighbours also arrive. Naked young children and women in sari on one side, men and boys on the other, in underwear. A brotherly discretion.

Each sun rise is a different sight and a new salutation to ones' own life. It feels like a rebirth with the awaited light honoured wholeheartedly.

The devotees take some water from the Ganges in their joined hands and pour it back in offering. Unity is offered and received.

The boys mutually spray themselves to compel each other towards courageousness. Buffaloes roam in search of thrown away garlands of flowers offered to the Gods of the area the day before.

I go take my first chai at the chai-shop set on the *ghats*.

Seated out of the way on one of the promontories, which overhangs the Ganges, a motionless sadhu contemplates. Blanket and bag on shoulders, three bearded and turbaned sadhus walk at the pace of resolute travellers. *Hari Om. Ram Ram*. The rising mist catches the light and diffuses it. One is dazzled from all sides. Without hesitation or remorse, a client drops his plastic cup at his feet. While I drank my chai, at least seven ways of tying a turban on one's head passed in front of me.

I have been meeting renunciant philosophers. You were right, they do not believe in the existence of the world.

In this religion, Gods are many but Being is only one, and is called Brahman or otherwise. It is impersonal, and the consciousness of the impersonal. The impersonal made life, movements, events, me, without ceasing to be impersonal. It is Oneself in itself and is all-pervading, omnipresent and immortal because it is without form; it is energy and substance, mind and manifestation before such distinctions. It is simultaneously the author and witness of everything.

This metaphysics does not need to invoke a God to compose a Genesis. The origin of reality is interpretation. And the beginning of interpretation is the noun and the adjective. This reminds me of Epicurus: 'It is always from opinion that error arises.' Or Marcel Duchamp: 'This is *not* a urinal.'

To understand the impersonal, one must experience it and there are methods for this: making efforts to see everything as an embodiment of oneself… Or like Epicurus again, adapting to the world as it is. Living in one's heart because there is nothing outside that. Directing one's consciousness to see all and everyone as one. Or removing name and form to everything to discover a dumb and awakened state. Or, like the Stoics, seeing the whole of the universe present in each part of it. Finding that, which was never born. Discovering the player whose game is the universe… Losing oneself in the present moment… Conceiving oneself as a fiction.

My Philosophers don't drink wine, but *chillums* favourably replace fermented beverages and there are no hangovers.

I have been reading. Ramana Maharshi, the Isa Upanishad in three English translations, Naipaul, *One million revolts*, Ramdas' *Pilgrimage notes*, a merchant who gave up his business and left for the roads penniless but with an intense desire to meet God. "The worshipped and the worshipper are separate and are one only. God is also his disciple, although he pretends to be different…" He was a love-crazed man who found love in everything and Ram in everyone.

At noon, at the parasol we agreed upon, I take my Hindi lesson with the wonderful Swami Nripendra who makes me repeat syllables very precisely – *Aap chai chahte hain?* Do you want tea? Is the train on time? *Kya gadi thik samay par hai?* Please excuse my incorrect pronunciation: *Mere ashuddh uchcharan.* But try to say this one correctly! We prefer to quickly move on to commenting on the Upanishads.

Your friend
Ludo

During my Hindi lesson, I saw a yogi wearing a minimal G-string practising postures of his art. He was doing headstands for long periods, he raised himself up on his hands, his head between his crossed legs; he was producing a bridge with his body tilted backwards… A snake like swelling ran up the length of his spinal cord.

'Maya is the manifestation of Brahman, the only consciousness,' explained Swami Nripendra that day. 'The unique absolute is One, but it exists as multiple appearances. An individual's consciousness is either united to Oneness – that is *samadhi* (gathering), or is overtaken by a fascination for the motions of the many. When this consciousness sees all as One in the idea and this One as all in becoming, it is said to be *vidhya*, conscious awareness.'

I was not attracted to the physical exercises of the yogi. I had more affinities with the *jnana marga*, knowledge of ultimate reality by means which do not exclude the intellect. I understood that it was about maintaining consciousness in a kind of fundamental and unifying point of view – a *Weltanschauung*, a comprehensive conception of the world – whose promise is bliss, *ananda*, nirvana and the ultimate youpi![2]

---

2 Youpi: French word equivalent for Yahoo! or Yippee!

Naresh, Laurie, Jane and Others

Naresh was completing a doctorate in Philosophy at Varanasi Sanskrit University. He stayed at Swami Krishnachandra Vedanta Ashram to work on his thesis in a quiet place but, in reality, it was to delay his return home to Bengal. I met him one evening in a circle of sadhus at Asi ghat. We sat apart from the others so we could have a chat. He liked to spend time with babas but did not smoke and was not in the slightest way a renunciant. He preferred to consider life through the prism of sex and pleasure.

He was tall and lean with the fair chestnut skin of high caste Indians, close shaven with his black vaselined hair parted in a precise line to the left, broad forehead, long face, intelligent gaze and a copious smile on his fleshy red lips; he wore the brahmin's *janehyu** – the three threaded string under his white, very fine cotton kurta.

'Your monotheistic religions have conditioned you to think of God on a prudish sexless high plane,' he stated. 'Even Christ, who is a man, is prized for his celibacy. As if sex comes under the order of good and evil, and is incompatible with the sacred! Our religion does not scorn sensuality. Indian Gods are sexed. They are sovereign in restraint, not in abstinence. Krishna made love to thousands of women and we sing his praises. Our symbol of the universe is the *lingam*, a phallus, erection, desire, the source of everything.'

'Foreigners come to India thinking that renunciation is the only Hindu truth,' he continued. 'They arrive hopeful to meet a Ramana Maharshi, Aurobindo, Ma Ananda Moyi… *Sanatana dharma* presents two paths for liberation: asceticism, the goal of which is the extinction of the senses, and the *tantric** path, which focuses on the transformation of sensory events into means of knowledge. Transcendence is reached through the immanent. Everything is an incidence of liberation. Vice and virtue dissolve. One does not want to liberate oneself from the world; one finds liberation within the world.'

'So what exactly is one liberated from then?'

'Do you have to invent sin to arouse desire?'

'And to create a sinner and guilt at the same time… I hope not.'

'Liberation from prejudices, then.'

'Excellent! You are a remarkable rhetorician.'

'In *tantrism**, the world is real. Energy creates matter, the earth generates life, the primordial sound becomes words; consciousness has voluntarily limited itself in my body. There is no renouncing. Everything is sacred.'

'I would rather agree with that.'

'The body is the instrument of bliss…'

'The problem is that our life is not only made of bliss. Even if I don't make any preconceptions about pain, I still suffer. You're forgetting that life is also burdened with worries, accidents, mishaps and monotony. Don't sadhus show a third path? The quest for a gentler way of life of contemplation and the sobriety of non-action?'

This conversation went on for several weeks. I would say: 'A swami taught me that desires are thoughts.' He would retort: 'So what! God also is a thought.' I tried: 'Sadhus are the only ones truly living Hindu spirituality. They embody the philosophy and its methods; the others only talk about it.' He protested: 'No, they are not the only ones! Pleasure is an offering to the Gods.' I put forward: 'Since the day of his departure each sadhu carries within him the story of severing his destiny. He left his wife, children, home, work, even his name and his place in the world, to seek bliss in renunciation. Has he not already conquered liberation in this initial leap? Isn't liberation this freedom? His ceaseless wandering re-enacts this beginning endlessly.' He refuted: 'No. Liberation is to find happiness in this body and in this life.'

And once again I agreed with him.

However, in this life, to reach the conditions of happiness, money has to be earned through the hardships of work, painfully accumulating it, anxiously preserving it, carefully spending it and thus only parsimoniously enjoying it. If you have to measure bliss, it is not bliss, just as when peace is threatened, it is no longer peace.

When we met in a circle of sadhus or if we walked on the *ghats*, Naresh spoke to me about his philosophy of pleasure and his sexed Gods. He was unbeatable when it came to the hymns the ancient sages had sung to the glory of body, sex and desire. The sexual relations of the Gods were no secret to him either – a three thousand five hundred year corpus. He had made it the subject of his thesis and said he practised a ritual at dawn in his room.

One evening in my *mandir*, by candlelight, Naresh read the most beautiful of Geneses!

"In the *Vishnu Purana*...

> Brahma was busy at his work of creation, probing the depths of his interior
> being and depositing on the shores of life the multitudes of
> forms modelled by his ardour. Then Kama appeared in
> the form of a young man. His face lit up by his imperishable
> youth; his chest had the colour of a fragrant sandalwood paste,
> his hips were smooth and the sweetest sensual delights slipped from his breath.
> Discovering himself, Kama called out to Brahma with a spark of
> mischievousness lighting up his gaze: 'Tell me Brahma, what is
> my name and my role in this world?' Brahma remained thoughtful for a
> long time, examining the creature that had come out of him. 'You are called
> Desire,' he finally said. 'You were born in me, born from yourself.
> I create worlds, but you give them life. I make things appear; you make
> them become. I give birth to forms; you animate them. You are poison,
> joy and intoxication. Whoever emerges from my consciousness
> surrenders to your charms.'"

'Blessed is the culture that addresses desire with such grace, cleverness and respect,' I appreciated.

I loved India.

The kindness, the vitality and the enthusiasm of Indians delighted me. It is a dirty, disorganized and chaotic country, over-populated with noisy and invasive people, but most of them are smiling and courteous. They expectorate with conviction, shout when talking, call out to each other from one end of roads and buildings to the other and private life overflows into public spaces, but their friendship is immediate and their sincerity spontaneous.

In the narrow lanes shared with pedestrians, careless of their nuisance, motorcyclists insist on the horn largely beyond decency and necessity. Whirrs of generators, bells and amplified rituals from temples, the backfiring of auto-rickshaws, political propaganda blasting out of cars, the latest songs booming from CD shops' loudspeakers, cawing crows: all this composes a continuum of cacophony, punctuated in rhythm by resounding percussions of all kinds of work; and then suddenly lit up by a muezzin who proclaims the hour of glory or the childish flat voice of a sadhu singing *Ram-Sita Sita-Ram* ad infinitum.

Holy Varanasi has discovered neon, plastic, posters and concrete. The visual realm is a mess. Electric cables weave a worrying net between the heavens and the earth. Nothing ever seems to be finished. Harmony and beauty, or simply order, do not seem to be worth even a shadow of concern. The general indifference makes a huge dustbin of the collective space. People drop anything they don't want here, there and everywhere, without remorse or complex and without making even the slightest superfluous movement. *India Ma* is a garbage dump. But these people can see beauty where others do not even have an inkling of finding it.

The air is unimaginably filled with levitating dust and the dioxin fumes of burning plastic bags and garbage. The acidic smell of spontaneous urinals pervades the alleyways. Sensory faculties are stimulated to their painful extreme. The food is like self induced arson that no amount of water can extinguish. Meals are torture. Each mouthful is a blazing inferno in which up to thirty-six types of chillies compete with flames roaring for fiery supremacy, imposing an exploration of the nuances of fire and burning upon the taste buds followed by the digestive tracts. At concerts, instruments and voices are amplified to the Larsen limit. 'If God gave heaven to the Indians, twenty-four hours later it would be no different from hell,' an Indian man once told me.

Half of the people cannot read or write and illiteracy is on the increase. Ignorance is deepened by prejudices, simplistic principles learnt by heart and by persistent superstitions. And certain traditions just prolong and amplify the misfortune…

At Chaumsathi ghat, an asylum practised the charity of keeping widows alive by offering them food and lodging, but nothing more because the Law of Manu prescribes *a widow must endure suffering until death. Curse to the God who kills husbands leaving wives dependant on their sons,* I read somewhere. Thrown out onto the streets by their families, condemned to be lost souls for life, these involuntary nuns wore white saris and shaven heads like a leper wears rattles and scars. Nobody approached them. Their common room opened onto the street and I saw them, half-heartedly mending, sorting lentils, praying and waiting… Rigorous orthodoxy, which prohibits widows' remarriage, produced this deplorable hardship. One of them begged in secret. When I passed by, I winked at her and dropped a few rupees in her bosom. She hastily conjured them away and made sure not to betray herself with a smile.

The Indian novels I read depicted a people as materialist as any other, filled with the same anguish and jealousies as any other. People more concerned with the illusions of this world than setting themselves free of them. Just like people everywhere.

"Blessed are the poor", we, Western Christians, repeat, thinking very hard "Let this cup pass from me" whilst already planning to buy whatever object we desire. Hindus do not seek adversity any more than others and have embraced consumerism according to their means. In the country of renunciants, the materialists are envious, covetous, show-offs and are in the majority, like everywhere else.

And I raged against filth and chaos, criticized conservatism, condemned its resignations, cursed the excesses, and thought that one must have carried out extremely nasty things in a precious life and produced terrible karma to end up being reborn in the land of karma. But with my heart of a benevolent anarchist, I was delighted there.

I loved India.

If we were to calculate the average time per day different populations of the world spend smiling, Indians would rank top of the list.

Wild and domestic animals live in cities. Not to mention wandering dogs, rats, tarantulas, lizards and cockroaches, one meets the monkeys of his local neighbourhood and offers them bananas, pats the passing buffalo on the street, gives a comforting smile to the neighbour's goat, strokes the washer-man's donkey, receives the blessing from the temple's elephant and greets vultures, perched outside slaughter-houses, that seem to ogle our future corpse. The crows come up close, blackbirds are not shy, eagles perch on street lamps and wild peacocks bow endlessly before each other on the highest balustrades. One feels less isolated in his species, sharing the city with other beings.

The muffled dampness of the tortuous lanes seemed familiar, as did their shadows. I savoured the coal fumes, frying spices and the omnipresent smell of cow pats. The whiffs of incense that came and lightened my steps afforded an exquisite charm. Expressing respect by bowing came naturally to me. Remaining squatted was second nature. I felt close to my remotest instincts, greeting the sun and honouring Mother Earth and her creations – the rivers, trees, mountains and fire. My genes had been doing this five thousand years ago, I was sure. I felt I knew the rituals and had sung in Sanskrit many times before.

At dusk, I often attended the open air *puja* at Dassawamedh ghat. On a platform overhanging the river, five bare-chested *pujaris* in synchrony elegantly raised their candelabrums of burning wicks to the Ganges and made them whirl. The yellow flames stretched in this movement and drew large circles of fire.

Accompanied on drums, cymbals, conches and oboes, the slow procession of hundreds of oil lamps glided on the water. In this *son et lumière* show, India met with the Babylon of my imagination.

Here I found a very moving densely packed collision of pagan temples from ancient times with the wandering philosophers of my fantasies of Greece, oxcarts from idealized images of Middle Ages, marble and mother-of-pearl caliphs' palaces from the Arabian Nights, Maharajas on elephant's backs on days of festivity, colonial Anglo-Mongol architecture with domes and broad verandas, English cars from the Fifties, snake charmers, troubadours, omnipresent cell phones and cybercafes where one surfed to the rhythm of U2 and Prince... A present with the thickness of three thousand years sliding along the eternity of a river.

I loved India.

In the evening, at Asi ghat, except for a distant electric light bulb and the motorcycle parked nearby, we could have been in a scene from twenty or thirty centuries ago. The appearance of these men in saffron rags, wearing dreadlocks and *tilak,* warming up to the fire would have been the same. So would our conversation. Who am I? Where are we? And why? Is this world real? Is there a consciousness other than mine? We were beyond time and space in these eternal questions that have shaken, inspired and pacified men since the beginning of time and produce a strange nostalgic feeling for the indescribable reality that precedes and encompasses speech.

Some days, an entire village of pilgrims invaded Ranamahal ghat: men, women, children, kitchen utensils, quilts, drums and sometimes even a small baboon on a leash. They would come from as far afield as Rajasthan, Kerala, Nepal... by train or on foot. It was their great journey this pilgrimage to the Ganges in Varanasi. In the evening, they began a prayer ritual in which the hums and murmurs, drum beats and conch shrieks continued all night long. At sunrise, they took the bath that cleanses all misdeeds. They would head back home two or three days later. Their company was pleasant. They lived in low voices low under their turbans and around their small dung fires.

The neighbourhood's youngsters were less timid. They came to check me out, venturing right up to my *mandir,* without hiding their surprise or their circumspection. Those who spoke to me began their investigation with prosaic questions: *Why do you live in a mandir? Don't you have any money?* Some of my visitors made no attempt to conceal their contempt for sadhus:– *Beggars, swindlers, dangerous sorcerers! – But I am not a sadhu.* Or saints... For they all claimed to know one who was an exception to their prejudices, who received their admiration.

'How is he special?'

'This baba, he sees God!' assured a computer student who had acquiesced in switching off his *ipod*.

'How do you know?'

'Me, I know religion a little. Him, he *is* religion!'

This country smells of incense.

I loved India.

I fell under the charm of the sadhus and their lifestyle. I often fantasized about joining these men who love life so much that they refuse to work for it, vow not to accept any wages, make a mockery of sweat and pain, and scorn productivity and competition in order to follow the various paths leading to God, love, peace, non-duality or nowhere... but from where they hope not to return, and in which each step is made of *blissful laziness*. The goal is the path itself.

I saw them as Epictetus' disciples, for this philosopher taught it was better to die of hunger having banished worries and fears, than to live in abundance mired in anxiety and sorrow. I saw them to be standard bearers of a kind of freedom and moderation which we have forgotten the taste of in our commercial civilization which preaches labour, consumption and economic growth, in a world which seems destined to short-term ecological disaster and demographic tsunami.

I did not believe in liberation. I did not hate life enough to want to get rid of it whilst still alive and rejected the theories of karma and reincarnation, which formed a vision of the world deprived of mercy. It is not from existence that I aspired to escape but from its gravity, its weight. I admired the lightness of theirs. I felt attracted to their impassivity, but did not find an ounce of the guts I would need to really leave everything in the hope that destitution would grant me a light heart and that philosophy would offer me a care-free life. I hung out with them as a dilettante benefactor. Between reading Diogenes and living in a tub, is health insurance and credit cards. One does not dare believe it is possible to live without them, even if one knows, from reading Epicurus, that attachment is the root of sorrow and pain the only fruit of incessant searching for happiness.

I glorified India as that civilization, which bestows the title of saint on renunciants, where contemplation is a divine attitude, non-action a goal and idleness a vision. She recognizes rapture in humility and the superiority of equanimity over the passions. Although eager for consumption, she glorifies simplicity. Despite her addiction to cell phones and social ambitions, she finds legitimacy in those who let go of everything.

I admired her culture, praised her philosophical works, and acclaimed her barefooted vagrant philosophers. I loved her huge temples; I was moved by the unostentatious fervour of her crowds.

And I also considered her broad-minded in spite of and because of her castes. For one can live there within the margins of common rules and more or less as one wishes, because she has created a space of emancipation in the very heart of her social rigidity, an *outside* that is not *pariah*, *dalit* or outcaste, but which is beyond the supposed scale of purity, which includes lunatics, lazy bums, wandering philosophers, ascetics and all the peaceful and wise men who voluntarily give her up, and that she honours and incenses.

And I would conclude that if one has to be insane to live there voluntarily, one cannot be less mad living anywhere else if one has the chance of settling there.

I woke up one morning with an erection which brought me back to basics: weightlessness can wait, I told the *lingam* in my *mandir*. Asceticism may be dangerous, even as a dream. Gods fantasize; men enjoy. I could never give *that* up anyway; I made my mind up as if that had been under debate.

In mythology, Shiva incarnates the perfect ascetic, meditating motionlessly and unperturbed for one or ten thousand years on Mount Kailash, but he is also famous for his one thousand years coitus with Parvati. That's a dream as well! The world is gentler when one has a girlfriend in ones arms. 'Shiva,' I ordered the oblong stone, 'take care of this!'

In the afternoon, two Western girls entered my *mandir* and joined their hands, giving the reverences due to a man of God.

'You speak English?'

One was Laurie and the other Jane. They were Australian. Both had blonde curly hair. Beautiful and friendly. God is great if he arranged this meeting… I mused in a rare friendly thought towards the C.A.O. (Chief Almighty Organizer).

'Why is this country which is inhabited by so many gods, so poor?' asked Laurie.

She had large green, aqueous, burning eyes. Gripping in the attraction of this contradiction.

'Gods are obviously not very rich,' I said, starting to understand that that was no longer the question.

My heart was clearly beating quicker.

'Or they must be miserly,' I managed to add. 'But to be honest, I don't know. You should ask a swami.'

'Aren't you a swami?' asked Jane.

'What are you doing here?' Laurie questioned.

Glowing and merry eyes. The skin of a blonde who gave herself to the sun without burning; amber, glossed.

She wore a light white blouse embroidered with small pale green flowers around the neckline. Her small feet protruded from baggy pants of the same cotton cloth, embroidered at the ankles. She was not so tall. Jane was taller and thin and also quietly provocative. A dozen plastic bracelets encrusted with shiny things glittered on her arms and rattled with her every move. But my heart had already taken sides.

'I have fun considering things from a *mandir*. But that does not give an answer to everything… And at times I think about the possibility of bliss in frugality. I'm interested in sadhus.'

The very moment I pronounced these words, I knew I was lying and that I did not have such a great appetite for the ecstasy of renunciants. In fact, my only thought was kissing her, seducing her, keeping her. I imagined that her sweat smelt of apricot.

'What are you looking for here?' asked Jane, making her bracelets tinkle.

'A wise man, perhaps.'

They were Bharatnatyam* dancers, learning and practising with their guru who lived close to Kabir Road. They did not stay very long, but they came back. And we went for dinner in a Chinese restaurant.

'… They have no idea of the difference between being loose and being seductive and attractive,' recalled Laurie in front of a very acceptable noodle soup.

Laurie and Jane had a female experience of India. They were chatted up by men who think that Western girls are easy and hope to fulfil, they said, their white woman fantasies.

'He wouldn't leave us and was not at all attractive,' said Jane about the man who had approached them a few hours earlier. 'He was stroking his privates in front of everyone saying in a deep voice and with a vicious smile which undoubtedly he believed spellbinding, *good, berrry good*. His eyes rolled up in their orbits, big like his promises,' she concluded imitating him brilliantly whilst cracking up laughing.

'How did you get rid of him?'

'We jumped in a rickshaw without bargaining. The bastard cost us a fortune!'

'Fathers are obsessed by the virginity of daughters and husbands by the fidelity of wives. So who do they get to…' said Jane understandingly.

'The same goes for Westerners,' I said making eyes to Laurie.

'For every 90 girls there are 100 boys,' Jane insisted.

'That creates an additional deficit of hope,' I observed without taking my eyes off my one.

They were curious, funny, mischievous, and enjoyed feigning that they believed I would dedicate myself to yogis' austerities. 'I am neither a swami nor a sadhu,' I played along. We laughed shaking our head the way Indians do to approve, accept, agree, stall, calm, beguile and send to sleep: *No problem, No problem*. We lamented all the poverty: *Baksheesh baksheesh*. They imitated the mannerisms and greasy voice of their dance guru: *Come on girrrlllls, concentrrrate. Twelve bits not less! Arrrle lyou dumb!* They were funny. They could laugh. It was a hot evening. It got late. 'I am going to bed,' announced Jane rising, leaving me face to face with Laurie and the scheming of our mutual attraction.

'Do you have a boyfriend in Sydney?'

'This question seems like an invitation,' said Laurie maliciously.

'And this answer isn't a refusal,' I noted on the same mood.

A little later, we returned as well. Laurie slipped under my quilt, in the deep end of my temple. The following day, I moved in with them in three rooms overlooking an interior courtyard on a third floor we rented in a private home.

They went to their dance guru in the morning. I would go for a stroll on the *ghats*. They would meet me after my Hindi lesson. Naresh would play truant from his work and join us. We talked with backpackers and sadhus, read leaning against each other, laughed at little things, rented a boat to have a picnic on the opposite bank, facing Varanasi, and on the way had a swim fully dressed in the clearer icy water of the middle of the stream.

Laurie and Jane were not cold-natured. They had the talent to lighten and embellish whatever they came about.

Their beliefs formed a romantic-mystic patchwork: karma and reincarnation made it possible to conceive Jesus as an *avatar*, Krishna was a God and Shiva, the Lord of dance… *there-is-no-accident* was their access to a search for meaning; everything bathed in love. The morals of their faith made them free, sparkling and even stimulating towards laziness. Every day, practising their art, they played Gods and demons.

'You know, one does not come to India by chance…,' Laurie ventured one afternoon, trying to include me in her karmic connection pattern.

'*Karma-de-de-da, maya-de-de-doo, Brahma-wa-pa-de-doo,*' I stopped her with the great gestures of a sorcerer. 'My karma has dragged me out here where you were also going. And we already knew each other in a former life… Do you think that I was a pretty boy or a dreadful grumpy one-eyed alcoholic who beat you? Eh? Can you imagine us a little bloated? Did you sell fish at the market or were you the Queen of Sheba?' I added bowing to her majesty.

'What do you believe happens after death?' she questioned with a rare gravity.

'I hope there is nothing on the other side of life,' I answered sincerely. We owe this modesty to eternity.

Whether everything returns to nothingness or becomes something else, they certainly enjoyed having this bodily existence. They charmed life with pleasure and determination. They fascinated everyone, had fun and were adorable. Whenever he was with us, Naresh rowed without getting wet and stubbornly eyed up Jane.

A brahmin, but not a priest, Naresh held on to ancient India's habits and prejudices. He walked with the straight back of princes and young village girls indefatigably carrying his black umbrella, which he used as sunshade but which he seldom opened. His caste placed him, in his own eyes, at the top of human hierarchy, a socio-religious aristocracy. It was a hereditary sort of pride. According to him, individuals of lower castes were inferior, even if they held a socially high status. He had found this reason for self esteem in his cradle; he believed in it. His *janehyu*, apparent through his kurta, constantly reminded him of this. And it reminded me too.

I was a son of my Republic: Liberty, Equality, Fraternity. I would speak to the boatman, the *bidi* seller and the *rickshaw walla** with respect, as it should be. I tried to make friends, have a special moment. If then I asked Naresh to translate some words, he would break the spell with his Duke of Incarnation style, and closed up these men like oysters. 'Speak more kindly,' I kept on repeating. Naresh gave them orders as if they were servants.

But he was also capable of touching gestures. He bowed before sadhus and questioned them with reverence: 'Will *Maharaj-ji* tell us what he knows about Brahman?' And would add: 'Will he allow me to massage his feet?'

His father and his uncles had a sandalwood wholesale business in Kolkata. Poor countries are not populated by poor people alone. I imagined a lineage of cultured and influential merchants. From his birth it was planned that Naresh would run the family business and that he would marry his cousin.

We were chatting on the roof of Swami Krishnachandra Vedanta Ashram, in the broken shade of a tattered parasol overlooking the Ganges between two decrepit palaces. It was an old, worn, grey building with two U-shaped storeys bordered with verandas. A small Shiva *mandir* with a conical dome was flanked by a *pipal* tree in the middle of the square court. At its ridge was a pole with a red flag.

'Do you love her... this cousin?'

'I have grown up with her. She is a sister to me. But I shall marry her. Better a partner whom I know and appreciate that an unknown girl chosen through caste, horoscope and dowry.'

'You know everything there is to know about Gods' sexuality, but you forget love!' I reminded him. 'Does it not bother you that your job, your wife, and just about everything you are, was planned from your birth?'

'No. Life is much simpler that way.'

'So, it's in this simplicity that you find it legitimate to simply reduce people to their birth caste?'

'You don't understand anything about castes, Ludoji. Your caste is your place in the world.'

'You scorned love and now you give up your right to innovate. There is too much past in the present of India. You drove out the British, but you did not make a revolution! Today, the sacred, the model, the spiritual ambition of humanity is that "all human beings are born free and equal in dignity and rights. They are endowed with reason and conscience and should act towards one another in a spirit of brotherhood."'

Idealist but universal.

A smell of boiling milk arose in whiffs from the curd store six meters below on the road side; the fresh cow dung pats stuck and drying on the walls gave the aroma a pleasing note, but wafts of urine broke the heady charm of it all. Very welcome warm breezes were coming off the Ganges. We could hear the curd merchant cursing a beggar who had threatened to pollute his cooking pots with his shadow.

'It is not age that gives a principle its value,' I persisted categorically. 'Or there would be no possible evolution! We do not have to drag our ancestors into our future. They were not necessarily right.'

Taking my lunch on the bench of a small bazaar restaurant with dirty walls and a gloomy light, I read in *The Teaching of Ramana Maharshi*: *The realization of atman (Oneself) is the most invaluable assistance one can bring to humanity.* Later on, in a random passage: *If you use sadhanas (methods which enable one to take a firm grounding in Oneself) to alleviate your mental activity, it will start again with force as soon as you cease your sadhanas. Know who you are. Discover Oneself (atman)*, were the counsels of this man of wisdom.

'What is that Oneself?' I asked a young sadhu the following day, who came every day to fill a jug from the Ganges.

He was a little over 20, wore a white *lungi*, was bare-chested, thin, sat upright with black hair coiled up upon his head. He spoke reasonable English and his voice was soft.

'Let us put down a principle,' he started. 'Call it God, Spirit, the Whole, Oneness, that which was never born, Brahman – Brahman means the oldest, the homogeneous. It does not matter. Everything comes from him. It is the Whole in its first form, as well as all the parts of this Whole and their interactions. Everything, every event and their actors, is his play, his *leela*.'

'We can suppose that,' I agreed.

'When you only identify with a fragment, (this is maya, the cosmic illusion) you ignore the other aspect of yourself, the Whole, the universal, the play. Who is the player? Brahman. *Aham Brahmanosmi*. I am Brahman. Atman, Oneself, is the awareness of that.'

'Are you a sadhu for lifestyle or liberation?'

'I studied Sanskrit in Rishikesh and I teach. I devote my life to *moksha*.'

When I was walking towards Dassawamedh ghat thinking of this Oneself, the player, a woman stopped me and said:

'Main yahan hi rehti hoon, aap kahan rehte hain bavajood iske ke aap

nahin jante ke yeh kahan hai.'

She was a little excited and could not comprehend that I did not understand her. Finally, I asked a man who passed by to translate: 'I live where you live, even if you do not know where it is, she says.' It didn't mean anything to me and I departed. The man also left, in the same direction. As we were looking at a line of six sadhus walking along the *ghats*, this man commented with contempt: 'Just beggars!'

There was a stink of self-satisfaction in this man which I figured must descend from a long line of ancestors sufficiently gifted to maintain themselves in prosperity. He was as fat as the others were thin. A *three-meals-a-day Babu*, say the poor of the area.

'These are the people that keep this country in ignorance,' cursed the chap.

'They think that you are the ignorant one, Babuji,' I answered without getting involved. 'Maya, etc.'

'Maya!' he snapped with derision. 'And if I prick you with a needle, will you still say *maya, etc.*?'

Metaphysics often stumbles on the question of pain!

But the question was: Who is the player?

Later, I read again in *Ramana Maharshi*: 'Just as the spider throws its thread out of itself and again withdraws it into itself, likewise the mind projects the world out of itself and again resolves it into itself.'

I found that this theory of the world had a certain intelligence. But I continued to resist it. If there is just one player alone, can it still be called a game? I liked the fact that another existed.

Give Up the Benefits of Illusion

'The Hindu statuary celebrates Gods and teaches philosophical principles, and we take this as a model in Bharatnatyam dance,' said Jane mimicking a Krishna hip-swaying, sideways enticing gaze, playing a flute.

The museum was almost deserted.

'This one will interest you,' Laurie promised. 'Look. It's *Nataraja!* In a circle of fire, Shiva does the dance of his five cosmic activities: creation, preservation, destruction, incarnation and liberation.'

Both of them bowed before this four-armed God.

'All of the esoteric teachings are present here in a single figure,' Jane stated.

'Although he has a human form, Shiva is not a personal God,' said Laurie. 'He is the Unique Uncreated. *Mudras**, the position of arms, hands and legs symbolize spiritual concepts that articulate and compose a *darshan*.'

'That's enough preamble,' Jane cut in. 'The right foot crushes Mulayaka, a demon dwarf, an allegory of human passions and ignorance. This character refers to a man who identifies with his own body, gets caught in believing in his own separate life and forgets that everything is illusion.'

'*Karma-de-de-da, maya-de-de-doo,*' Laurie repeated. 'We are this ugly little man.'

'No, you are very bright!' I said with appreciation.

Both raised their left leg, their feet crossing their right knee in the position of the dancing God.

'Raised, the left foot indicates the highest state of consciousness,' explained Laurie, 'transcendent united consciousness, without object and without support.'

'So, the two legs demonstrate two states of consciousness,' Jane summarized, 'the dwarf-dualism, which differentiates between subject and object, identifying with one's body and one's mental experiences... and the other – divine, which is free from the separation between the perceiver and the perceived. *Sivo'am So'am*, I am Shiva; *That* is me!'

'The upper two arms are active,' Laurie went on, raising hers. 'The right hand plays the *damaru**, a small drum that vibrates the primordial *Om*, the essence of all sounds of the three times, the vibratory cause of the universe – the divine word, speech. *Om* creates the world.'

Jane's bracelets applauded this beginning.

'The left hand holds the flame of knowledge,' she slipped in.

'Knowledge that destroys the world,' said Laurie playing its apocalyptic impact. 'The torch rotates around the body of the God who represents the universe, giving the impression that he is surrounded by a circle of fire. But there is only one flame! The circle is an illusion. Shiva is the master of maya.'

'Ah!' finally I understood. 'During the evening *puja* in front of the Ganges, the *pujari* runs a torch around this way... He reveals the illusion of a circle!' I discovered. 'The dance of fire.'

'The movement creates the illusion,' Laurie synthesized.

'The *damaru* and the flame: creation and destruction, the vibration from which the universe manifests and knowledge which allows you to see it as it is – a magic circle, a cosmic illusion – and to be set free from it,' Jane summed up.

'How?' asked Laurie taking the posture of the God in his dancing bronze incarnation. 'The two lower arms, motionless before the body of Shiva, indicate it. The right hand, palm lifted suggests the absence of fear, peace, equanimity, immediate acceptance of what is, the extinction of emotionalism. The left hand, pointing down, shows the earth, takes her as a witness, and reminds one to rest consciousness on what is, rather than on what the mind interprets, builds and plans with desires, fears and hopes.'

A young Japanese couple went through the hall. The boy wanted to take a picture of the Australians in the pose of Shiva. Laurie hid behind Jane and lent her two arms.

'Send photo me.'

'Yes yes,' said the Nipponese.

Exchange of email addresses.

'When Shiva stops dancing,' Laurie concluded, 'the object and the subject dissolve.'

'And what happens then?'

'Nothing. It's the end of the world. At least, the end of your world.'

She took my arm and followed my steps.

'Look at this one, he is so cute,' Jane whispered.

She meant the young and beautiful sadhu whom I had asked about the atman or Oneself a few days before.

That day, he was wearing a *gomcha*, a short loincloth that did not hide much of his hairy legs and let the eyes wander up a long way on his shapely thighs. With an upright back, muscular chest, brown skin, jet black bun, three white marks on the forehead, a straightforward gaze, he was the image of an ascetic Adonis.

'Behave!' I reprimanded between my teeth, always more uptight than the other two when it came to good manners.

As soon as she spotted a living example of chastity vows, Jane had to challenge it. For fun, she was carrying out a kind of personal study on the resolve the abstainers had in their abstinence. And Laurie assisted her. The figures of the two girls, their skin and their smiles could whet the appetite of even a model renunciant. Their taste for provocation, their daring, and the eyes of Laurie made them a devastating challenge for ascetics, young and old, along the *ghats*. Many of them showed a willingness to adapt their vows in view of the enticing circumstances.

That day, Jane was aiming her sights at this young sadhu sitting alone on the bank of Ganges. Afterwards, she called him Maya Baba.

She asked for permission to sit with him. He granted it, surprised that we had taken an interest in him. And soon, Jane was making eyes and was looking for his answering gaze, whilst slightly leaning forward.

'Is the world really an illusion?'

She played candid but she knew how to express the substance of her thoughts with her body without verging on vulgarity.

He drew back. Already portraying virtue.

'A kind of illusion,' he answered cautiously, 'like a dream.'

'And if I prick you with a needle, will you still say that pain is an illusion?' a man asked me on the *ghats*. 'What do you answer to that, Swamiji?' I asked sincerely.

'It is because of pain that we begin to seek a meaning to our lives,' explained Maya Baba, 'then we search how to avoid suffering. The other side of pain is pleasure, but the reverse side of these two, i.e. the reverse of feeling, is immobility. And immobility is only achieved through renouncing.'

Desiring only to give up... I thought. And yet, not even... bringing desire to a standstill to find satisfaction...

'Is there another kind of dream after death?' Jane asked.

She was wearing tight jeans and a chiffon blouse, through which one could make out her small Mickey-Mouse nose breasts. Her long blond hair waved freely on her chest. She smelt deliciously of her fragrant soap.

'We try to overcome hallucinations,' answered Maya Baba.

A gaze that held on to nothing.

'If life is a dream, let us dream instead of trying to wake up,' Jane snapped back, with a few promises in her eyes, leaning slightly less forward.

He drew back.

A sculptor would have taken him for a model in an allegory of virtue. In a world of seduction, the most attractive have more merit in temperance than those who have no chance of seducing anyone! We are not equal before saintliness either. Maya Baba was running with this handicap. On the mode *life is a dream*, it was easy to imagine charming him, touching him, grasping him or becoming the shadow of his shadow at least... and Jane fell to it. She diverged widely from the usual scenario.

'It could be a wonderful adventure!' she insisted. 'Why should you decide it's not worth dreaming about or experiencing?'

'Joys and sorrows that fulfil or overwhelm us are transient. You will age, you will become much less desirable, and your senses will deplete, prophesied the Ephebe. Even pleasure will lose its flavour.'

'What do you know about it?' I whispered.

'It's only then that renouncing will be worth it,' Laurie promised, more relevantly.

'Shut up!' Jane commanded.

She turned to Maya Baba: 'Why do you renounce?'

'Because one has to relinquish the benefits of illusions to escape illusion,' he answered in his own particular logic.

'I want to teach you the art of love,' she offered without taking her eyes off him.

He was watching the pavement in front of him.

'You cannot give yourself to a stranger,' he said with frowned eyebrows, moralizing in disbelief.

One had to find some imperfection in him in order to free oneself from fascination.

He turned towards her.

'For you I will be a guru,' Jane said encouragingly, looking straight into his eyes.

'I haven't chosen you for a guru,' opposed Maya Baba, smiling at last.

'Although transient, pleasure is good. And happiness that Gods grant us, we must accept it. Only, do not get attached to it,' Jane professed already in her teacher's role.

'Transience attracts and enslaves you in its movement. Look for what is permanent,' replied the ascetic Sanskrit scholar.

'A man lives with his wife for a lifetime,' reacted Laurie to the rescue, 'if his wife dies, even if he suffers from her loss, he still has experienced a lot of nice things with her. Do not lament having lost what you loved, do not deny yourself knowing what will disappear, rejoice having known it, said the Dalai Lama. Whether it was one night or a lifelong love.'

'The purpose of life is not to know everything it offers,' opposed Maya Baba, ' – what it offers is infinite – but to discover how to get freed from it.'

'No!' Jane sighed. 'Imagine I am Rati and you are Kama.'

She raised her arms as a goddess who has at least four and then gathered in her hands in a *pranam* and added, bowing: 'We are both born of Brahma so that pleasure and desire meet.' Prostrating before him, her hands in offering, she begged: 'I am your consort.'

Gods become flesh when they are taken as models. Offering herself as a *Shakti*, she was inviting Maya Baba to become a God.

He drew back.

Even if I did not share his principles, I admired the ascetic and philosopher who had learned, like Epictetus, to change his desires rather than the world. And stuck to his values. I felt a little ashamed to participate in disconcerting him. But Maya Baba did not let himself be disconcerted.

'You are Pramlotchna, the temptress of Kandu,' he fought back with a smile. 'This nymph was sent by Vishnu to Kandu to disturb his *tapasya*, and the ascetic succumbed to her charms for nine hundred and seven years, six moons and three days.'

A myth against another.

'Our desires do not necessarily turn into obsessions,' I balanced out.

'To love is to put yourself in danger, open to life, get involved,' Jane emphasized. 'You want to get over life without living it, and hope for a cure for love without knowing what love is. Don't be afraid of pleasure, it's only a moment!'

135

'We must one day decide we want to reach the point beyond the ocean of becoming,' said the monk. 'And get out of *bhava sagara*, the world of change.'

Should we really want that? I wondered. Or was it a matter of accepting it?

Jane called him Maya Baba thereafter. She told, mischievously and mysteriously: he smelt of smoke. Nostalgic: His lower body was hairy, the upper smooth: a faun. Chatty: He had no experience. He was experimenting. He repeated *maya maya* and made love like a medical examination. He knew nothing of his own body. He watched his penis coming in and out of me a lot. And I liked him looking at himself that way.

'He is looking for the point beyond the ocean of becoming,' I recalled. 'Maybe he has found immobility in motion or transcendence of sensation...'

'Everyone has their own G-spot,' Laurie concluded.

'Stretching his vows in this way makes him even more admirable,' I appreciated.

'One cannot go beyond what one has not experienced,' said Jane as if she gave herself, with this justification, a final absolution.

'I would like to have ten arms like Vishnu to hold you all over and caress you a thousand times more,' I whispered that night to Laurie in my arms. I watched my penis coming in and out, and the prickly, delightful, spicy-sweet, self-stimulating sensation of the friction of union. A paradox neglected by abstinent mystics. Embracing elusiveness. Uniting fever and abnegation: tenderness, a human creation. The Big Bang is probably the orgasm of a greater being. The question is: with whom does he have it? Me?

Agony follows death in coitus. Back to oneself. The penis shrinks, the blood moves away from the flesh, the body once again returns to itself and weightiness. And already Laurie is lighting a cigarette. She is hot. Each of us back in our own world. Lying next to her, I imagined an ascetic meditating on a mountain, on the other side of *that*, closer to the beyond of everything. In motionless and everlasting delight. I opened the *Avadhuta Gita*:

> When there is nothing to seek,
> And nothing to desire, nothing,
> Where neither thought nor speech can happen,
> Brahman, the homogeneous, shines.

The light went off. The breath of the fan slowly died. And heat settled, compact. Our bodies oozed.

'In nothingness, to enjoy is to shine,' I summarized for Laurie.

'In cigarettes also,' she told me.

'Give me the lighter.'

The flickering glow of a candle flame.

She took the book and read, then…

'Glorifying nothingness so much, it's crazy, don't you think?'

'Yes, crazy and admirable.'

The power came back and the light and the fan took momentum.

We did not see Maya Baba on the *ghats* again.

'Listen to what the wisdom of your tradition says on caste, Nareshji…'

We were having a chocolate on the bank of the Ganges, chairs, tables and umbrellas on a terrace. I read him this stance of the *Avadhuta Gita*: 'There are no *Vedas*, no worlds, no Gods, no sacrifices, and certainly no caste, no family tribes, no birth. The ultimate reality is Brahman, the homogeneous.'[1]

Laurie and Jane joined us.

'I accomplish my *dharma**,' said Naresh.

'*Dharma* is maya as well, in your culture!'

'No. maya, illusion, i.e. your nature, is determined by *dharma*, i.e. your destiny, your place in the world. A rose is not a carnation. A donkey is not an elephant. I cannot be other than what I am. My *dharma* is to be a brahmin.'

Once his *dharma* had been established and his caste recognized, Naresh was a normal boy who had no hesitation in transgressing what he had ascertained as holy and immutable. Snobbish and traditional, but also open-minded, especially with regard to sex, he was the embodiment of pre-independence India living in the days of cell phones and on-screen kisses. And he tried to flirt with Jane, a *mlecha** – a barbarian, worse than the untouchable *dalit*, for his caste, who after all things considered, were also untouchables. But Jane did not respond to his charms. She only liked renunciants.

'Being many, the Gods that are not *one-and-only* have learned tolerance and relativity. Relativity is exactly what is lacking with the God of Abraham, as you say,' I remarked to Naresh to distract him from ogling Jane.

---

1 *Avadhuta Gita* I 32.

'*Non-unique* Gods have understood that it takes two to join in pleasure…' he flung back. 'And they can laugh! That has not happened to *your* God since he had the idea of creating *your* world.'

'But before that we don't know,' Laurie reflected.

'From the beginning of me, I'm sure he has a lot of fun,' Jane tossed in to bring us relief.

'It is said,' Naresh told, 'that when Hanuman, the king of monkeys, wanted to build a bridge between India and Lanka to attack King Ravana and free Sita, Ram's wife, he asked Ram to accomplish the miracle of making stones float on the sea. He then laid the foundation stone of the bridge and it sank.

'"Ram! Can't you make the stones float!" Hanuman called out.

'He had the idea to write the name of Ram on the stones before putting them down on water, and they floated.

'"The name of Ram is more powerful than Ram," proclaimed Ram observing the miracle.'

'Self-mockery should be a compulsory divine virtue and a constitutional obligation,' I suggested.

'It is an attribute of power,' agreed Naresh.

'It makes Gods much more likeable,' Laurie put forward.

'*Our* God prefers thunder and lightning,' said Jane.

'Because he avenges the unjust and destroys the unfaithful,' I explained. 'Whereas here, karma takes care of justice and punishment and so, freed from this role, Hindu Gods can be kind.'

Naresh took us to Vishwanath temple at the time of the *puja*. The *pujari* poured a pot of melted butter on a one meter high *lingam*, and then spread the lubricant with both hands, chanting prayers.

Divine masturbation!

The priest then flooded it with a bucket of fresh milk.

Where, from my republican and atheist point of view, I saw a salacious waste, the *tantric* brahmin understood a union of male and female flux:

'Nectars produced by the intoxication of desire,' whispered Naresh.

The milk then spread over the *yoni*, the cosmic vulva, and poured away through a penis-shaped gutter.

'Monotheism produces an asexual metaphysics. You're right, Naresh,' I commented, outside the temple. 'The *one-and-only* God never has sex, by definition.'

'But here, there's a lot of sex,' Laurie whispered, with a teasing wink in her voice.

'At what time do they give it a blow job?' Jane asked, opening her mouth very wide to make us all laugh.

'Let's go smoke a *chillum*,' I suggested.

Walking to Asi ghat, Naresh preached:

'The *Bhagavad Gita* teaches that for the yogi's practice, pleasure is a test to verify his soul's equanimity: "Whoever endures pleasure and pain with an equal mind is a wise man ready for immortality," it is said.'

'You see sex and fornicators everywhere!' I retorted.

'No, *tantrikas**,' he corrected me.

'And you are very brave at confronting the trials of pleasure!' Laurie said mockingly and holding my hand.

'Some hesitate for a long time,' Jane remembered.

'Wise men undergo these tests,' insisted Naresh.

'Wise men, I can believe, but for you that's just where it starts!' Jane pointed out.

And we all exploded laughing.

'Apparently, one has to give up the benefits of illusions to escape illusion,' I recalled.

'A principle of renunciants! I am no renunciant. "*Virtue and vice, pleasure and pain belong to concepts, not to you if you are the Omnipresent!*"' He quoted.

Bom Bom Bholenath! proclaimed a sadhu before lighting his phallic shaped pipe...

Around the campfire, one of them said in fairly good English, yet addressing only Naresh and myself:

'I never trust a woman... Women are terrible creatures of the animal realm. They are very effective for material matters but they cannot reach God. Women are fire and men are butter. When there is a woman, a man melts.'

Jane was about to explode. I hurriedly said:

'You don't know anything about it, Swamiji. When a man melts, it produces beautiful flames!'

'Marriage is a knot that binds a man and a woman to illusions and grief,' he continued without remorse.

'There's no point in getting married!' I replied in self mockery.

'I don't know if women are animals, but for you, a man is just a dick,' Jane was bursting with contempt.

'I am 78 years old and in good health. I have always been single. No worries, no savings book, no car,' the ascetic made his list, pleased with himself.

'There is no merit in renouncing what you have not known!' Jane provoked with irony.

'Who is Krishna without Radha!' uttered a sadhu of the circle who had grasped the meaning of our discussion because he knew what a bore this man was.

Naresh translated.

'We are all Radha!' stated another.

'We are not women,' protested a third.

'What is a God if there is no world?' added a fourth.

'In mythology, Radha is the wife of Krishna,' explained Naresh. 'In metaphysics, she is his consort, his power to manifest. She is Krishna himself in the appearances of what exists. Thus, everything is Radha. And we all are Radha in the unity of this idea. This is *tantrism*.'

Naresh remained constant in his defence of desire and praises for pleasure. The following evening, we were lying side by side on the stone slabs of the banks, breathing in the stars and inhaling the cool breeze. Sitting up, he whispered:

'It is said that neither God nor father nor any man ever equalled Kama, Desire, the first born, born of himself, existing by himself.'

'A Beautiful Genesis!' I appreciated, examining the stars scattered like dust in the sky. 'In the beginning, before all of that, self created: Lord Desire.'

'What happened next?' asked Jane.

'According to the *Shiva Purana*, Creation is a thought and the seed of this thought is Desire, the first God, the first force that puts the mind in motion. It says: There was desire and then the power that provides it.'

'But it doesn't work every time!' I observed with sadness.

'In Vaisnava Upanishad, it is said: "Eager for pleasure, he becomes dependent on desires, but the wise man who takes sensual pleasures as they arrive, with a detached mind, becomes free from desires.'

'Your religion is wonderful!' Jane exclaimed. 'You get cured of desires by succumbing to pleasures…'

'Provided that it is with a certain detachment,' Laurie cut in with irony.

'I look forward to reading your thesis. With you, it sounds like they only talk about *that*,' I kindly rebuffed. 'However, I read in an Upanishad the human body described as a revolting aggregate of flesh, bones, phlegm, urine and faeces, and existence being portrayed as the pursuit of desires that are only illusions involving jealousies, cravings, diseases, sorrows and death. There are puritans in your tradition that are trying to make you lose your hard-on, my dear Naresh.'

'One point for Ludo,' counted Laurie.

'If you love, you don't see things that way,' he reproved with disdain and sadness.

'So there! One point for Naresh,' approved Jane. 'Freud described a kiss as a union of two erogenous oral zones. Cold and objective. Without affection or fantasy, making love is just doing somersaults,' she added pulling on his shoulder to get up.

'But with them, it's ecstasy,' he promised.

'One point for Naresh,' I arbitrated in turn.

One morning we visited a sadhu who lived in a small house-boat moored at Asi ghat. The small cabin was a shambles of dirty pots and plates, bowls, a gas stove, an oil lamp with books and blankets laid everywhere. This floating ashram was presided over by an image of Bhairava, a wrathful figure of Shiva, with anger in his eyes, tiger's teeth and hair on fire. Kailash Puri Baba had established his *asan* on a plank placed on stacked bricks. We did some cleaning and washed the dishes before we sat in front of him. During the conversation, he said:

'In the subtle reality, a bird in the air leaves no less traces than your feet on the sand in the sensory reality.'

Naresh translated.

'Guruji, would you tell us what this means?' he asked.

'Everything that appears arises from what preceded it and yet which no longer exists,' he answered.

'So before me, I was already there!' Jane exclaimed.

'It's worse than that – you're already no more, Darling,' replied Laurie.

'I am never anything more than an anticipation of myself,' I said with a humble bow.

The baba burst out laughing. He slipped his hand under his blanket and took out a large cobra adorned *chillum.*

I Live Where You Live

For several days, every morning, Ramasharvan Baba spread a saffron cotton cloth on the concrete footing of a lamppost at Ranamahal ghat and placed upon it a small white marble Ganesha lying on a sofa. With his temple set up, he lit a stick of incense, offered a little dish of water, and remained quiet. He was a *bhakti* baba, one of the unconditionally devout kind, struck dumb with love. I left a ten rupee note at his feet when I greeted him in passing.

I sat down with him one day.

Orphaned at the age of ten, he fled from his uncle who had taken him in but abused him. He met three sadhus and asked for their protection. He had been roaming the roads for the past twenty-three years. He was wearing a green vest over a saffron kurta and a *lungi*. His black oiled hair fell to his shoulders.

'What are you looking for in this life?' I asked him.

'*Bhagwan!*'

'Have you found him?'

Ramasharvan Baba favoured me with an ecstatic smile and whispered:

'He is everything!'

'Then, why do you endlessly walk towards him?'

'To meet him everywhere. You are God!' he added, looking at me with bliss.

Polytheists are so sweet, I thought.

'Did you return to visit your uncle?'

'Much later, he went there.'

'How did it go?'

'He is everything. All is well,' concluded Ramasharvan.

One by one, four sadhus came to sit with us. A passer-by approached and dropped a rupee at the feet of Ganesha.

'In this *kali-yuga**, devotion is the only way to achieve liberation,' said

Ramasharvan Baba applying a *tilak* on the devotee's forehead.

'I don't really believe in God,' I confessed.

'Why do you not want to love him?' he wondered.

'Last week, heavy rains triggered a landslide that engulfed twenty-five thousand people, near Dehradun. If Gods had any respect for their devotees, they would have saved them…'

'In a war, soldiers are killed, and yet they are not the king,' argued Ramasharvan Baba with a mysterious logic.

'The path leading to higher realms is often opened by miseries and frustrations,' broke in one of the babas.

'If God could do something, wouldn't he lighten living beings' burden of pain? I would imagine the Almighty might be more friendly! And his justice more merciful,' I replied.

'Being a process, Creation cannot be perfect. That's why it must contain pain,' said another baba.

'Perfection is possible only on return to God or in the motionlessness of Oneness! We must get used to suffering,' confirmed the first.

'Sure! But these are ideas, theories,' I refuted. 'Pain is not an opinion.'

'Your life doesn't seem unhappy. Providence did not forget you. How then can you blame her?'

'I feel solidarity for the billions of beings who experience great torments even though they pray morning, noon and night!'

'*Atchaaa!*' Ramasharvan Baba assented. 'Love him for the awareness you have of that pain. It is said that the awareness of the pain there is in existing may lead to *samadhi*. You possess this awareness, Prassadji.'

It was the first time someone called me Prassad.

While we were talking like this, a sadhu who was passing by stopped to watch me carefully, then ran to me and touched my feet.

'*Hari Om, Gurujiiiii!*'

'*Mujhe?*'

'*Haan*.*'

'*Nahi!*[1]'

'*Aap hamare guru hain.* You are my guru. You are Shri Saraswati Prassad Bhagwan Shivo'am Baba!' he seemed to say as he stood back up. 'You gave me the name Balamani Baba.'

---

1 Me? Yes. No.

Somehow, he made me understand that, as a child, his first guru had been Shri Prassad Baba. But he had died. And just before my own birth. Crazy! But Balamani Baba also stated the name of my former girlfriend, and my mother's, her age, my address... He told me facts that he could not know.

'How do you know that?'

'You taught me to see these things! Then, becoming very solemn, he said: *Main yahan hi rehta hoon aap jahan rehte hain bavajood iske ke aap nahin jante ke yeh kahan hai*: I live where you live, even if you do not know where it is.'

The same weird words as the crazy woman, a few days earlier! This time, it had a stupefying effect. The world disappeared for a moment as if the sun had closed his eyes.

'Babaji, you are my guru,' insisted Balamani Baba when I regained consciousness of his existence.

'No,' I said categorically. 'I don't want a *dharma* (destiny).'

And I ran away while he prophesied: 'You will come back in five years, Guruji...'

This country talks to me! I discovered with amazement. And her Gods guide me... I tried to decode this bizarre phrase in every possible way to conclude that it meant nothing, but this very quality, which made it noticeable, and its recurrence, changed it into a sign. Should one resist the dictates of fortune when, by continually insisting, it takes the disguise of destiny? One would become insane believing it.

This man could not know what he knew of me. I tried to forget this meeting so full of mysteries that exploring them would disturb too many certainties. And furthermore would add opaqueness to gravity. I did not mention it to the Australians nor to Naresh.

'*Aap patra Hindi me likh rahe hain*? (Are you writing a letter in Hindi?)' Swami Nripendra asked me.

'*Ji haan, aaj-kal main Hindi seekh raha hun* (Yes, these days I am learning Hindi),' I replied.

'*Mujhko pani chahiye* (I want some fresh water),' said my teacher.

'*Ganga sabse badi aur pavitra nadi hai* (The Ganges is the largest and most sacred river),' I replied, feeling quite proud of myself.

When we had studied enough useful phrases, conjugations and declensions, I questioned Swami Nripendra on the Isa Upanishad that I was reading in three different translations.

One said: "They are doomed to darkness those who worship only the body, and to greater darkness those who worship only the mind," the second vowed to darkness those who worship rituals, and to larger obscurities those who worship knowledge only. And the third preferred "manifested" and "non-manifested". Swami Nripendra examined the *sloka* in Sanskrit.

'No, no, it's neither one nor the other,' he confirmed. '*Avidhya* and *vidhya*. Those who dedicate themselves to non-knowledge, non-discrimination, maya, are in darkness. And those who worship discrimination or knowledge and spiritual practices are in greater confusion.'

'Why are they doomed to greater confusion?'

'Because spiritual knowledge, which does not lead to the transformation of oneself is not true. It is complacency. Just as understanding the rules of a game is not playing it, knowing only the teaching of the non-dual path is not having reached oneness.'

'What is the difference between *vidhya* and *jnana*?'

'Knowledge and non-knowledge are two sides of the same unique transcendent. The game of the *vidhya marga* is to assert something as true as its opposite so that you believe neither of them, abandon beliefs, dethrone knowledge, foil servitude of dogmas, avert hope for truth, free oneself from the duality of true and false, put an end to conditioning… *Jnana* indicates a direct experience, an intuition of the ultimate reality.'

In the afternoons or the evenings, *bhajans* were organized in ashrams on the banks of the Ganges or in temples close to the University. I would sometimes go with the Australians and sing my head off with a dozen renunciants – simple repetitive hymns burning my voice and making me giddy.

Sankara Shiva, Sankara Shiva,
Shambu Mahadeva Sankara Shiva.

Names of Gods, their epithets, words of love… Between two songs, after having screamed in a row of loud voices, beating of drums and cymbals bursting eardrums, all was quiet in me too. Like in the eye of a typhoon, there was a sudden and vertiginous tranquillity.

Laurie and Jane sometimes danced a few steps, impersonating Krishna and Radha, Sita and Ram, Hanuman and Ravana, in Bharatnatyam style.

We would order chai in street chai-shops, munch on chickpeas and puffed rice, associate with sadhus and their *chillums*... A yogi explained his *asana*: "Focusing the gaze on the subtle opening of the forehead, he sees a light. It is Shiva's, the boatman! Contemplating this light beam, he becomes the form itself of the light he perceives from his inner vision."

A kind of abyss for consciousness to dissolve into.

While we were dining in one of the *chowk's* restaurants, standing in the lane, two boys, around ten years old, did not take their eyes off us.

'They're counting my blackheads,' Jane supposed, as if starting a game.

'They're trying to figure out the mystery of the white man,' tried Laurie.

'They're neither hungry nor beggars. They're dreaming of the happiness they presume others have. They just need experience,' I guessed.

Jane invited them to eat with us. Their few English words and my novice Hindi were enough to make a memorable conversation.

'What will you do when you grow up?'

'Tourist.'

Life is a dream, it seems.

Eight other boys between the ages of six and twelve came and stood in front of the restaurant, staring shamelessly. They were talking among themselves with loud voices and laughing wholeheartedly.

'One says I look like a pink pig,' I translated, guessing the meaning from recognizing one or two words and the body language.

I listened:

'Another says: "not a pig, a monkey's ass!" And what the tall one is saying is roughly: "White men, with their whiteness, they always look like they are on the verge of puking."'

It made them laugh a lot. Their skins were different shades of brown, eyes sparkling with intelligence and teeth white as pearls. School children, after school.

'It's healthier to make fun of Westerners than to envy them,' said Laurie – positive stand.

'They're asking if I'm sleeping with you or with Jane,' I continued translating. 'They find you too flat. "Not melons. Not even tomatoes... very small tomatoes..."'

'Chai?' Jane offered.

She ordered tea and biscuits. Naresh, who had eaten in his ashram, now joined us.

'Do you sleep without marrying in your country?' asked the tallest, in school English, and using unambiguous gestures to make himself understood.

He already knew the answer.

'Yes. But not with anybody,' said Jane.

They all burst out laughing boisterously.

'Would you agree to get married to a girl who isn't a virgin?' I asked Naresh to translate.

'*Nahiiiiiii*,' they all replied in chorus.

'As long as that is so, you will not make love before marriage,' I informed them.

'Virginity is not worth abstinence, believe me,' Jane preached.

We did not convince anybody but we had made some friends.

'What does not change, can you tell me?' he asked to start the conversation.

He was wearing a white *dhoti* and a cream-coloured cotton shawl; his head had been freshly shaven. His caste string was ostentatious.

'Nothing,' I replied, fatalistically.

The man smiled at me like someone who will finally assert his science.

'No Sir, not nothing. Change itself does not change. Everything changes except the stream of changes.'

He was proud of himself.

We were hanging around on the steps of Hanuman ghat. Laurie and Jane were not listening; Naresh was explaining *tantrism*: 'Sex is a practice to achieve psychic unity, ecstasy and enstasy. The entire body is an offering. The mind gives itself to the vitality Brahma used to create multitudes. Sex is divine!' and he quoted: 'In the *Bhagavad Gita*, Krishna proclaims, "In human beings, I am desire..."'

I had to put up with this bore that I suspected to be begging in roundabout ways. It was not the case. Ganesh was a *pujari* at the Chidambaram* Temple where *Nataraja* – Lord Shiva dancing his cosmic activities – originated and is worshipped. But he was not interested in fine arts nor dance or metaphysics. He preferred to feel sorry for himself. It started with:

'I was born a brahmin. Brahmins are the purest. We have been very good in our past lives.'

He granted himself a status or a privilege that no one had reasons for envying. He was small, with a big belly, had an oddly triangular face, eyes set far apart, sticking out ears and a very long nose. Particularly inharmonious features that suggested a long lineage of inbreeding.

'For us, it is our last life,' he said.

Maybe it's better that way, I thought somehow in spite of myself.

'Nothing escapes the cosmic law. Shiva is everything,' he ended an endless explanation.

But then he recited an even longer litany concerning a land reform, in Tamil Nadu, which had confiscated the large agricultural estates owned by the temples. This change had significantly impoverished priests, depriving them of a substantial part of their income and influence. It was a scandal, which had affected Ganesh for life because what he was referring to had happened decades earlier. He expressed no sympathy for the millions of serfs who, thanks to this revolution, had been emancipated from near slavery and now enjoyed land ownership.

'We are two hundred families having to share the temple duties,' he groaned. 'People only come rarely nowadays. Thirty years ago, devotees gave one rupee for *darshan* and *tilak*. One rupee had some value then. Today, they still give one rupee. And sometimes, nothing! We barely earn enough to avoid starving.'

'*Pujas* are very important to purify karma. Gods pay attention to devotion. Even if hell is not forever, it's better never to go there!' he carried on as much out of conviction as of threat.

These anxiety-creating Hindu theories justified his salary. He believed in them so much that he predicted those who overlooked worship would suffer abysmal adverse effects. Karma would avenge him. Temple business.

'Swami, you said change never changes. You're not flowing with the stream, you're hoping to stop the river!' I told him, to have a little fun with him. 'Your world has changed but you remain petrified in nostalgia for your caste privileges. Your religion is a superstition: a *tilak* on the forehead, a rupee to the priest and one is protected from misfortune. It does not work! Everyone knows that it's useless.'

'It works! Of course it works,' Ganesh protested. 'Shiva is a powerful God.'

'Doubt a God who cannot ensure that his priests make a living!' I urged him. 'India is changing. Your customers are your former slaves and they are wary. They have been to school. They know that it does not work. God does not protect them from hardship. In the market your rituals are worth a rupee. No more. The market itself is telling you. You need to accept this or change. Adapt what you have to offer if you cannot generate demand.'

And I was surprised that I was giving an audit to a priest.

'Are you in advertising?'

'No. In business strategy.'

'*Atcha!*' said the Brahmin, with interest. 'What do you think we should do?'

'The Almighty taking care of everything – it's over. God does not protect against adversity. For this, there are insurance companies: more expensive but relatively more reliable. And people do not expect wealth and happiness from his benevolence either; for that they either buy lottery tickets or they work hard. They no longer want to be told what to believe in: for want of liberation, for leisure they have TV. They long for a wisdom that will give them well-being in this life, whatever the circumstances. Either you can offer it or you no longer exist. The customer gives the orders and he is free not to go to the temple.

'*Nataraja*, your idol, holds the flame of knowledge that destroys the world,' I added remembering what Laurie had said about it. 'We see a circle of fire, but there is only a flame and motion. How do we get out of this merry-go-round? If you can answer this question, you are in business. If not, you are out.'

Ganesh was an antique, a perfect replica of knowledge dating back to the most ancient Upanishads concerning convoluted and mandatory rituals passed down by his forefathers; yet in truth these rituals were not so essential. The unbelieving-believers had managed to do without them. Apart from rites, he had nothing to offer. The fidelity his caste devoted to its traditions would become its funeral oration. Those who do not evolve, disappear. Often, those who have disappeared have known that.

'Teach love. Love sells well!' I suggested, wearily.

In the shadow of sadhus, the priests did not shine.

He was as tall and as strong as you would imagine a Viking, and he was not short of projects… 'I'm from Arkansas! Bob's ma name. Microbiologist! Work for Monsanto. D'ya know Monsanto?' A very strong American accent from near Nowhere Very Deep, as the coastal US citizens say of their Mid-West compatriots.

'It's the multinational laboratory that sells genetically modified sterile seeds,' Jane replied. 'Soya-bean, maize, tomato, cotton…'

What remained of his long blond hair was now both yellowish and grey and was gathered in a meagre ponytail. He was in his fifties. We were in a restaurant for backpackers and broke tourists. He drew out of his pocket a piece of hashish as big as an eraser.

'Exactly Man. A disgrace! A horrible idea! And'am part of it! But in ma free time, I also work for maself.' He widened his eyes like a little rascal, and then focused on the flame of his lighter that he placed under the piece of hashish. He crumbled some from a corner in his palm. 'Ya know what I do?' He finally asked, mixing the resin crumbs with tobacco.

'A joint, Man, I know,' laughed Laurie with a heavy voice straight from an Australian suburb tavern.

'No, Man,' Bob replied. 'I've located the sites that control the production of THC in hemp's genes. I'm a microbiologist,' he reminded us. 'I've grafted them on the DNA of nettles, tomatoes and hops. Get it? You plant nettles in your garden and if you smoke'em, you've got the same high as if you'd planted cannabis, marijuana, *ganja*, pot, grass, dope, weed… Get it now, Man?'

'Fantastic!' exclaimed the girls.

Absolutely brilliant! I thought too.

Without hurrying, he stuck together two sheets of cigarette paper perpendicularly and tore the remnants…

'I'll offer the seeds on the web. They'll be called *Princess*. Those who plant'em will reap good THC and millions of seeds,' he said almost as a song, 'they'll give'em to others who'll give'em to others… It'll spread exponential, Man! Cops won't understand nothin.'

'Actually, you are both alter-globalisation and pro-GMO at the same time. A rarity!' I admired.

'Maybe we should not totally reject GMOs after all,' said Jane.

'They are quite interesting from this point of view,' approved Laurie.

'In appearance, they are normal nettles or tomatoes,' Bob went on to explain. 'Who can prohibit tomatoes, Man? Who can control nettles? Who can outlaw pulling them up! They want everyone to think like them, square, business, profit. When the whole world will be stoned, Man, there'll be no more wars. And neither spreading sterile seeds, which is a war too, in a way.'

'You're an undercover agent in enemy lines,' praised Laurie.

'After the next revolution, you will receive medals and there will be streets and bridges named after you,' I prophesied.

'*Amen!*' Jane proclaimed like a born-again.

He put the mixture on the sheet and rolled it in a cone. Then a lick on the cigarette paper...

'Many people will end up smoking nettles which will only be nettles,' Jane suddenly realised.

'Shouldn't we test hop's smoke on a few rats...' I suggested.

'The revolution must take place in our minds, not in the streets,' concluded the American without acknowledging our comments. *Amen! Bom Shankar!*

He wet the tip of the *joint* rolling it on his tongue, lit it up, and inhaled.

'To change the world, we must change its karma, my friend,' he added holding his breath.

He breathed out a cloud of brownish smoke; then emphasized: 'And to change its karma, you change what it trips on. Shit calms. And makes you creative.'

'You're a missionary actually!'

'Yeah!'

He handed me the cigarette.

'Is it hemp or nettle?'

'*Charas*, Man, good Parvati *charas*!'

The authentic equivalent of Chivas Regal in another culture – 18 years of maturation and genetically untouched.

'Soon, at the market, we will ask: One kilo of "trip" tomatoes and two "ordinary", please,' Laurie began.

'And in twenty years, Chivas flavoured THC modified hops, aged in barrels with care and love...' I proposed.

'This nettle on your balcony, is it Colombian?' 'No, it's Afghan crossed with Arkansas. They sting less,' improvised Jane.

'Without dreaming of hallucinogenic potatoes and opium gherkins,' thought Bob.

And pink elephants.

It's time to invent post liberalism.

In the Times of India:

Suicide of 40 000 farmers
Following the acquisition of Mahyco, the largest Indian seed company, by Monsanto, 40 000 cotton growers riddled with debts have swallowed pesticide to end their life.

Having destroyed the local reserves of cotton seeds, Monsanto forced cotton farmers into debt selling them genetically modified Bt seeds which are much more expensive than traditional seeds, along with the fertilizers needed for them. But their crops are below expectations. Unable to repay the debts, farmers have to forsake their land. The seized plots are then bought by large farms from the food industry.

Post liberalism is really urgent.

Mahavir Baba was taking in the wind breeze, alone on a promontory of Dassawamedh ghat. I had already spoken to him. He is the one who said he did not stay in the same place very long. The sun was already high that morning. It was pleasantly warm. I sat down with him.

'Basically, are you a sadhu for the lifestyle or to seek liberation?'

He wore a sleeveless red safari jacket with a dozen pockets over a T-shirt and a faded pink *lungi*. He had soft eyes.

'Between knowing the world is an illusion and freeing oneself from it, there is a difference: indifference and renunciation.'

'With Maya, you only deny reality, you do not transcend it,' I opposed.

'You do not want to deny your existence as long as you feel you are winning,' said this quiet man who expected nothing and seemed content with that.

'It's probably true,' I admitted. 'Yet, do we have to undergo pain to discredit the world?'

'You must want to get freed from it, whatever the reason.'

'Karma, maya and liberation are as illusory as everything else because everything is. Why do you want to free yourself from links which do not exist?'

'Maya and karma do not bind you to a destiny,' said Baba Mahavir, 'they enthral you in a game. Maya is the seduction of forms and motion. Indifference and renunciation set you free from it.'

What should I renounce, to renounce? I asked myself at Manikarnika ghat. What urgency, what disgust, what despair, what challenge or what doubt does one have to respond to? I wondered. We were watching the night covering the river and fires consuming dead bodies. Naresh was probably contemplating the reverse side of desire. Laurie was holding my arm with both her hands. Jane was quiet.

Indifference, I remembered. Is it a way to defeat death, by giving up the fight? Or just another way of fighting? Who does not imagine himself for a moment in place of the dead man, tied with cloth strips, being just placed on the pyre?

No. Here, there is no more problem. We must imagine the final moments of lucidity of a drowning man… In a flash, I realize that I'm exhausted, I am giving up, I breathe in water, I will soon black out for good and never be me again. A blade of anguish scrapes my stomach. I wonder one last time if there is a player behind the game of seduction of forms and motion… Before I prepare to accept whatever will come. Indifference and renunciation. And then the great sleep of emptiness. With or without a dream?…

No. At that moment, it's already too late. We must look to the hospital when being informed of having a deadly disease: *three months at most*, the doctor would finally come out with. *It's happening to me*, I would tell myself stunned, but still incredulous. *It must happen one day*, I would try to reason in vain. I would recall everything I have put off till tomorrow during my entire life. *Not now, not me, not here, not three months, not so short… and why?* I would try to resist; but resist what, death or believing in my death? *I am dying*, I would contemplate intermittently in terror, dizziness, denial, contempt, grief, derision, fear, horror, helplessness, rage, resignation… in every possible order. I would try to conceive of a world without me. I would picture some of the people I have known learning about my death. I would explore again if there is a "me" without a body. *Let's go*, I would agree from time to time with courage. The last day, I would say that I would like to live until tomorrow. *But tomorrow, I'll still want to be alive…* Renouncing is to abandon the ideas of struggle, bargaining, compromising and planning. To cease wanting…

Meditation, I discovered later, reveals that state in which we struggle against struggling without doing anything other than observe. There, outside impulse and necessity, there is no more fear, denial, grief, contempt, rage or resignation…

Travel encounters of the romantic kind are as fleeting as a season and lighter than a plane ticket… We loved each other, conceived no children and split without remorse or resentment. It was better than a fairy tale. The two Australians offered to continue the adventure with me in Goa. Sleepless nights on the beach in ecstasy and techno. I wanted to understand immobility, or what cannot be other than oneself but does not control anything and has the shape of the light that is perceived by inner vision… something like that.

'See you in Sydney maybe!' said Laurie.

'*Que sera sera!*' I promised.

Naresh was sad. But he also had to leave. He took a train to Kolkata the following week.

On the *ghats*, a yogi taught me *Pranayama**, a yoga *sadhana*. Breathing in: 1 length of time; holding breath: 4 lengths of time; breathing out: 2 lengths. Through the right nostril and then through the left. Next, one doubles, triples, and quadruples the pattern. 'It calms the mental activity, the source of all illusions,' he promised. I tried. It does calm indeed, and quickly. There are so many calculations one has to do, I could think of nothing else! What was I supposed to find in suffocation? Learn to relax… slow down… concentrate… Just be, maybe.

Another sadhu told me that the symbol of *manas*, the mind, is a miraculous pearl… 'because it grants wishes; and because it interprets perceptions and sensations, it holds the key to happiness and sorrow.' What troubles men are not things, but rather the judgments they make about things, Epictetus also ruminated.

I read in the *Uddhava Gita*:

> It is not the body the source of pleasure and pain,
> Nor Gods, nor the soul, nor planets,
> Nor action (karma) nor time (kaal).
> It is the mind, the absolute cause
> Which sets the wheel of *samsara* in motion.[2]

---

2 *Uddhava Gita* 18, 43. *Samsara*, life, the cycle of lives, the cycles of life; the succession of birth.

Peace

One day, as I was strolling around the lanes behind Kedar ghat, I discovered a little square encircled with black stone houses two storeys high covered by a large and old banyan, whose foliage made a broad canopy perforated by glints of sky. In the interlacing of its aerial roots, somebody had recognized the head of Ganesha, his large smooth cranium, his trunk turned to the right, his broken tusk… and had painted him an orange face, drawn eyes, marked his forehead with a *tilak* and his cheeks with a *trishul** and a *swastika**. The God, thus revealed, was honoured with fresh flowers, a banana and scattered grains of rice.

A few steps away, leaning against a windowsill, an old sadhu was quietly smoking a cigarette. A woman was doing her washing on a flat stone beside the pump; struck by the full glare of the sun, her scarlet plastic bucket was shining like a ruby. Two naked children were running after each other, shouting at the tops of their voices. Two other children, wet hair and shivering, were hugging each other under a shawl in front of a door. A tied up goat was hopping about on the spot impatiently… The soothing sight of an idyllic scene.

I sat on the steps, a little distance from the sadhu, picked out an orange from my bag and waited until the monk had finished enjoying his cigarette to present it to him. He greeted me with a gaze that was both profound and gentle, then enhanced by a smile filled with love.

'*Wherlle arle lyou flrom?*' he asked me.

He was a little stooped and short, and his white bun was falling forward.

'I come from your heart,' I improvised pointing to the old man's chest.

'*Aaaaah*, Ram!' he sighed, lowering the eyes.

He raised them at once to observe the one he had just called with a name of God. '*You arllle in love willlth India!*' he declared without hiding that he was delighted.

'Yes Babaji, that is slowly happening to me.'

'Come to live here,' he said indicating the door of the house. 'There is an empty room. It is better than a guesthouse.'

He showed it to me, on the ground floor, then introduced me to the owner who lived in the back, around a small courtyard, with his wife, his mother-in-law and two children. Three other families lived on the upper floor.

I moved in the following day.

Ram Tilak Baba had his own room across a corridor from mine. There was no furniture at his place either. He spent the days and a good part of the nights sitting on his two blankets in front of his window opening out on the square, like mine.

We established a kind of arrangement: I brought rice, *daal*, some vegetables and spices, and in the evening, with loving care, he prepared a meal on a kerosene stove he had borrowed. We ate together without speaking much and often without a word. I also bought him oranges or some pastry.

Three days passed.

'What do you do, Swamiji?' I asked him, coming back from the market and passing the groceries through the window.

'In the shady coolness bestowed by the banyan, he looks where thoughts come from,' he answered.

I laid down my quilt folded in four in front of my window, and tried to find where thoughts come from, but I got tired of this rather quickly and went for a chai on the *ghats* which is pervaded by a burning and radiant peace when the sun is high. The paved walkway is deserted, the Ganges glistens, sliding along silently, a few barges go downstream, buffaloes ruminate and meditate in the strip of shade at the wall's edge, the breeze hisses softly in one's ears… this kind of solitude was very pleasant.

'You start by passively watching your passing thoughts,' explained Ram Tilak Baba as I was returning.

The following day, I devoted my time to observe my thoughts; now spied upon they talked alone, intimidated by the observer that I was they now lacked motivation. Ram Tilak advised me to take this very thought as a target. I examined it. It did not take a whole day. I discovered an ordinary feeling that I called boredom. The life of a goat tied to the stake but without a rope.

It was not pain strictly speaking, it was… like the tears of the newborn on the floor above, insistent and pressing. Nagging. A feeling without a cause or rather whose cause is the absence of something, a warning function of consciousness to itself, a hollowness, like hunger: the neurons are demanding, and not only oxygenated blood, but adventures for the dendrites to bite on, for electric activity to be disseminated in the head, for stimulation, motion. They are in need of acetylcholine, the substance they release through their synapses to communicate with each other. And which brings them pleasure. But which sometimes also agitates worries, frustrations and other inconveniences.

My attention held fast to whatever I saw: amazed or lost, worn-out tourists, sometimes holding on to a bottle of water; the frustrated goat which did not grow tired of pulling at its leash; white shirt and blue tie, the elder brothers returned from school… The newborns spent the better part of the day deploring being born endlessly groaning in the background against the first frustrations of the human condition.

A squirrel went down the banyan to go and sample the rice offered to Ganesha. It was joined by another. They were nervous and apprehensive like robbers on the scene of their crime. With reason. A skinny black cat that seemed to prowl around unconcerned suddenly darted for one of the rodents which rushed up the tree. The cat attempted to follow it, but squirrels are unbeatable on a trunk: they can move horizontally, make rapid U-turns and go up vertically and much higher than a cat. It escaped easily. But at once, in a cackle which increased and spread everywhere, all the squirrels of the square had informed each other. And they were shocked!

An ant carrying a vegetable scrap a hundred times bigger than itself tried to climb up the wall. It fell but valiantly went for the ascent again. And again. Ten times, twenty times… on its fifty-fourth attempt, it succeeded in reaching the small round opening above the door, which ventilates the excess heat. A lesson in tenacity.

Boredom: an indefinite craving. Anything but idleness.

And sometimes I did not see anything; my vision disappeared into my thought, and images, ideas or feelings wandered around.

'Don't fight boredom. Accept it,' Ram Tilak Baba recommended. 'Try and try again.'

'I am not interested enough in myself to concentrate on myself only. It does not work.'

'Then take the *Ram-mantra*. Come near.'

Ram Tilak whispered three times in my ear: "*Om Shri Ram Jay Ram Jay Jay Ram*" in a singing voice.

'Repeat this *mantra* constantly, sitting, standing, walking, washing, eating, dreaming. It will concentrate your thought and will reveal to you who it is that actually acts.'

'What does that mean?'

'Ram is consciousness. *I greet the Lord Consciousness, Victory, Victory to Consciousness.*'

I agreed to repeat it. To see, as poker players say when they place a bet. I forgot to repeat. I remembered to repeat. I could even say these syllables and think of something else. *Om Shri Ram Jay Ram...* I did not make an obsession of it, I tried an experiment. *Jay Jay Ram...* It often made me yawn.

As I was walking, my *mantra* on the lips, a brahmin seized my wrist to try to tie a wool yarn around it and in this way, sell me a blessing. When I understood what was going on, I withdrew my arm vigorously. *I am God!* I said with authority enlarging my eyes. *Bow under my feet!* He was unable to utter a word and fled. 'He is God also,' said a smiling man who had seen the incident. *Jay Jay Ram...*

I went for walks...

In the window of *Indica Bookshop*, ten copies of a best-seller: *God is my C.E.O.* It's a guide of *ethically correct* liberalism for the use by God's concerned World Corporation Ltd. employees tormented by the devastation of globalisation. New Age flying to the pension and hedge funds' assistance or how mystics can rescue economics, or in other words how to please God without displeasing shareholders and more practically, without sacrificing profitability. There is no other God than the shareholder and Dividend is his prophet, Gregory would have parodied. I haven't written to him for a long time, I thought. I bought the Katha Upanishad commented by Sankaracharya, and two novels: *A terrace on the Ganges*, by Pankaj Mishra and *Kanthapura* by Rajah Rao. *Shri Ram Jay...* I flipped through *I am That* by Nisargadatta Maharaj: *There is no exit. The exit is also a part of the dream. All that you have to realize is the dream as being a dream.*

Shri Ram Jay...

The *cycle-rickshaw walla* takes a nap, rolled up in a grey cotton blanket, head on the bench, coccyx on the saddle, and feet on the handlebar. With a little more effort, this fakir would be levitating... *Shri Ram...* The *minch chilli walla* slips chilli fritters into the boiling oil. His customers do not speak to each other, they shout out. Mouths full of fire. An energetic woman wearing a silk sari haggles over the price of rice. In front of the confectioner's stall, muffle high, a buffalo pretends it is thinking of something else. The confectioner doesn't believe it. He is already leaning to seize his stick. A tourist takes pictures of a bare-chested boy in beige shorts full of holes. A grimy vagrant, wearing a dirty *lungi* and his brown blanket, crosses the lane with the vacillating stride of a drug addict. *Jay Ram...* Lured by music and chants, I entered a small white marble temple dedicated to Hanuman, the monkey God. It was empty. A CD was constantly repeating the *puja. Om Shri Ram...* Leprous, cripple, simple minded, depressive, lazy or tired beggars and other victims of karma camped and held their hands out along the steps of Dassawamedh. *Ram...*

Om...

'Where from?'

'*Bhagwan!*' I replied, raising my index finger towards the sky.

'*Bhagwan! Bhagwan!* God is a human creation,' answered this still young man who was not a sadhu but nevertheless homeless, a practitioner of non-action and an atheist. 'It does not mean anything to say *Bhagwan*. I know that I don't know, said Socrates; that's a beginning. This moment is *Bhagwan*.'

'OK.'

'All this is nothing.'

And nihilist.

Jay Ram Jay Jay...

The Nepalese temple, of which travel guides point out the remarkable erotic sculptures, was built by King Virendra at the beginning of the nineteenth century. It is now a museum temple kept by a small miserly faced brahmin who opens it only to squeeze rupees out of rare tourists and pilgrims. He swooped down on me like a crow sweeping on the eyes of a cadaver. In his elementary school English, this man spoke only about money, needs and costs... Between two pressing appeals, he took on the knowing look of complicity in concupiscence whilst pointing out Shiva and Parvati on a cornice, in three or four acrobatic sexual postures. 'This temple is the shelter of your cupidity,' I told him, refusing to give anything. Not sure that he understood.

Ram!

A wooden crate was turned into a small portable altar placed in the middle of the street; a chalk-drawn face, on a small garlanded plank made an indefinable God; a burning wick reflected in an oil cup where passers-by dropped coins and then brushed the flames with their finger tips before placing them to their hearts and eyes. Two incense cones smoked on each side. *Jay Ram!*

Ram Tilak Baba sometimes bent over a large, old and worn-out book which opened like a laptop. His only book. He would decipher some of the printed lines, then straighten up to examine their relevance or their wisdom. Slowly. Very slowly. He had undoubtedly read it a hundred times already and was in no hurry to finish it again. Whenever he talked to me, he would only say a few words. Nothing on *how are you*, never *hello* or *goodbye*. He would quote an Upanishad, point out a principle, formulate a thought in his shrill little voice. 'Ram! Maya, it should not be hated, it should be loved.' In passing. Or: 'The inner reality, Ram, is the world perceived as oneself.' That fed the neurons a little. That gave me an insight. *Jay Jay Ram...*

He took his bath in the Ganges at dawn, slowly and silently. And when he started cooking or washed his clothing, I only heard the water flowing from the tap. He seemed to slide on the ground and brush against things. The careful and always precise way he moved, collaborated in elaborating the quiet harmony around him. His daily cigarette was a weakness which made him even more likeable.

'Would you translate some lines of your book for me, Swamiji?'

Ram Tilak Baba read: 'It is there, in dreams that *manas*, the mind – this divinity! – enjoys its majesty. The senses are then withdrawn within to this *manas*, which is the internal sense, and at this time, the only sense. It re-examines what it already saw, re-hears what it already heard, and experiences once more what it has experienced in various places yet differently. It perceives what was seen and what was not seen, heard and not heard, experienced and not experienced, that which has existed and that which does not exist. It sees all of this; it sees this in its quality of everything. By perceiving everything it is everything.'[1]

Shri Ram...

'Kashi* is the most sacred of India's sacred places, because in Kashi all your past is washed away,' Ram Tilak Baba said one evening, during dinner. 'Kashi is the threshold. When you immerse yourself in the Ganga, she absorbs your form; you dissolve in her. Three times. The third time, consider that you have just been born.'

Om Shri...

The following day, I went to take my first bath in the sacred river in which so many things drift and rot. It is holy, but it is also used as bath-tub, washing-place, waste bin, cemetery and sewer by a hundred million people over a thousand kilometres. I tried not to notice what was floating around me, praying – to nobody in particular – to be spared infections and also hoping a little in this promise to soon be born anew. But without dying for real! Imitating Varanasi's locals, immersed to the chest I pushed away the detritus floating around me, joined my hands, greeted the sun, smiled at him and plunged vertically. Once, twice, three times... I felt nothing special, no dissolution, no radical memory failure and no new innocence. It was noon. The water was freezing cold. And if there is any rebirth, it is from believing one would die. *Om...*

I rubbed myself and then returned to the shore, taking care not to slip on the thick viscous filth stagnating on the steps. I dried out under the sun, got dressed and sat in the shade on one of the large stones that reinforce the wall, facing the broad vibrating bluish band.

Shri Ram... I watched my thoughts suggesting desires or desires suggesting thoughts... I remembered the smile of quite a nice looking girl who was walking out of Trimurti Guest House this morning, when I was coming back from the market. I should go and take a stroll around there... In Sanskrit, I mulled over, man (*manu*) derives from mind (*manas*). *Humus* makes *homo*, man, in Latin, but *humus*, the soil, the earth, is the source of all life; the specificity of man is the mind, I considered, giving my approval to the Sanskrit. *Shri Ram...*

Ramasharvan Baba, the pious devotee of Ganesha, gave me such an appealing grin that I felt a burst of joy, which I became aware of later. I thought of Mahavir Baba: indifference and renunciation. I wondered what strategy Nicolas was conjuring up and what he would be selling in Paris. And which merger Gregory was working on, studying his balance sheets, graphics, press releases and analyses? It is claimed that the world has opened up to free trade but it has been omitted that merchants and profit rule over the world to prevent us fearing the dreadful consequences of making greed a universal value! I ruminated. *Jay Jay Ram...*

My past had not dissolved.

I smiled to Gregory. India does not exist, you had said. You were right, she talks about it a lot, I answered him in space-time lag. Reality is an idea, also said Plato. But how can one live with this idea? *Om Om Om...* I tried to concentrate my thoughts on Ram Tilak Baba's peaceful aura. *Om...* but I came up immediately with this self-evident truth: a renunciant does not want to escape poverty; he has decided that he does not need anything. To become lighter.

To free himself from gravity. This lightness… perhaps that is what levitation is. *Shri Ram…*

I thought of Laurie with tender nostalgia. And Jane with a friendly enthusiasm. *Ram Naam Satthya Hai!* A procession carried a client towards Manikarnika ghat. *Shri Ram…* 'He goes, homeless, scorning gold and the glances of girls,' a baba prided himself yesterday at Asi ghat. I could understand his indifference for gold… but as for girls, he is wrong, I commented to myself. *Om…* A lateen sail barge attracted me in another rhythm, a very different universe of desires. I imagined myself sailing down the river on one of these boats. Whole days sliding along landscapes… But I remained there, motionless, looking passively at what appeared, then disappeared in front of me and in me. *Shri Ram…*

I cancelled my Hindi lesson and spent the following day on the *ghats*. And also the day after. Three days contemplating about the river which promises new birth caressing my eyes. A luminosity arises from the gentleness of the gaze that is placed on things. For full three days, after taking a bath, I observed my thoughts change from a network of agitation in the morning to an inexplicable feeling of peace in the evening. *Jay Ram Jay Jay Ram…*

Peace! It is nothing like boredom which is more of a beckoning, albeit indefinite. Peace… the passivity of satisfaction… A yielding, as if to a caress. A nuance of blandness within lightness. A spongy astonishment. An acquiescence. The desire or fear of being someone else, suspended. *Om…*

The fourth day, peace was there in me from the morning. And it told me it's secret: Nothing is to be done, nothing has to be done and there is nothing one has to do. Ambitions, responsibility and duties are vain. There is nothing to be, to have, reach, find, prove, become or gain. Neither destiny, nor God, nor merits of sorts… Nothing to do. *Om Shri Ram Jay Ram Jay Jay Ram…* Existence does not have a goal or a price. One can do whatever he wants with it…

And everything became light.

The *Avadhuta Gita* confirmed…

> There is neither reason to act, nor action to take,
> How then, O my friend, would I speak about victory or defeat?
> And there is nothing to venerate,
> So how would I speak about knowledge?

What are you looking for? Chandrahas Baba, my first sadhu and guru-for-a-day had asked me. *Peace*, I had answered.

This country spoke to me.

And where is home for you? this Baba had again questioned me. *In this peace*, I could now answer. *Nothing has to be done* became my *mantra*. These words, this thought, this reminder brought me back instantaneously to these moments at the banks of Ganges. I had never known such a profound well-being. The Ganges offered me this gift, inspired this intuition… I was born that day.

I went to bow before Ram Tilak Baba and told him my discoveries.

'Atcha!' he exclaimed as if he had achieved a great thing. 'Persevere and then come back to India.'

The following day, my guru and neighbour said good-bye.

'Where are you going?'

'Where my steps will lead me,' he answered as if this were obvious.

I gave him an offering. He left, carrying his small bag and his two blankets. His room was rented to a couple and their two children. I returned to my *lingam mandir* at Ranamahal ghat.

In the evening, I would go and listen to *ragas** or see a dance performance in a temple, or join a circle of sadhus, or withdraw into my cave… at such times I would offer a candle to the *lingam* and then contemplate the encounters of the day. Sometimes imprisoning thoughts would arise, that suggested life objectives – above all, prescribing it to have some. *Nothing has to be done,* this *mantra*, this certainty, this freedom, immediately relieved me from the burden of the compulsory mode of existence and brought me back to serenity. Out of reach, at times, of the tyranny of ideas and desires, ego and super-ego, fears and ambitions. Nothing to do, reach, prove or find. But I would forget. And when disturbed, peace is no longer peace. I would then go to take the *darshan* of a quiet man dressed in saffron and, in his aura, enjoy moments of causeless bliss.

I spent an afternoon in the Durga temple, a unique place of worship where one can sit down. I reflected on: "Nothing is enough for the man to whom enough is too little," a saying of Epicurus. Sadhus don't just talk about *it*, they become *it*. Isn't this the way to spend life? But I would die in three days… replied the little voice of reason.

Except for a few monkeys, I was the only visitor for whom the meeting with this sacred site lasted for more than three minutes. Devotees followed one another in front of the listless *pujari* and his fixed eyed idol. They received a *tilak* and a spoonful of holy water in their palm, drank it, dried their hand on their hair and left an offering before setting out.

I opened the *Avadhuta Gita*. The wise man proclaimed: "In truth I am reality eluded of such blemishes as destiny." To dare to elude… this stuck in my mind. Isn't liberation firstly the freedom one grants himself? One must relinquish the benefits of illusions to escape illusion, Maya Baba had reasoned. But I would die in three days… the leitmotiv of caution.

I summoned Shiva to inspire me…

Maya, karma, moksha… Is there a world, a reality? Maybe that is not the right question. Should one aspire to set oneself free from it? That one neither. Am I or am I not? Not that either. The only question worth exploring is: how should I live? The answer I found was… as a baba.

Sadhus are not instruments or guardians of theological principles. I had observed that they are neither moulded in a single faith, nor fixed in compulsory ambition. They believe what they want to believe, like each and everyone. Some perform severe *tapasya* but the majority do without. How many spend years meditating in mountain solitudes? How many reach the pinnacle of immobility or cross over the ocean of becoming? How many keep an arm raised up until calcification or lie down on a bed of nails? Very few. And to achieve what, was my own answer. If one considers his body as a prison for consciousness, there may be some value in these painful disciplines which promise liberation. Otherwise one lacks motivation. There are many more who more modestly give up the world without completely leaving it, contemplate its movements, practise non-action in contentment, roam the roads, flaunt satisfaction as a principle, bathe in cheerful peace, and their desire is not to desire anything else. And their company is often pleasant.

My fantasy was not about aiming for the Everest of asceticism. I did not believe I was going to learn to levitate, or to be in two places at once, nor did I hope to reach immortality. I was not anxious in my metaphysical curiosity; I did not have the heart of a hero or the spirit of an athlete. I would be content remaining in the planes of contentment. In the peace offered by the certainty: *there is nothing to do.*

What does the *Astavakra* say today? Page thirty-four, he raises a question:

> The one whose mind is freed from desire and from desiring to be free from desire,
> This magnificent soul that has found satisfaction in self-knowledge.
> What could he be comparable to? (III, 12)

To draw satisfaction from self-knowledge appeared to me an ideal. Was it accessible? It had not to be an objective however, but rather an absence (of struggle, action and reaction, comparison), a weightlessness, a leniency in being. I admired that in baba-life. But I would die in three days, whispered the coward.

I thought I had come to the end of my thinking when a young sadhu came up joined hands and asked for permission to sit down with me. I granted him that.

He wanted to speak with a Westerner, but after having stated that he didn't say one more word. I questioned him on wandering monks' daily life.

'I serve my guru.'

'And what else do you do?'

'I practise yoga *asanas*… meditate, pray, love, give…' he enumerated.

'Where do you sleep? How do you find your food?'

'In a temple. Or we beg.'

'Is this hard? Are you ever hungry?'

'Not often.'

'And cold?'

'Not often.'

'Do you sometimes rest?'

'Yes.'

'And when it rains?'

'During monsoon, we stay on the mountain.'

'Are you never bored?'

'Sometimes…'

He was continually laconic. This boy had never learned to speak about himself. What happens on the roads? Your *asanas*, what do they produce in you? Uday Baba did not understand my questions. He was nineteen years old and had lived this way since childhood. Wandering was normal life for him, and his *asanas* were somehow his version of school work. After a while, he asked for permission to leave.

We met again at the parasol where I took my Hindi lessons. He would sit in front of me and look at me. He would not say anything if I did not question him.

'What do you find sitting with me?'

'There is nothing to find,' he answered.

Young sadhus go from one circle of renunciants to another during their free time. I saw some of them on Asi ghat. This one had chosen me. He took my *darshan*. I took his. His presence was respectful and familiar. His company forced me to observe myself, and to observe myself being observed.

One day, Uday Baba took leave and asked for my teaching.

'My teaching? I don't know anything!' I exclaimed. 'I am not qualified!'

'Real gurus also answer this way,' Uday insisted. He saw me as someone from a distant country, strange and not so strange after all, who though different, had surely acquired some knowledge.

'There is nothing one has to achieve,' I told him. 'When that is known, everything becomes light.'

Satisfied, Uday bowed to the ground, offered me a bundle of incense sticks and left.

'Sadhus do not die in three days!' I retorted to the obsessive voice of reason and caution.

I was adopted by a group of about fifteen sadhus who were camping out with their old huge and lenient guru on the hardened silt left by annual floods at Asi ghat.

The younger ones built a *dhooni* while others swept with straw. They found two large branches and lit a fire with dried cow dung, laid out plastic covers around the hearth and then their blankets, forming a broad circle. The fire was high and vigorous. They considered its intensity as a blessing. *Om Namah Shivayah!* The Naga babas stripped off. We smoked *chillums*. We sang hymns. They honoured their guru lifting him up in the air several times. *Guruji ki jai!* It was a feast for these divine vagrants.

'It is a feast everyday!' Ramanand Das Mahatyagi told me. He had a broad smile and responsibility for the supply of *ganja*. He asked me: 'What did you come here for?'

'Wisdom,' I answered in joy.

This 22 year old Naga baba straightened up and, raising an arm and his chin, he professed:

'The final wisdom is: all is One. One is all. And now, what do you do? Become a sadhu?'

I quivered with longing and fear.

I spent the night between two babas. My first night under the sky.

In the morning, I bowed before Ramanand Das and put down a *dakshina* at his feet. My young guru accepted it with pleasure, honoured and proud to have been useful. I gave an offering to his guru as well, and he at once announced its amount with satisfaction. And then I watched these free, simple and generous men disappear, frolicking about villages and cities as I somehow imagined the disciples of Saint Francis of Assisi.

Final wisdom is all is One. And now? I already missed them.

I considered the civilisation that raises renunciants to the rank of saints, respects them during their lifetime and supports them, as being admirably wise. What a miracle that a country exists where this way of life is possible! I would not die in three days! I refused to listen to the shivers and fear and I promised myself to return one day.

I understood that whatever my professional achievements, no matter what I would manage to acquire or elucidate, I would still be missing the essential: Peace. And this is how I discovered how not to be a materialist...

There is nothing one has to do, this point of view, this *Weltanschauung*, this *darshan*, this awareness generated peace but did not maintain it. I wanted to spend my life in its aura.

And the prophecy of Balamani Baba came true.

Five years later, I left my apartment, job, income tax, world news and other compulsory concerns, I left my friends, gave up wine, cheese, Pastis, *saucisson* and many other sweet pleasures like monthly wages and annual bonuses, spring mattresses and private cars, central heating and my books, and I followed the advice of Ram Tilak Baba: I returned to Varanasi. And I met Ananda Baba, my guru.

Part Three

Initiation

*I*n front of a shoe store, a man greeted us with joined hands: *Ram Ram!* A short russet-red henna tinted beard and a white cap marked him out as a Muslim. *Allah Allah!* whispered Ananda Baba, turning his palms upwards. They smiled at each other. Further along, three women, enclosed in black *burkhas**, slid along in a mute file behind a stocky man. Cone shaped, uniform silhouettes with no legs, no face, no eyes. Shadows of their shadows. *Shri Ram!* shouted a sadhu behind his short clay *chillum. Jay Ram!* shouted back my guru while the other inhaled through the pipe.

And finally, the light of the Ganges and its breath of fresh air. When the morning sun was hot enough to lift the dampness deposited by night, Allahabad was clothed in a hot dazzling veil of mist.

Hindus regard confluences as sacred. They see them as a symbol of union and they bathe there to purify themselves. Allahabad is a Holy City, for in Allahabad, the Ganges, – daughter of Himalayas, albeit muddy – and Yamuna – the sparklingly clear daughter of the Sun – unite with a third river, invisible, mythological, the Saraswati, the river of illumination. Also the name of our order. We immersed ourselves in this auspicious symbol and then Ananda Baba decided to build a *dhooni* close to the cremation ghat. We gathered some stones and bought wood.

We had lived and slept there for two days.

Two days contemplating five pyres swallowing bodies before collapsing in themselves, leaving only heaps of ashes. Two days governed by the rhythm of funeral processions announcing: *Ram Naam Satthya Hai!* Four men carried a corpse covered with a yellow silk shroud on a bamboo stretcher. Parents and friends followed behind proclaiming: The only truth is the name of God!

The yellow fabric is consumed by the first flames and then the body is naked, but it does not burn at once, first it boils, then cooks, grills and blackens. The penis becomes a torch, a wick; it shrivels and then disappears. While roasting, muscles tense up. When a sizzling leg or arm rises, then falls and rolls away, a *domra*, using two long sticks, puts the stray limb back on the remains. The stomach explodes, the entrails overflow. Sons break the skulls of their blazing fathers with a heavy stone. A smoking pulp comes out of it. The eyes have long before evaporated, the cheeks are ablaze. *Ram Naam Satthya Hai!* The wreaths of smoke form greyish silhouettes undulating in a last dance before utterly dissolving into transparency. Yet we still breathe in these grilled smelling ghosts. In the distance vultures and crows quarrel over the corpses of dogs, cows, saints, children and the poor, given to the river and slowly drifting down it. The fish share the leftovers. A fisherman throws his net. *Ganga Ma* is a food chain!

How can I fail to imagine for a moment myself in the place of this dead man… or as the ashes which the *domras* collect, carried in buckets and thrown in the river without any particular care. Nothing. But thinking of oneself as nothing is still a lot of being, Ananda Baba had told me.

One day, after having smoked a lot, I felt a dizziness, which turned into an intense tiredness, which became a massive weakness. I yawned repeatedly. Sitting up became impossible. I lay down but even then my body weighed me down. I understood that I was going to lose consciousness, but resisted with my last strength. The world seemed to crumble. The effort required to keep it all together was too great. I thought that death must beckon in a similarly irresistible way. I thought that I would die if I lost consciousness. That I would stop breathing… But I even consented to die as I gave up the struggle and then fainted.

We really don't know anything about death and yet it is the only absolute certainty we have. That day the sun will not rise for us, but for the others he will remain loyal. We are afraid of it, although death is the only event in our life that we will have no knowledge of; the episode that we will not live through. Consciousness cannot experience its own non-existence. Death is the moment after; after agony and demise, after consciousness. When I was unconscious, I did not exist anymore. When we do not exist anymore, we do not exist. What can we be afraid of in nothingness? How could nothingness do us wrong? Where is the problem? There is no problem. And I found this thought more liberating than the promises of an eternal me stuck between remorse and hope.

The grieved ones came and asked us to make wishes in favour of their deceased. Charity being among the conditions that make a rite complete and effective, they left us offerings. Several times a day, processions of pilgrims accompanied by a brahmin went to the water's edge to accomplish a ritual, concluded with a distribution of alms.

'Go have your head shaved and take a bath. Tonight you will receive *diksha*, initiation,' announced Ananda Baba.

'*Atcha!*'

I saw my hair fall in tufts around me. I closed my eyes and opened them only when the barber had passed his hand on my bare, smooth head. Then I leaned on the small mirror set down between a brick and the ground. Thus exposed, my ears took on much greater dimensions! And for the first time in my life, I saw this naked, greyish oval lump which shelters "me". But in a certain way, however, I discovered someone else. Initiation had begun.

When I came back, Ananda Baba invited two *samnyasins* passing by: Mama Baba and Krishna Baba.

'Cover your head and go fetch wood for the fire,' he ordered me.

The night came. It was moonless. The pyres were only heaps of ashes now. The cremation ground became deserted. The flames of our *dhooni* made disturbing shades bounce on our faces and behind us.

Of the two *samnyasins,* Mama Baba was the guru. He was about forty. His long black hair fell undulating on his bare chest and merged with his beard, hiding half of his broad round face. He was wearing a faded saffron *lungi* smudged with grey stains. His nails were black. He liked to pick up burning embers and keep them in his palm. Krishna Baba was fifteen or seventeen. He was a servant-disciple. Mama Baba taught him devotion through obedience and submission.

My guru cast a log in the fire and said in a burst of sparks but without bombast: 'You will die and you will be born. No more having to appear today as the one you were yesterday. Initiation to *samnyasa* is this liberation. *Diksha* is the ritual of the second birth.'

Smoke stung the eyes and heat burnt. Krishna Baba prepared a *chillum*; we smoked it in silence. On a yellowish cloth beside Ananda Baba, a coconut waited with a few handfuls of rice, wheat, barley, in plastic bags, an earth cup of milk and a saffron *lungi*.

Like every other evening, a pack of starving mangy dogs dispersed in search of an arm or a foot which may have escaped the blazing infernos. They did not come for nothing and fought brutally over the remainders of those who had had too small a pyre. Scabbed, covered with flees, human flesh eaters, untouchable, they came too close to us and our offerings. To keep them away, Krishna Baba regularly threatened them with an imaginary stone and Mama Baba with his *trishul*.

'If you subject your senses, you are covered; if your senses are out of control, you are like a naked man,' declared my guru. 'Undress!'

He poured some water from his *komandalu* on my head; then spread a few handfuls of tepid ashes on my shoulders.

'Man is the sacrifice! When everything is burned, what remains is immortal. Ashes will be your clothing and you will mark your forehead with it.'

He nevertheless gave me the orange *lungi*, explaining:

'Those, who belong to the Saraswati Sampradaya, do not go naked; they wear the colours of fire, but they don't distinguish between the castes, wealth, the sexes, pure and impure because the creator of the multitude is himself one only. And you are Him.'

He broke the coconut on a stone of the *dhooni*, and then poured its milk on the flames.

'Look at what is left of your ego,' he said, showing me the two pieces of shell before throwing them into the fire as well.

Mama Baba poured water in the hollow of Ananda Baba's united hands who poured it in turn into mine proclaiming in a rare use of the first person:

'I entrust you to water, plants, sky and earth. I entrust you to all living and non-living creatures and to Prajapati, the Creator, Savitri, the sun, Chandra, the moon. *Om Namah Shivayah Subham Subham Kuru Kuru Shivayah Namah Om.*

'I entrust you to the three *Vedas*, the Upanishads, the *Vedanta*, the *Purana*, the Brahmana, to the line of *rishis* and gurus, the *acharyas**, Kapila, Pradipika, Patanjali, Sankaracharya, Swami Vidyaranya, Narayana Guru, Vivekananda, Maharishi Dayanand, Vishvatma Baba, to *vidhya* and *paravidhya* I entrust you. *Om Namah Shivayah Subham Subham Kuru Kuru Shivayah Namah Om.*

'Do you wish to take refuge at the feet of your guru?'

'I take refuge at my guru's feet,' I responded.

'Who is your guru?'

'Swami Ananda Saraswati Baba.'

He wrote on ashes from the *dhooni*, and then announced:

'By the authority bestowed on Vishvatma Ananda Saraswati Baba, by the lineage of Saraswati Sampradaya's gurus, Ananda gives you your name: Ananda Prassad Saraswati Baba. Babaji will call you Prassad, the offering.

Agni*, the fire God, is your Master. In the divine realm, he is power, and in consciousness, he is will. May ignorance and habits of ignorance burn in the fire of discrimination.'

I threw the cereal seeds in the flames in pinches, repeating *Om Namah Shivayah*. In its cracklings, the fire also sang *Shivayah, Shivayah...* 'May the sickness of life, death and suffering disappear in this offering,' wished Ananda Baba.

He brushed his index finger on the milk, sprinkled on the fire, then handed the cup over to Mama Baba who started preparing chai.

There was nothing to steal anymore and the dogs wearied.

Ananda Baba sunk three fingers into the ashes, and then marked my forehead with three horizontal lines. He opened up a slip of newspaper which contained a crumb of vermilion paste, then dipped a match into it and traced a thin vertical line between my eyebrows pressing thoroughly: 'Look through the inner seeing, which reduces multiplicity to nothing,' he said applying it carefully. The feeling of this mark lasted a long time. Inner seeing... what is it? I wondered.

'Although the visible Whole has appeared from the Invisible Whole, the Whole has not been altered,' says the Isa Upanishad. The one who realises this, knows himself to be the Immutable. The nature of Brahman is *SatCitAnanda* (Consciousness, Existence and Bliss). The nature of the world is *namarupa* (names and forms). Brahman appears in the names and the forms but that does not change it. That is what inner seeing is.'

It was time to take vows: to be truthful, not to kill, not to hold on to anything...

'And you will not accept any wages. You will beg for your food...' listed Ananda Baba as he was recalling them.

He talked about abstinence: You will regard all beings as brothers and sisters. And modesty: You will adopt the same attitude toward honours and insults. A superb modesty: Whoever blesses you, will be praising Shiva through you. Among renunciations, there was the one about appearing desirable... And not to wash nor to comb my hair, to let the beard and moustache grow. To restrain from any act tinted with desire, lust or passion. And to practise *tapasya*. To sleep on the ground. And still very many other details... He finally threw a log in the fire, and a spray of sparks punctuated my oaths.

For me, these vows were the means of entrance into the babas' brotherhood: a formality. I wanted to be earnest about them, but I was taking them as a trial rather than seriously. I am not made of the stuff that the dogmatic, signing up for a cause kind of people are made of. My free will could never be mortgaged, even by myself: granting myself the right to make mistakes, I also had the right to change an opinion at any time; my promises remained subject to my evaluation for perpetuity.

Ananda Baba knew that I did not bestow great value to religious fuss. But he conferred initiation to me to connect and include me in the mystical current of a lineage of gurus, to give me a place in the company of sadhus, and to allow me to beg without becoming a beggar.

Here I am *born again*! I told myself.

From then on, I adopted the turban.

We set off again the following day.

The orange garb gave me the appearance of a little saint in the eyes of benefactors. I was not a Westerner anymore and not even a man. They called me Babaji. I was a renunciant, a symbol of moderation and freedom. Old men came, touched my feet to praise detachment and take part in its bliss. I received gifts like *lungi*, shawls and blankets… Sometimes a shopkeeper would allow me to choose whatever I wanted in his store as an offering. Life could be free.

In the 8th century, Sankaracharya founded the Orders of the Ten Names of Renunciation (*Dasnami Sampradayas*): Giri (mountains), Puri (town), Bharati (All-India), Tirtha (holy places), Vana (forest), Aranya (grove), Parvata (high mountains), Ashram (place of refuge), Sagar (sea) and Saraswati (teacher). He thus channelled and organized the wandering monk tradition into various institutions which differ in terms of their ascetic practices, their lifestyles and the philosophical points of view they adhere to.

Two centuries later, in order to fight the Muslim invaders, Ramanuj-acharya founded the first *akhara*, a training camp of warrior ascetics, the Naga babas. Later the invaders were British and the regiments multiplied to seven. They changed into schools of asceticism and developed their own spiritual ways: Ananda Akhara, Niranjani, Juna, Avahan, Atal, Mahanirvani, Agni.

The Nagas practise yoga, do not wear any clothing and, it is believed, are masters of startling powers. Some Naga babas are castrated. Generally around the age of fifteen, they roll their penis around a stick and stretch it for several weeks. The erectile tissues, which retain the surge of blood during erection, and some nerves, are thus irremediably damaged. Erectile stiffness is physically impossible. These babas were proud to have preserved the innocence of a child and to be insensitive to the tyranny of sensuous desires. They regarded this mutilation as liberation and by no means a disgrace.

In addition to the *akharas* are the *Nath* Sampradaya*. The Matsyendranath Nath asserts a tradition much older than the Ten Names (*Dasnami*). Their ancestor was swallowed by a fish so as to go and listen to the very secret teaching Shiva gave Parvati on the ocean floor.

Other sects of *Nath Sampradaya* claim Dattatreya, an *avatar* of Shiva, for founder. Their purpose is to enjoy peace, freedom and happiness in this life and not to be reborn.

All these institutions evolved into sub and sub-sub orders. Disciples practice and then transform their gurus' teaching and pass it on in turn. There is no dogma.

The unique capitalized Being, whatever name it goes by, is an experience rather than a discourse, but that does not prevent it from also being transmitted in discursive theoretical terms written down in voluminous treatises. This intellectual and philosophical perspective is divided into five large currents and is subdivided in almost as many doctrines as individuals. The title of Swami is given to those who study them.

Udasins (order of the melancholy) are itinerant Sikh preachers. They vow to avoid earthly pleasures and defend justice with the sword; they celebrate it telling the martyrdom of their lineage of gurus with many bloody details – dismemberments, decapitations, pyres and resurrections. Deogirs ("the ones who speak") live in cities and villages and teach… Gorakhnathis claim that their order is as old as the world and that Brahma, Vishnu and Shiva were the first disciples of Gorakhnath, their guru, immediately after Creation. They practise yoga and *mantras.* Brahmas worship the wind and often fast. In the XVth century, Kabir mocked both brahmins and imams for their stupidity and their narrow-mindedness. *Ramanandrins** are not numerous but they sing Kabir's hymns and improvise new ones, know the Ramayana by heart and repeat like an advertising catchphrase: "In this *kali-yuga* (the dark time in which we live), people can find liberation only from singing the name of God and telling legends." These troubadours who do not lack a sense of humour put their contempt of priests into verse with praises for non-duality, and their loathing of rituals with a glorification of the merger with the Unutterable.

Do you believe you purify yourself in holy water?
And washing wood before lighting it?
If one found salvation by plunging in water,
The frogs are saved taking plunges all day long!

There is neither day, nor night, neither Koran nor Veda,
Where the Formless dwells!
Do not let yourself be disturbed by the madness of the world,
Says Kabir, and worship nothing but him.

In the XIXth century, Vivekananda founded the Ramakrishna Mission, a network of monasteries comparable with their catholic eponym, – with schools, orphanages, dispensaries, hospitals and publishing houses, to serve the poor and to help those who wish it to attain liberation.

Kept away by the others, covered with ashes, *Aghoris* practice the darkest ways of *tantrism* and are famed for their psychic powers. They dwell on cremation grounds, drink alcohol in human skulls, eat cow meat and also cadavers and, it is rumoured, their own faeces and those of dogs. They find liberation in breaking as many taboos as possible, adopting the most contemptible behaviours because Shiva loves those who are freed from the distinctions of pure and impure, likes and dislikes, ghosts and devils and are afraid of nothing. Some of them spoke loudly, drank to the point of delirium and smoked enough hashish to knock out an elephant. Other sadhus kept a distance with them because they are quick to be rude and constant in their provocation. But in their eyes, I sometimes saw a man who had faced the extreme of disgust and had risen above everything through this path.

Certainly more delicate, the *Kaneyas*, sometimes bearded men, love Krishna so much that they think they are Radha, his wife. They wear saris and jewels and adopt female postures to allure their God.

Their distinctive features are innumerable: Vaishnavites and Swetambaras are dressed in white, Bhaironaths and some *tantrics*, in black, different Shivaists share hues from ochre to red and from saffron to flame, Udasins and other *tantrics* wear black and red and Gorakhnathis, an earring. *Aghoris* hide their genitals in a twisted cloth which looks like a snake. For Kali-Durga worshipers as well as *Ramanandrins* the *tilak* is black, for Hanumans' it's orange. Digambaras* and Naga babas go naked or covered with ashes. Nirvanis tie their bun on the right, Niranjani in the middle, Juna on the left and practice the *dhooni*... Some sadhus carry a sword, a spear, a *trishul* or a staff. Vaishnavites display a variety of fourteen stigmata and have thirty-six different frontal marks. They also have their Nagas, their regiments of warrior ascetics and theirs sub-sects and reformed orders.

The Ten schools, seven *akharas*, the *naths*, the *maths** and the lineages of masters and disciples, but also Krishna lovers, friends of Hanuman or Ganesha, sons of Kali or Ganga, slaves of Ram, Shivaist, Vaishnavites, and the Jain*, Sufi and Sikh variants – each sadhu belongs to multiple orders and sub-orders and loves many Gods… but all of them proclaim uncountable the paths leading to the goal. If one remembers that there is no goal, one understands that there is nothing to understand, although we still become *it*. It is a matter of making a lifestyle out of *truth*.

It is practised alone, or in duos, trios, in groups of a dozen on the roads, alone in a cave or a hermitage, alone or with many others in a *kutir* or a temple, an *akhara* or an ashram around a guru.

One can be a Dandi *samnyasin*, carrying a staff and teaching, or a *tantric*, using body, senses and mind to transcend them. Or Virakas, aiming to lose individuality in meditation and study. Or a *Muni* – silent. A few women slip into this male universe, but these *sadhvis** are isolated, in the background. They rarely roam the roads; most often they stay in women ashrams around a Mataji.

Some sadhus continue caste discriminations, others have dropped them. I had a double status of *Mlecha* and White, two synonyms which do not have the same meaning. *Mlecha*, the caste below the untouchable *Pariah*, is a barbarian. He is more than impure, he is very different. A *Pariah* is an outcaste who accepts caste discrimination and obeys its rules. There is, within this *non-caste*, a very precise hierarchy of sub-castes: a shoe-repairer is purer than a sweeper, a milk-man purer than a *dhobi** (launderer), and the aboriginal is untouchable even for a *domra*, who touches cadavers. But the barbarian is an outcaste who does not recognize this caste hierarchy.

When, to avoid receiving something from my hand, a man indicated to put it down, or when another avoided conspicuously touching me, I used to point out to them: '*Maharaj*, I distinguish neither castes, nor social conditions, neither family ties, nor races, nor any particular purity in you.' For I was also a white man, belonging to a historically dominant race, educated and demanding, and that made me another kind of caste which required a certain level of consideration. But not everywhere. At the *bhandaras*, they tended to place Western sadhus at the end of the line of babas, last with the lunatics, and just before the *sadhvis* and the beggars.

From the lone, illiterate, wandering renunciant to *avatar* – a living God or *Maha-mandaleshwar* – the supreme leader of an *akhara* or a school who travels on elephant back on the day of the Kumbh Mela, the range of ways of living a life of renunciation is very broad as are those of making a career and reputation out of it. In transit or settled, standing up for twelve years, remaining motionless in meditation for a thousand, founder of ashrams, village saint, *acharya* (scholar, teacher of Gods), *swami* (learned man), *Mahant** (a kind of bishop), guru, yogi, Principal of one of the four Sankaracharya *maths*, *jivan-mukta* – a liberated soul of any condition… Some are fashionable, attend power circles, spread their word in television shows and are worshiped by millions of devotees. Some dwell high in the mountains' solitude and anonymity. Renunciants sometimes receive important donations and take it upon themselves to accommodate and provide for sadhus or support dispensaries, schools, shelters…

There are hypocrites, of course. It is an institution like any other, whose scandals have punctuated history and the news. Each generation has produced saints, sages and swindlers who were not either solitary or worshiped by the masses.

The status of a sadhu depends on his administrative rank, his titles, but also on countless other considerations: the number of years he has been a sadhu, the reputation of his guru, his own spiritual achievement, the severity of the *tapasyas* he has performed, the *siddhis** (psychic powers) that he claims, his wisdom, his fame, his age, his caste, his influence and the wealth of his benefactors, the authority of his order, the number of his disciples, their reputation, what he has built, the charitable organisations he has founded, his TV air-time… It is extremely complicated. Quarrels of precedence are innumerable and find their epilogue either in protests of modesty or in the muffled confrontations of magic powers, or in raging scandals and thugs fist-fights. *Ram Ram fight*[1], we said. Humility is a sign of achievement, but the living liberated can exempt them of it without losing face because they are beyond everything.

At the Kumbh Mela in Prayag, a confrontation arose between the *Mahant* of a group of Udasins and Tapaswiji Baba about the height of their flags. It found its outcome in the night with the, mysterious as it was convenient, death of the *Mahant*. A few days later, a sadhu who had insulted Tapaswiji Baba was found cut in pieces at the other end of the camp.

Frictions forge legends and fame more surely than the quiet anonymity of

---

1 A fight between Ram and Ram: Nothing really happens.

a *kutir* lost in a forest. The heroes of these quarrelsome babas were the *rishi* from the beginnings of time, the seers who pit themselves against the Gods, cursed them, for they dwelled in the realms where events are forged.

It was said that Bhairon Baba of the Juna akhara had pronounced a *tantric mantra* against Hari Puri because they were in disagreement about the Datt akhara's succession to the throne. Hari Puri fell into a coma the next day and died a few weeks later. Hari Puri's medical cause of death of was a massive embolism, but killing-*mantras* make legends and legends immortality. There are many sadhus who dream of psychic powers, hope to become renowned rather than famous, memorable if not glorious. Or a reviled assassin rather than being utterly forgotten. Two years after I first met him, Kaushal Giri had his two legs broken by a paid mob because he wanted to be elected *mandaleshwar* of the Juna akhara.

Babas, yogis, wizards, therapists, shamans, fakirs, swamis, *acharyas*, philosophers, scholars, hairy or shaven heads, dressed or naked, walking the path of devotion (the realm of form) or that of knowledge (the realm of illusion), diligent with *tapasya* or relaxed with everything, handicapped and beggars… and they spoke Gujarati, Bengali, Kannada, Tamil, Hindi and their dialectal twists… these few hundred thousand anonymous souls haunt the roads from North to South India and along the fifteen hundred kilometres of the Ganges valley, the shores of Yamuna and Narmada.

They were renunciants, indifferent-to-the-world, conquerors-of-desire, and lived off almost nothing… But in the *almost* of nothing, a little greed, cheating, bad moods, obsession about precedence and indelible animosities could manage to slip in. Bliss had tears, but the effort was not in vain. It produced reasonably free, reasonably good and easy men, living day to day, by the grace of an ideal, or for the love of God, for a gaze, a point of view, a lifestyle, or even by contempt… a love of contempt for the world. A challenge. Sadhus are men like any other. One does not start wandering with a diploma in modesty. And some end up tangled in the bureaucratic games of renunciation.

It is a world in which silhouettes arrive at dusk, to have disappeared by the following dawn on another road. Friends for two or three days, but sometimes more. A fraternity of chatty, crafty, quick-tempered, thrifty, silent, nasty, quiet, harmonious, wonderstruck, merry, focused… men. Men like any other. One does not start wandering with a diploma in saintliness.

But most are generous, and spend, share and offer without motives or remorse, like God who, they say, gives everything and does not keep anything for himself. They regard hoarding as inelegant. And it is often a feast day when everything is spent.

One becomes a sadhu to walk across the path of liberation or just to untie family bonds, get away from social conditioning, break out of a caste, or because one needs adventures or in order to follow, in one's elderly years, this ancient recommendation. Or in childhood surrendering to God's irresistible vocation, or latter by a call of renunciation, or without having chosen it, because as a baby, father and mother gave you to a sadhu as a vow. One can be baba for fifteen days or a month's vacation, between two jobs or trying it out following an ordeal or a period of mourning, and one is nevertheless respected as a full saint. There is no final break between one lifestyle and the other. A sadhu told me one day: 'If I find a woman to support me, I will drop baba-life.'

Some sadhus set themselves up as *paanwalla**, establish a cigarette outlet or sell rosaries, holy images and copper rings engraved with a powerful *mantra*! An orange wool thread carries their blessing and brings in an offering… A refreshment stall, a portable clock repairing workshop, reading *Bhagavad Gita* aloud on a road side, enables them to make a quiet existence close to a holy place, keeping God in their heart or in mind. Some trade semi-precious stones. Others sew pouches with secret pockets. And some deal, at various levels, *charas* and *ganja*.

Dhaval Puri Baba was a real-estate agent before, and at retirement, became a sadhu. In just five years, he had obtained the title of *Mahant*. Rather charmless and sour, his body was fatty and grey, marked by years of leniency and his tone and manners were brutal and gloomy. He held court in the small *akhara* his hierarchy had entrusted to him, surrounded by half a dozen chillum-babas of no interest and two servants. They read the newspaper and commented on the news, slandered like locusts and were dealers like *pros,* in no way worried about being caught by the police.

Dhaval Puri's cell phone often rang. He would then rummage through his bag and withdraw a plastic bag containing four packages, each containing several twisted bars of hashish. He would take out the order and give it to one or the other babas or his servants to deliver. Upon returning, a servant handed him a few bills. Dhaval Puri pulled a wad of 500 rupees notes out from his belt, and counted them, counted them again, added the amount of the last sale and then carefully put it back in.

A world of very ordinary crooks, with spirituality non-existent.

'How was I supposed to regard that, Babaji?' I asked my guru when we had left.

'The world is changing. *Dharma* is weak. People are materialistic,' answered my guru. 'Those in charge of institutions seek and favour disciples whom they believe gifted to perennialize the institution, and preserve its influence. Presently, they find value in a real-estate agent. They value a disciple's attribute rather than the disciple himself. In this way, they carry out their duty to maintain this tradition alive, managing things for the next generation, which will be less materialistic.

Akhara business.

Begging

'Have you been to the Krishna temple in Gokul? I can guide you there. Your pilgrimage would be incomplete without this visit.' Holy cities are teeming with temples and self proclaimed guides who are commissioned by the priests, whose real God is the rupee. They tell them the appropriate offering they should fork out according to whatever social status they deem them to be from and by asking a few seemingly innocent but clever questions about the reason for their pilgrimage, the vow that brings them here or the prayer they wish to make. They get half of the offerings back in commission.

Having come here to worship Krishna, the pilgrim is then guided towards the vault of Radha, the God's consort, then his half-brother, his father, his cousin... And each time he is invited to pay the *darshan*. Temple business. 'Only one God is enough, Babuji!' I told one of these devotees who was getting fleeced. The man immediately understood the economic significance of my remark, and perhaps also the main virtue of monotheism, and headed for the exit. The *pujaris* rebuffed me: 'Do you think your way to God is the only one?' I am not going that way.

We entered a large temple to take shelter from a shower and then we stayed there. We put down our *asans* in the hall of a thousand pillars, open on all sides but enclosed with new, high orange painted railings.

A plump and chubby-cheeked brahmin with a hairless torso wearing a *dhoti*, came to greet us. He gave us some of the trivial news from his world, as though we were members of the same club. Amongst suitably religious people.

His head was shaved except for a wick of hair at the back, tied in a plait and folded up giving him a small penis behind the head. He pointed towards the railings: 'Some people were fornicating in this hall,' he told us. 'We had to close it. Vice has cost us one hundred thousand rupees!' He was being specific with delight, thinking himself heroic amongst worthy company. I could see it on his face; he was expecting congratulations and came to receive them from some renunciants, a public he believed to be sympathetic to the cause of virtue. Ananda Baba simply made uninvolved *Haans* and *Atchas*.

Finding myself categorised amongst the self-righteous and called to lend my support to a reactionary crusade against the erring ways of love and pleasure immediately put me in the mood for blasphemy.

'I hope that the lovers found another place, Swamiji. Where will they go now?'

I was transgressing the rules of reverence... He was my elder and I was only a novice.

The brahmin put on an expression of not understanding tinged with sadness but did not react. Ananda Baba swivelled slowly towards me, smiling as if to greet what was happening.

'One thousand pillars... that makes a forest,' I insisted. 'And if one does not have a home, a forest is the next best place to make love. Do a good deed, *Panditji*, sell the railings. Think of those who still like *it*.'

Ananda Baba burst out laughing. I love making him laugh. It was my way of resisting him. The brahmin wondered to himself watching me closely as if trying to read my face to know how to understand what I had said, so scandalous or strange my attitude had appeared to him. He turned to my guru but could not find any noticeable support in him.

'It is a sin...' he finally he responded, stuttering in English. 'It is a sin to make love in a temple!'

'But Gods do it, don't they!' I retorted.

The brahmin's eyes were once again looking questioningly at Ananda Baba.

'Everywhere there is a man, Shiva is, and everywhere there is a woman Parvati also is,' my guru told him, stating this principle as something indisputably obvious.

'You are a *brahmachari**, aren't you?' he asked me, looking me up and down trying to detect a sign of something to the contrary.

'Me, yes, Swamiji, but not the rest of the world!' I answered bowing. 'These things only concern those who do them.'

'*Sarvam khalvidam Brahman*, all this is Brahman,' tried Ananda Baba to cool down the game.

'Krishna was a heavy fornicator, *Panditji*,' I recalled.

'Krishna is Krishna!' spouted the brahmin impatiently.

'But all beings live in Krishna!' I insisted.

'You are not serious,' he concluded decisively.

I was about to let him have the last word, but as he was shamelessly claiming victory, I retorted, grasping my *Avadhuta Gita*:

> Prescriptions and prohibitions are transcended,
> Purity and impurity no longer exist,
> Mind freed from differentiation,
> What is prohibited is permissible to him,
> He is beyond rules.
> All is accomplished.

'Is *this* your *shishya*, Babaji?' he asked my guru.

'*Haan, haan*,' Ananda Baba answered shaking his head. 'He is a little insane and he jokes about anything, but he makes him laugh. He is a good disciple.'

And he added, still in the universal third person singular, which indicated each one of us in every possible role: 'He regrets that he does not appreciate his *darshan* (his image or his point of view).'

'*Atcha, atcha*,' said the brahmin rising and going away.

Good disciple, I was not. I did not honour my guru with as much ostentation as other *shishyas*, but I amused him. And I endured the hard times with patience and never felt sorry for myself.

'Why did you call me Prassad, Babaji?'

'Because you make Anand laugh.'

I knew this, but I liked to hear him say it.

'Five years ago in Varanasi, a baba also called me Prassad. He said I was the reincarnation of his guru…'

'Do you want to live with that?'

'No. I don't like railings.'

I studied the treaties of Sankaracharya or the Upanishads, which came into my hands in the space-time coincidence of a day of wealth and a bookshop. I found an anthology of the *Puranas,* which I exchanged against an anthology of the Mahabharata with a second-hand bookseller. These old legends, written by the first *rishis* tell that, in the beginnings of time, the *rishis* had achieved heroic austerities, which had shaken the cosmic order and alarmed the Gods. Nymphs conceived by the Gods tempted them and disturbed the ardour of their *tapasya*. And from them girls were born, and other stories... The Gods who were waging war against demons, took *rishis* as referees, begging the authors of these legends to grant them victory! And they married their daughters. The wise Lilliputians threatened Indra, who had made fun of their weakness, to generate another Indra. And because Shiva kept him waiting (he was making love with Parvati), Bhrigu put a curse on him making his destiny one of being worshipped in the form of his penis. This sensitive and rancorous *rishi* also cursed Brahma, the Creator God, who had not condescended to return his greeting. 'Since you have no respect, you will not be worshipped on Earth.' Bhrigu spread the rumour that praying to Brahma brought bad luck! It worked; there is only one temple devoted to Brahma in all of India. Durvasa, an atheist, cursed Dharmdeo, Goodness, condemning him to be reborn as the son of a servant girl, a *pariah* and then a king. These *Puranas* ended with the promise that those who recounted them would be granted the highest merits.

In the Mahabharata:

- What is the highest refuge of virtue?
- Generosity.
- What is the most secure shelter for fame?
- Goodness.
- What is the most reliable sanctuary for thoughts?
- Truth.
- And for happiness, what is a safe place?
- Patience.
- Of all shelters, which is the highest?
- Giving.

I also read newspapers, which came before me. In the short news column: A twenty-two year old man tried to murder his mother by binding a bare electric wire around her neck. He coveted her job as a sweeper at the Railway Station. A new swindle: a couple ring the bell at the door of a house, holding an urn containing an ancestor's ashes, claiming to be distant cousins. Once they get inside, it's a traditional hold-up. One crime often came up: A husband sprinkles kerosene on his wife and sets her on fire; or alternatively, with his mother's assistance. He claims it's a kitchen accident. He hopes to remarry and pocket a fresh dowry. Some denied it, accusing their wife of having committed suicide, in order that they would be accused of murder. They must have been particularly odious to bring their wives to this end! Every six hours, a woman dies this way.

The government had granted production licences of Viagra generics to ten laboratories. Hard-ons at hand for all budgets! I thought. I was pleased to still be capable of bawdy considerations. An effective thermometer for measuring my own mental health when I felt encircled and badgered by the sanctimonious and the saintly.

And Ananda Baba kept on teaching me the *advaita* philosophy, mapping out for me one or another of the mental paths that lead consciousness to experiencing Brahman.

Everyone accepts that music inspires, evokes and triggers emotions. Words are no different. An insult, even undeserved, causes a shock, a love declaration also; in the same way, an intellectual construction can produce effects.

'One cannot know something which does not exist in the realm of names and forms. Anything that exists for oneself exists in the realm of names and forms. Even non-existence. But still one cannot say that non-existence exists, for then there would be no difference between existence and non-existence.

'Nobody doubts his own existence. Questioning one's own existence is an unreal question, because there must be someone who asks and to whom it is happening!

'Before there was the projection of maya on consciousness, before a question on existence could arise, consciousness (*cit*) is, and it's on this consciousness that the question of existence is asked.

'The One-without-a-Second Being (*Ekam eva advitiyam*) and consciousness exist permanently and forever. One cannot describe it without giving it names and attributes which it cannot have, since nothing is outside of it and it is sole. Oneness does not imply any positive qualities.

'This consciousness is like a screen upon which maya is played and can be known when mental activity ceases. If mind is thought free, the Witness consciousness is the perception of immobility.

'This is a *darshan* (an immediate experience) of Brahman as consciousness (*cit*). What is aware of something cannot ignore this thing, especially if this thing is awareness. There is no knowable exterior to consciousness.'

It was not a dry rhetoric; it was a speech which could drive the mind into an abyss. Leaving it in a void of word and concept that is not nothingness, but is empty. And aware.

Rows of women with feet in water and bent doubled over, transplant rice shoots in paddy fields, laughing, saris pulled up to their knees. On the outskirts of villages, poor people camp along the railroad tracks. Horses graze on an already close-cropped grass. A cowherd leads his animals to the municipal pasture. *Hari Om!* A young *pandit* learns his lesson in the shade of a mango tree, his books opened in front of him. In the centre of a roundabout, an ascetic in white marble, wearing glasses, infinitely contemplates the traffic. *Namah Shivayah*.

Small red edged clouds at sunrise. Then, the round, orange, burning star face to face. Alone with this light. Going through Mirzapur: a horizon of faces. Thousands of gazes, moments, destinies. And one hundred thousand colours. But a single Being. *Om Namah Shivayah.*

One evening, we arrived in a cave occupied by six sadhus. One was cutting the calluses off the feet of another with a razor blade, a third was tidying up his bag, and a fourth mended his shirt. Pots smoked on a wood fire. *Namoh Narayan. Hari Om. Namah Shivayah...*

'Sit, *Maharaj-ji*, please.'

'When do we eat?' asked the chiropodist.

'Can't you see it is not cooked yet!' the cook shouted.

'Do you have some *charas* with you, *Maharaj*?'

'They've got some!' Ananda Baba reassured him.

He then gave me the *chillum* to prepare. During that time, the man who was tidying up his bag said that, in the afternoon he had begged, calling out to the fattest passers-by: 'Hey Babuji! Give me some of your cholesterol.' And he burst out laughing with all the others.

'How much alms did you receive today?'

'Twenty-five rupees. And you?'

'Thirty-five!' flashed Cholesterol, proud of his victory.

A gang of villains dressed up as sadhus. Or an assembly of Gods embodied as babas disguised as villains... *Namah Shivayah!* I greet Shiva. The universe is one single being but in a set of mirrors and representations.

I sat beside one of them who was quieter than the others. He took a small plastic pocket out of his bag and handed it to me, announcing with the delicious joy of a little boy in front of a big treasure: *Lakshmi Ma!* (Mother Lakshmi). In the small pocket, a piece of ruffled aluminium foil.

Bom Bom Bole Bholenath! From hand to hand, the *chillum* went around the fire-pit.

Further away, we made a stop at a large ashram ruled by Swami

Bhramavichara, a rich and famous celebrity guru. Surrounded by a dozen unconditionals, with two cell-phones at hand, he received calls from disciples all over the world and we heard his lavish advice. A shrink, matrimonial counsellor, financial expert, soothsayer and coach all at the same time; he predicted the short-term fall of the market, recommended patience to a cheated wife, prescribed a *mantra* to a depressed man and encouraged a correspondent in an intricate affair of office politics. A young disciple served his chai in a gold cup.

> When one perceives the universe as One with nature and
> consciousness, One should not praise or blame the personality
> and the acts of others.
> [*Uddhava Gita* XXIII, 1]

In Saidpur, Ananda Baba gave all the money we had to a beggar and his three children who had an urgent need for it. We did not find any *dharamsala*. We had to fast or beg. We rarely had to because *grihasthas* usually gave us more than we could wish for.

Begging was both a role to play and a vocation: a *sadhana*, the observance of a correct attention and state of being. In India's history, kings abandoned their thrones to go out on the roads, bare feet, a begging bowl in hand.

'Do not beseech. Do not ask. You do not need anything,' warned my guru. 'You are Bhikshadom, the King of kings, Shiva who disguises himself as a beggar. And your benefactor is *Bhagwan,* Shiva manifesting as a protector. You offer the opportunity to know this Oneness.'

Ananda Baba stood in front of a shop and did not move until the owner saw him. He then blessed the place and those who were there, with an invocation he addressed the meals: *All this is Brahman, offered by Brahman and taken by Brahman.* And he set out again, whether he was or not given an offering.

We quickly got the twenty rupees, which would pay for a *thali** in a restaurant. Happy are the people who take sadhus for saints and find pleasure in receiving blessings.

With the passing of the months and the begging bouts, there were sometimes exceptions.

'*Kali-yuga* hypocrites! Parasites! False renunciants! Obscurants!'

'*Namah Shivayah!* He greets Shiva,' answered Ananda Baba bowing. 'None other than him could know it so well.' He laughed. Nothing could affect him.

One day, from the far end of his fan store, a bloated man poured scorn on me in front of his friends: 'Look at this vigorous man who's begging! That's why India is so wretched! And a he's foreigner too!'

'Do not answer,' Ananda Baba had cautioned me. 'Calumny and insults are a test. Remain firmly in Oneness.' I remained.

Another time, a sari retailer said at the top of his voice, and with no decency, in front of employees and customers: 'I am myself a beggar, *Maharaj*! Every day I pray to *Bhagwan* to grant me more money. Go on your way.' This time I answered:

'I am not a beggar! Babuji needs it more than I do.'

I emptied my pockets on his counter, told him: 'God is answering your prayers,' blessed him and went away. And regretted it. Not so much the money but the fuss a little. The shopkeeper caught up with me. His contrite face split in a half smile as he joined his hands before me: 'Don't feel angry with me, Babaji. I see that you are a true *samnyasin*. You gave me all you had. You are a father to me now.'

He took me back to his shop, ordered a bottle of *Campa Cola* and gave me two hundred rupees. A lucky day after all for matters of material supports! I did not disparage wealth in renunciation. But when important alms turned up, Ananda Baba advised me to redistribute more than half of it to the sadhus of the area. The other half of the fortune was spent to pay for meals, buy some *charas*, offer chai to brothers, get incense sticks, or acquire a book. I found *The Poems of Tukaram*, and *The Rubaiyat of Sarmad*, a Sufi saint of the XVIIth century who lived naked in the king's court and ended up decapitated because he refused to recite the entire *kalma*. He was content simply saying *La Ilaha* – no God. "I cannot say that there is no other God than God without lying," he explained during his trial, "because I do not know God." One should not mess around with these things, even out of modesty. Condemned to death, he declared on the scaffold: "A noise occurred, and from the sleep of non-existence we opened our eyes and on seeing that the tumultuous night remained motionless, we fell back to sleep." A scrupulous, foolhardy, delicate man. As a Hindu he would have been venerated.

Bang Handi Mandir

A burning ochre coloured wind swept the Ganges plain, carrying a dust and sand cloud from Rajasthan that seeped in everywhere and which one breathed in. The *looh* was announcing the torrid season. The temperature rose several degrees in a few minutes to reach the forties.

During the suffocating month of June, preceding the monsoon, we stayed at Bang Handi Temple, a baba *mandir* in Delhi, facing the Old Railway Station.

Behind a temple, at the far end of a large courtyard surrounded by high railings, two half-meter high, large, concrete terraces, closed on three sides with low walls and roofed with corrugated iron sheets, were used as shelter and sitting room by about thirty sadhus.

The cemented courtyard was dusty and littered with small yellow rotting banyan fruits, bird droppings, dead leaves and plastic cups tossed about by the breeze. To the left, an oval stone the size of a watermelon, erected on a flat stone celebrated the encounter of Shiva and Parvati: union of consciousness and its manifestation, this world, a temple. Alongside this *lingam-yoni** honoured with a garland of red, yellow and white flowers, was a hand pump on a paved area large enough for two babas to take a bath. At the other end was the kitchen with its two cooks bickering loudly, and to its left, a two storey circular pavilion on the ground floor of which, around twenty more sadhus were crammed. On the smaller first floor, alone, resided Mahant Borot Puri Maharaj, the saint and master of Bang Handi. Here and there were seven old trees offering shade and surrounded by welcoming platforms where we met in small groups. Far away on the right were well kept latrines. In corners, old heaps of rubbish were slowly disintegrating, drying out to dust. A few broken bricks gathered at the bottom of a wall…

Against the outer wall, a small shelter made of plastic sheets attached to bamboo poles and roofed with a rusty metal plate, was Rujula Baba's place;

he was a very old man who was awaiting death and no longer wanted to speak. When he untied them to take his bath, his dreadlocks were so long that they dragged along the ground; and his body was so thin and knotty that he looked like his locks.

On the terrace where we settled down, Niranjan Baba had made an altar of a tray set down on four bits of bricks and covered with a purple velvet cloth. A bronze of Ganesha presided, surrounded by coloured pictures of Shiva, Parvati, Vishnu and Dattatreya in red aluminium frames. Some fresh red and orange marigolds glorified godliness. Hair hidden in a yellow turban, trimmed beard and moustache, round wrinkleless laconic face, Niranjan Baba chanted and prayed from morning to night in front of a book resting on a small lectern. When he had completed a prayer, he shut it, put it down on his right and took another from a pile on his left. In the middle of the afternoon, this devotion lover lit a bundle of incense sticks and offered it to his altar, and then the scent of smoked flowers mingled with that of *bidis*, *chillums*, carbon monoxide and whatever was lying around rotting. He did not travel anymore. Many devotees knew his fervour and came to him to seek blessings.

Bala Baba, the youngest, was seventeen. He had very short hair, wore jeans and a caste cord slung across his shoulder under a *gomcha* he used as a shawl. He was a tall boy in a juvenile body, thin and straight as an "I". He came from Ahmedabad, had fled from his home a year earlier and lived in Bang Handi since. Casual but respectful, Bala Baba seemed to be gliding high above his life and rejoicing in this. He chewed gum and his words together, but spoke never more than five in a row, if they were not only approving or exclamatory onomatopoeias. He liked *chillum*, went from one group to another to take a puff, and massaged the hands, arms and feet of the elders.

Naga Baba Ginesh Giri was wearing a silk ivory kurta on a new bright orange *lungi* and a beautiful wrist watch. He was thirty-five, had been a sadhu for twenty years, and spent much of his time soliciting money from foreigners who came for *darshan* or those he would pick up outside the station. With his fifty English words, this tourist-baba taught them the bases of Hinduism: karma, reincarnation, and the incalculable benefits one gets in giving alms to sadhus in order to receive their blessings which purify past karma. 'Bad karma back. Baba giving good karma. Baba me good. Baba life me love. Me Work not. Food simple, *chillum*, *prassad*, *puja*, meditation, chai, peace, *shanti, shanti…* me love, me love. Giving – good karma.' To those who did not know them, he displayed a sordid image of sadhus. But if he had four bananas, he would share them out. 'We must give everything for *Bhagwan* to replace it,' he once said. It worked. *Bhagwan* replaced amply. Our benefactors regularly put down offerings on our blankets, touching our feet. 'What does *James Bond granola* means?' he asked me. He was trying to read *Zodiac* by Neal Stephenson using a dictionary as his only assistance.

An old *muni* baba was staying on his *asan* in a corner of the terrace and seldom moved; he watched and listened and only came up to a group when he wanted to receive the *chillum*. His *darshan*, seeing him, always made me consider how much I created and defined myself by talking. And I was more aware of what I was saying when listened to by an abstainer from speech.

A sadhu in his thirty's, Mahobat Baba, wore a pink T-shirt, a Nehru collar jacket and a green iron bangle on the wrist. A permanent grin in his tow-beard made him adorable. He had settled under a tree near the fence with the squirrels.

'How do you see the world?'

'The world is good for me,' he answered quietly.

'Since when are you a sadhu?'

'Since tomorrow.'

Tapasji Baba had vowed not to sit or lie down for twelve years. He was completing the third year of his efforts. When a tourist was around, he would lift up his *lungi* to show his infected abscesses on his legs, which had swollen and become like two towers. A pitiful sight. He would then try to squeeze one hundred rupees out of them for medication. The ointment he used cost only thirty.

'Even on a scooter or in a bus, I stand!' he said.

He still sat on the edge of the terrace, but seldom and briefly, and slept harnessed to a pillar. When I looked at him, my blood oxidized and my stomach knotted with terror out of sympathy with the agony of this tortured body. He was for me an image of hell. And stupidity, because he was there voluntarily.

The ascetic champion who hangs a ten kilo weight to his penis, the *tapasya* maniac who keeps an arm raised for twelve years – what do they find? Glory and admiration, just like an Olympic athlete.

'Will you be wiser because you have been standing up all this time?' I asked him.

'My guru ordered me to perform this *tapas* to prove to myself that this body is nothing. After that, I'll have will power,' he answered with faith. 'And I will become famous and respected.'

But pain made him cranky, and promised fame, already proud. Our body can endure a lot; it does not mean it is nothing. He made me feel like sitting for eternity. Ananda Baba and other adepts of non-action had an asceticism that was less dramatic but no less authentic and more acceptable on a daily basis.

A native of Bengal, Saarvan Giri owned a small baba ashram in Haryana. Subsidized by the Government, he was building another one in Gita Colony, a New Delhi south suburb, and he stayed in Bang Handi when inspecting the construction work and to consult doctors about his heart. He was sixty-two, had slanting eyes, a Mongolian moustache and a Druid's beard. His small *lingam*-shaped coil fell to the right. Long ago, in another life, he had been a town councillor and supervised the creation of a library in a small town in Bengal. He liked to recall that his family was related to Tagore. He was a man of integrity, self-respect and tolerant, even if he sometimes let himself criticize a younger baba. He remained seated on his white blanket all day long, leaning his back against his bag.

Vinay Baba, a very showy renunciant, wore two diamond rings, a pearl necklace, a Rolex and had an iPod. These outward marks of wealth publicized that he had one or more rich and grateful disciples.

Those who despised objects did not despise those who loved them.

'What are you listening to, Guruji?'

'There is no Guruji,' he protested. 'We are all the same. All souls are one soul. Whatever you do, affects all the others and the entire reality. There is no other karma than this one.'

He handed me the headphones. He was listening to the latest Bollywood songs.

There also was a real drag of a baba I called *Mister Preacher.* He introduced himself as belonging to this breed. He reasoned a horrific vision of existence: 'Life is a punishment. If you must live a hundred years, it is a punishment. Best is to die as a child. You must hate life to love God. If you pray to God, you are redeemed. God is eternal. Eat vegetarian, repeat *mantras*, control mind, remove all desires, that's what you have to do...'

Fifteen babas were living on the terrace where we had settled down. The corrugated iron roof was opportunely protected by the high and wide foliages of a banyan and a *pipal*, both centenarians. In mid-height three fans produced a warm breeze in the dry and intense heat, but only when the electricity was not cut off. Scattered shoes and *chappals** lay in a corner.

A grimy baba, about thirty, was always alone under a tree at the far end of the courtyard. His clothes had long since lost their orange colour and had now acquired the various shades of filth. His face, hands and feet were coal black, his long hair tangled and dirty. His *tapas*, not to wash, assured him solitude. He displayed the fixed, anxious and fierce gaze of a schizoid contemplating his obsession. I was told that he had not stepped outside Bang Handi for twenty years. Everyone regularly tried to speak to him.

Bom Bom Bole Bholenath! Chillums were passed around here and there.

Ananda Baba generally laid down his *asan* on the periphery of situations, rarely at the centre, and he moved little. From there, he contemplated his environment with the benevolent gaze of *ananda* (bliss), the main quality of the substratum of Being, the challenge of any circumstance. However, he sometimes played a part in conversations and disclosed his wisdom. Benefactors came to him readily; his hirsute and jovial style was welcoming. His *darshan* and his teaching brought him important *dakshina,* which he immediately redistributed. Which earned him the respect of his peers.

I laid out my blankets close to him, but would not stay. At Bang Handi, after the morning meditation, days passed with more or less spontaneous meetings of two to twelve sadhus and some regular benefactors who had chai delivered from the corner chai-shop. Lay residents and travellers also passed by...

The city was swarming with noise and activities behind the railings. Faithful crowds visited the various *mandirs* of the temple compound and they rang the bell and deposited the offerings which enabled us to survive in non-action.

The beggars and the poor were numerous around Bang Handi and Old Delhi Railway Station. But they were not envious of our choice. Hope – maya squared – held them tight. They relinquished neither sex nor money and in their prayers they did not want liberation but sons. They asked our blessings and left us offerings we could not refuse.

'A foreigner came yesterday,' said Mahobat Baba.

'Someone who talks a lot,' confirmed iPod Baba.

'I have not seen him. I went out last night,' said Ginesh Giri.

'He is from Germany.'

'I'm going to Ana ghat tomorrow,' announced iPod Baba.

'So, let's prepare a *chillum*...' suggested Pramod Giri.

'Wait, chai is coming!' curbed Saarvan Giri.

'I am a sadhu to save the world and make it beautiful,' Mahobat Giri Baba told me. 'To help people,' he went on, 'show the path to the heavens, pray to God. Praying to God makes you happy. God makes you happy.'

He did not pray much in a formal way, but God surely made him happy.

Soon a kid arrived with five glasses of chai in a wire holder.

They discussed everything and nothing, gave one another addresses of well kept *dharamsalas* and *akharas* whose presiding baba is a friend, gossiped a little, shared their point of view on the Prime Minister, were shocked at the quadrupling price of onions and the increase of the kilowatt, told episodes of the Mahabharata or *Puranas* and recalled a philosophical principle in the detours of a sentence.

Disputes were not uncommon and their reasons were quickly lost in abuse and name calling. A sadhu hangs up his shawl on a rope and it's an outcry:

'We no longer see the sky!'

'It's dark now!'

Ram Ram fight. A dispute of Oneself in himself.

'Why did you take this place?'

'And why not this place?'

'Move over a little, you're too close. Leave at least two hands width between us!'

But love at first sight, often happened. 'Where there are good manners, love dwells easily,' said Ananda Baba.

One could also keep quiet and stay on his *asan* and, as a spectator, like Muni Baba, let oneself glide along the stream of tranquillity of witness consciousness.

Naga Baba Sukumar Giri arrived with his blankets wrapped around the waist and a large backpack on his shoulders in this overwhelming heat. He set his *asan* up to the left of Saarvan Giri's, taking care to put two bamboo mats down between them as bedsides. He was a handsome man and he knew it. Twenty-nine years old, a sculpted chest, black shiny eyes, cheerful gaze, and a gleaming smile which uncovered his beautiful white teeth. An icon of Shiva as Yogiraj, the king of ascetics. His father had been an officer in the Army, but he was also a gambler and one night had lost his regiment's payroll. Tried and sentenced to three months of prison, he was dismissed from the army and could never find work again. Sukumar Giri Baba, then ten years old, left home to become a sadhu. He still lived in his native Uttarakhand, in a small temple in the Corbett jungle reserve surrounded by 15 lions, 8 tigers and 3 bears, as he precisely remarked. Tourists were welcome and went, probably attracted by wild nature and his particular feline charm more than by liberation. Sukumar Baba was a sophisticated tourist-baba. He gladly showed pictures of his temple and his Western *girl-friends*, an Australian and another Finnish, who would soon arrive in Delhi. 'They are my *shaktis*, they have dollars!' he said. 'In this *kali-yuga*, the present dark age, power is in money. But I never ask for any. I am careful about my image.' He had made a portable altar in a *catogi**, a little cup he used as a lid for his *komandalu*. He had placed a statuette of Yogiraj there with a shell, a few stones and a flower.

On our terrace, the man of power was Mahant Kaushal Giri. He dwelled in Bang Handi several times for several weeks each year. He sat at the centre, on a thin cotton mattress doubling his blankets.

'As a child, I already had God in my thoughts,' he told me. 'When I was six, I used to sit with sadhus. At seven, I met my Babaji and I left home.'

That a child would take his destiny in hand in such a radical way never ceased to appear miraculous to me. Socially, Kaushal Giri had done well: the title of *Mahant* ranked him two steps away from the top of his hierarchy. He had built baba-ashrams in several villages of Haryana and Rajasthan, in Rishikesh and still elsewhere and had left disciples there. He was rich. He had an expensive wristwatch and kept his cell phone at hand. A full beard and short hair under his turban; he was forty and had a rather small body, but great ease and manners of the mighty. Even his smile reflected authority. He was a political baba. He was ambitious, he was making a career.

He travelled with a disciple who served him with love and grace. Naga Baba Partib Giri was about twenty-five. He sat up straight and had an intelligent gaze. He wore saffron colour kurta and *lungi,* and several rosaries and amulets around the neck. His turban made a proud fire colour crown. His swift and effective moves always happened in harmony with the stream of events. He silently put down a chai cup and biscuits at hands for his guru and waited for the right time to be useful. If a visitor arrived, he left his place close to his master but remained attentive, prepared *chillums*, listened, intervened appropriately, praised his guru telling a flattering story, but could also keep quiet. Every morning, on his *asan*, Partib Baba bowed in the direction of Kaushal Giri's *asan* and left his forehead to the ground for ten minutes repeating the disciple's vows. Kaushal Giri then blessed him distractedly.

I did not practice this kind of ritual with Ananda Baba. I was not that kind of disciple. I expressed my respect not in submissiveness but in admiration.

'Are you a sadhu for the lifestyle or for *moksha*, liberation?' I asked Partib Giri.

'I am a *jivan-mukta*, a free soul,' he answered proudly.

'*Atcha!* But if you suddenly inherited several hundred million rupees, would you renounce renunciation?' I insisted.

'In the days of the founding of the universe,' he answered, 'Kali*, the devil, asked Parikshit, the king of the Earth, where his place was to be on earth. Parikshit offered him bars, brothels, gaming rooms and slaughterhouses. Kali bowed and thanked but still wanted other places that he could inhabit. Parikshit gave him lies, pride, passion, ignorance and hostility. The devil bowed but insisted, "Won't there be for me a prestigious place in this world?" "Dwell in gold! Gold ruins men," finally conceded the king of the Earth.'

I bowed.

Chai and two lay men, disciples and benefactors of Kaushal Giri, arrived and held council with their guru. A poor *dalit* appeared afterwards. He did an *omkar* touching the edge of the terrace in front of Kaushal Giri and hesitated to come in, watching for a sign of approval. The *Mahant* looked at him coldly as he questioned him with his chin, leading him believe that he did not know what he wanted, but responding in fact in the scorning astonishment he showed by this movement to keep him distant. If he was above all, he showed it a lot. Having come to lighten his heart, elevate his spirit perhaps, the man went away crushed by contempt. My democrat and Human-Rights committed blood pounded wildly in my temples.

'For you, Guruji, are men unequal?'

'A single soul but for different services; one father, several children; one hand but five separate fingers,' he answered in brahmin stock phrases. 'Prior to this life you have been good to become this human incarnation.'

'Before, I was a good dog, then a good monkey, then a good cow!' I said more with disbelief than sarcasm.

'Yes. Cows, lions and monkeys naturally become humans afterwards,' he approved. 'When you do something stupid, the second time you learn. It's the same with rebirth.'

Partib Giri was reproving in silence, but getting restless, my irreverent tone with his guru. Kaushal Giri made a calming gesture.

'If caste justifies pride or contempt, it is Kali!' I said turning to his disciple.

Probably to interrupt this conversation, Kaushal Giri suddenly phoned his

German disciple and handed me his phone... Kalpeshwar Giri was in Rishikesh... He would come to Delhi in a week or two... He planned to build an ashram for retired cows. 'Cows are sacred, but farmers want returns!' he summed up. A village in Punjab had offered to build him a little *kutir* and a land.

'... But I told him it was a 7 gram bag!' Ginesh Giri suddenly burst out on the defensive.

'But 7 grams for one hundred rupees! It is wrong! It's a rip-off.'

While I was speaking on the phone, Saarvan Giri had scolded Ginesh Giri for having sold a tourist a sachet of *ganja* ten times its price. The other babas had known about it. 'He will think all sadhus are as greedy and sly as you are...' they all tried to tell him at the same time. 'What you do concerns us all!' He had unanimity against him. It pressured him to leave.

'*Hari Om*. Sit here, *Gurubhai*.'

Mahobat Baba was inviting me to make a stop at the foot of his *asan* as I was walking towards mine. 'You see Rujula Baba...' he told me as if there was a secret and looking at the shed the old sadhu who awaited death lived in, 'three months ago, he flew to this tree, and stayed there all night.'

Atchaaa! He had smoked a lot, his eyes were red, and at that time, everyone had their feet on the ground. Except him perhaps.

I went to pay my respects to Rujula Baba.

'*Hari Om*, how are you, Babaji?'

'*Manonasha*,' he only answered.

Na means no, *sha*, him, *manu*, man, *man*, to think, but *mano*... I ran to ask Ananda Baba: '*Mano* is the ego.' Ego-not him, was therefore telling me Rujula Baba. Which meant "I am not me" in the impersonal singular.

'What difference do you see between us?' I asked him.

'No difference!'

Suddenly, in the gaze this *no different* man rested on me, in the surrender it offered me, I became conscious that I belonged to his consciousness as much as to mine, to his smile as much as to the surrounding sound city and to myself, to the old banyan of the courtyard, to the broken brick which lied about for days, to each being who shared my existence... Suddenly, a kind of liberation in the feeling to belong to whatever was around, to belong to the object of my vision, as Merleau-Ponty said.

In the circular pavilion, a group of sadhus was watching the world cricket championship on television but the power went out and they dispersed, some went to the kitchen, others to take their bath, wash their cloth, have a nap…

Two sadhus arrived from outside. Radiating love, one pointed out the other saying: "God!" He was his guru and his friend and he grinned in silence, but not the least disapproving.

Far away on the terrace of the *pipal*, a sadhu was teaching a *mudra* to his young disciple. He patiently corrected the fingers' position of his pupil, invited him to relax breathing, body, arms… and tried to infuse the elegance that was to accompany the accuracy of the posture. When the lesson was over, they looked like two lovers, gazing in each other's eyes lengthily.

Two servants came with buckets filled with rice, *puris* and *daal*, announcing that a benefactor was treating. Most of us turned down the offer, but Lal Giri felt like eating and accepted. He opened a newspaper as a mat before him, put down the *mahua*-leaf plate full of *puris* and *daal*, leaned over it and examined it carefully, bowed and, raising his eyes to heavens, blessed God, the benefactor and the servants who were taking such good care of him.

An old baba arrived after sunset.

'Not here, Babaji, there,' Saarvan Giri told him.

'There, you'll be better,' further went Partib Giri.

Five babas encouraged him to put down his *asan* on the left rather than on the right of the terrace. The old man hesitated.

'Not here, Babaji, there, there,' insisted Kaushal Giri.

But he finally settled on the right.

On the left he would have been in the shade. On the right he could benefit from the electric bulb and be seen.

'Do you have a cigarette? There was a cigarette here and I can't find it anymore.'

'And my soap? You forgot it!' Mahobat Baba called out to Bala Baba who had just taken his bath.

'Gopal Giri is a calm baba; he is wise. He is never overtaken by anything,' said Saarvan Giri.

We were regularly invited to *functions*: commemorations, inaugurations, weddings, city hall receptions, launch of a product by a company, birthday of a powerful baba, festival of a God in a temple, a *bhandara*… A successful celebration requires many blessings and for this, saints in multitude. Their organizers came to invite us; otherwise, the rumour reported the event.

We sat in line on hemp mats and were served by our host followed by a procession of young volunteers or servants who carried aluminium buckets full of rice, *daal*, *chapati*, vegetables in sauce or chickpea. *Chawal*, Ramji? *Daal*, Ramji? *Chapati*, Ramji? More than enough. Ram is he who serves as well as he who is served. Non-duality is this in-difference.

And we received gifts, money and *charas*.

'They will distribute *lungi*,' pointed out Paritosh Baba who spread the news.

'I already have plenty,' replied Shubash Giri.

'I need one, but I cannot go,' cut in Niranjan Baba who droned out prayers, dotted with bell rings, from dawn to night.

'I'll go for you and I'll bring you back whatever they'll give me,' promised Shubash Giri.

One received, one gave. Money and objects circulated. The others were oneself. Giving was that pledge.

When he got back, Pramod Giri shared his gifts with Ginesh Giri. I offered a *lungi* to Bala Baba.

In the circular pavilion, a few babas were watching *Krishna leelas* on TV: It's a pastoral series on the child-God's silly tricks and marvel games played rather naively in gold-thread costumes and cardboard decor. Their air-conditioner hummed. Several sadhus had gone out to spend a few hours at Hanuman temple. I was reading on my *asan* behind Ananda Baba. Kaushal Giri was speaking with his two disciples. Four or five sadhus contemplated transparency distractedly… A young man entered, greeted each of the babas respectfully and asked for Ananda Baba's permission to sit in front of him. As chubby as serious, and cold, he introduced himself as an engineer student and announced that he did not believe in God and considered religion as a poison.

'I want to confront this problem with a guru,' declared this truthful and scrupulous young man.

Ananda Baba invited him to express himself. Mansukh said: 'Religions and their Gods are tales for children and illiterates… Science is the only faith which produces what it claims…'

'It does not claim the disasters it produces,' corrected my guru amiably.

'But why are you so concerned about Gods and religion? Search Being! That will immediately show you the heart of the problem and without risks of poisoning. Concentrate your mind, which is scattering, on a single idea which excludes any possibility of duality, and Oneness will be revealed to you. You can create your own *mantra* and your own religion. You have the right to be creative.'

'What idea, for example?'

'Your mind must dissolve the world in the same way that you know you cannot grab an object in a mirror. Say for example, *this world is like an image* or *I am the mirror of this world.* Or *neither the image nor the object.*'

'Another example, Babaji,' I suggested...

'The existence of objects (*satta*) and knowledge of these objects are perceived by the ego-sense (*ahankara*, "I") which is a reflection of Self-consciousness (Atman-Brahman). Be that which sees in forms, different forms of the same phenomenon,' proposed Ananda Baba. 'Watch what this produces...'

'*Atchaaaa!*' Mansukh exclaimed as Archimedes eureka!

He had found something. He did not say one more word and we left him in his serene illuminated contemplation. He set out again as the happiest of men.

A poor man came in and twirled a stick of incense in front of Muni Baba's face, joined hands and bowed; then sat down.

'O *Bhagwan*! Look at the swelling on my neck,' he said in a childish voice. 'It's a cancer. I'm only thirty-four and I have a wife and six children to feed. O Vishnu, you heal all, look at me. O Bhairava, O Mata Kali, O Purushoatman...'

The man bowed to the ground and left.

The lay visitors who came to us with a wish first related a pain, explained a worry, before handing in their hopes... A barren woman plagued by her stepmother, the lazy daughter-in-law that bad luck had brought in, the son who had to be successful... They asked for wealth, health, a successful conclusion, the diploma which opens doors... A young girl was thirsty for life with a great heart and hoped for a husband. 'A boy! A son, *Bhagwan*!' wanted a woman not so young... 'Give me a boy.' And the confession of her shame, lowering her eyes: 'I have six daughters.'

'Six girls are enough,' Ananda Baba told her, delicately.

They implored an inspiration or hoped for a miracle. 'May my husband recover kindness!' And did not expect an answer.

'If the other's misfortune is your own misfortune, your peace is peace as well,' Ananda Baba told me.

I met Mister Preacher in the courtyard, on the platform of the banyan.

'When I was twenty-seven, I got tired of the world,' he told me. 'I am awakened… accomplished. I know God.'

He was at the same time sour and reasonable. Austere. Overly bleak and gloomy. And he insisted on speaking to me in English, for he was a Gujarati.

'I am 58 years old. I was civil servant in Mumbai and I am now a preacher,' he declared as if I had asked.

'What do you preach?'

'God gave instructions. All religions are telling the truth. The Bible, the *Koran*, the *Bhagavad Gita*… the scriptures are there. They are old. Millions of people couldn't have been deceived for so long.'

I was about to contest this claim, but Bala Baba joined us and started massaging his arms and neck, listening.

'How you arrive in the world is not important,' continued Mister Preacher. 'The world is a prison. What's important is to know how to get out of it, how to reach eternity.'

'It's a prison that we love,' I slipped in. 'Very few want to leave it.'

'Hmmm…' assessed Bala Baba, good mood as a principle.

'But you must leave this life. You cannot find pleasure in what does not last,' decreed Preacher Baba.

'Oh yes, you can,' I assured him, trusting my own experience. 'Saying the contrary is a lie. Do you want to be alive one more minute? Be honest. If you answer yes, then you do find pleasure in the transient thing that everything is.'

'To live one hundred years is a punishment!' he opposed, dodging aside. 'You should always be sad, artificially sad. Never laugh, and eat discreetly not to wake up envy. And love God. God loves his devotees. Let us bless God to be sad,' he added with no enthusiasm.

'Why would not pleasure also be God?'

'Pleasure spoils you. You forget God.'

'You say that we must love God who made this world that we must hate. You describe a hypocrite!'

'It is a trick of God,' he said cunningly.

'No. It is *your* trick!' I underlined.

'Hmmm,' punctuated Bala Baba.

'*Hari Om Shanti*, it's enough!' said the Preacher pushing back Bala Baba who made an exaggerated yaw, laughing and exempting him an ultimate affectionate caress before releasing his arm.

'Hmmm. Babaji is sad,' he joked.

'If you adore God, you go to eternity,' resumed our untiring preacher.

'The eternity of what?' I asked as an untiring pain in the neck.

'Eternity of what is most desirable.'

'Actually, Babaji, you are a sensualist, but in the future and in the absolute. Eternal delights or nothing. As if eternity could be later!'

'You should not joke with that.'

'Believe me, *Maharaj-ji*, if you must obey rules and constraints, it is not liberation; it's slavery.'

'*Atchaaaa!*' burst Bala Baba, to change.

What does the *Avadhuta* say today?

> Renounce the world anyway.
> Renounce renunciation as well.
> The poison of eternity is renunciation and attachment.
> What nothing affects is our immutable nature.

Reassured, I joined Ananda Baba. He was now speaking with a man about thirty, a teacher probably, who wore kurta and jeans.

'How to know oneself?' asked the visitor as I arrived.

I sat down behind my guru and listened.

'Allow your consciousness to follow the path, Anand will draw for you,' he advised him. 'Don't be distracted.

'Maya is all *that is not*. And Being is what is not maya, which means: that which is not what is not. Look for Being. Who actually is? Does existence exists in your body only or outside also?

'Part of Being is inconceivable by the "me" mind. *Neti neti*. This atman is not this, not this, says Brhadaranyaka Upanishad. That which knows the atman (Oneself) is of the nature of the atman, says Mundaka Upanishad. It is not the arm, because a one-armed person still has a "me". It is not the garment, it is not the temple. Everything can be rejected, he who knows it would still be. Even "me" changes, he was a child; he became a man.

'Being is common to the supreme Brahman, to Gods, to men, to animals and to objects in all times and dimensions.

'Penetrating the world, Brahman seems to be atman (Oneself) and atman seems *jiva* (a person). The indestructible witness is Oneself (atman) as a Being rather than "me". But these three states are the same one and only Being. To Know yourself is to know that.

'Nobody can believe he does not exist. To believe or not to believe is to exist. Anyone who would doubt his existence would be the proof that he exists. We must accept the idea that existence exists.

'Something appears to consciousness through the interaction of the body and nature (the objective world). External objects give form to mental changes which create the mental world of the waking state. It is one order of reality.

'When you dream, you create a world which is only in the mind. There is no objective world, and yet you perceive one. It is another order of reality.

'The objective world is different in dreams, and completely disappears in sleep, *samadhi* and fainting, therefore it does not exist continuously. However, this absence is known. When you wake up, you know that you slept, you know that you fainted. The witness of changes in consciousness exists, and it is permanent, because if it was not, who would know? To Know yourself is to know that.'

Another day, a German couple spent the afternoon with Ananda Baba. She was blonde, dyed blonde, and sophisticated; he was more natural with his old safari jacket and his shaven head. But both were fun, had good manners, knew India and her customs well; they just wanted to talk for a moment. He carried his own *chillum* and used it.

'Hindus say that everything is an illusion, Babaji,' he said after the third *chillum*, 'but hundreds of beggars hold out their hands. All is illusion, but I nevertheless travelled in a plane to come here, and if I had not come, I would not speak to you in this moment.'

Ananda Baba considered him kindly and did not answer. 'Everything is an illusion, but I have a good situation and I am quite happy in the illusion,' he continued in English with a pleasant German accent. 'When I smoke *chillums*, I easily agree that everything is an illusion… more or less, but when I'm at work, in Munich, I must be convinced that what I do is real, that my decisions and my actions really result in reaching a profit. We need the business running, otherwise the illusion will be a nightmare…' he soliloquised a little longer. 'Babas live quietly, not working, not worrying, and they say that everything is *maya maya*! But others work hard!'

'When you're at work, be at work. It is leaving work which seems to raise difficulties,' finally answered my guru.

'*Ja, sehr gut*, you point out the problem, Babaji.'

'Give up *me*-centred thoughts. And you will know what there is to know: to whom does it occur.

'The power to reveal objects to consciousness belongs to consciousness, not to objects. In the same way as there is no difference between the bubbles and the ocean, there is none between the sight of objects and the light which reveals them, nor between objects appearing to consciousness and consciousness itself. So consciousness cannot be denied. By whom would it be? There is no exterior to consciousness that is knowable.

'The photographer is in the picture. Don't separate.

'The power which creates this pot has neither the shape nor the qualities of the pot. That is why we cannot describe maya.

'Maya is neither real nor non-real, nor real and non-real. It is indeterminable. Thoughts and feelings change, consciousness remains unaffected. Because we experience it, maya is not non-real. But because it is constantly changing, it disappears in deep sleep and can be transcended, it is not really real either.

'Consciousness on which something appears still exists after this thing is gone. What happened? Maya has shown something to the immutable. When the duality knower-known disappears, what remains is the undetermined Self of consciousness.'

The German thought about it, then exclaimed: '*Sicher! Sehr gut. Danke,* Babaji. You teach mind yoga.'

Horns hoot behind the railings, the generators roar, two transistors and hundreds of starlings gather on the *pipal* to shriek out the last twenty minutes of daylight. And yet all was calm. A sadhu was blowing into his pen refill to push ink towards the ball. Another praised the qualities of his watch to his neighbour: '40 rupees. It also gives the date which automatically changes every twenty-four hours!' And sadhus in small circles here and there on the terraces.

'Go get some change and give twenty rupees to the first ten babas you will see,' ordered my guru holding out his *dakshinas* of the day. And I received ten blessings.

In front of Old Delhi station, a man introduced to me his little boy, eyes lined with kohl:

'Bless him,' he asked me.

What can be better than wishing the best for someone? I blessed father and son.

Mr Pivel

A French man, about fifty years old, wearing a kurta and linen trousers, turned up one afternoon and then came back over the following days. Mr Pivel was not one of those tourists who steps in to smoke a *chillum* or buy some *ganja* and disappear an hour later. He bought chai several times a day, gave offerings and supplied *chillums* with hashish. He knew how to win people over. He asked questions and took notes. He was a *Lekhak*, a writer. Everyone got to know this and wanted to talk to him. Several secretly hoped that their names would appear in a book. He sometimes came with two translators. On other days, I interpreted for him.

'What is your interest with India?' almost all the babas asked him. 'Everywhere I go, I look for wisdom,' he would readily reply.

'What is your religion?'

'Everything that belongs to humanity belongs to me.'

He had Jewish origins, but for the babas that did not mean anything. 'Jesus was a Jew, just like Buddha was a Hindu,' he explained. He claimed he was an atheist. He wanted to learn, but also talk, discuss, argue and refused to accept when his interlocutors thrust forward ready-made beliefs out of the local catechisms that he already knew very well. I identified with him a little. He used a tactic to break the sadhus' propensity to play the guru whenever they have a Westerner in front of them. Dragging them off the faith beaten tracks, inviting them into dialogue and bringing in other ways of being wise, he sometimes argued starting with… "*in my tradition….*" 'In my tradition, we answer a question with a question. Thus, anyone who asks a question can find his own way.' He impressed the babas with his arguments: 'An answer may be right or wrong, a question is always true. Truth is in the question and not in our answers.' 'In my tradition, we say that God and the world exist because I question them. If I stop questioning them, they dissolve. Our questions are the foundations of the world. To know himself, God needs our questions.'

I made use of his idea thereafter to say that all the men are born free and equal in dignity and right. *In my tradition...* I would start, and I evoked an evangelical parable, quoted Plato or Nietzsche.

During a conversation about the earthquake that had killed seventy thousand people in Pakistan, Sukumar Giri commented: 'Nature is not evil. It is always right. But Man abuses nature.' He showed his ecologist seducer's colours, opportunely moralistic and expert because he lived in a nature reserve full of wildcats. But Mr Pivel contested:

'There were tidal waves, earthquakes and volcanic eruptions long before there was man on earth or the slightest human produced pollution.'

Sukumar Giri gave up ecology for a while.

'If you completely surrender to God, God looks after you,' he promised.

'There are many things to believe in, in this world... that the government will really fight corruption, that by using Ariel your washing will be cleaner, that Pepsi makes an artist of you, or that God takes care of you...' replied Mr Pivel. 'It's advertising!'

'Do you believe in God?' asked Sukumar Giri.

'Does God believe in God?' retorted the writer.

This question made Sukumar Giri thoughtful. Saarvan Giri intervened:

'You know the answer since you are God. Can you not believe in yourself?'

But Sukumar Giri left him no time to react.

'Do you believe in the Hindu religion?' he asked naively.

'In my tradition,' said Mr Pivel, 'we sit around a table and the guru asks the others: "does anybody have a new question today?" In my tradition, we ask questions and we try to find new ones. And if, somehow, we find an answer, we question it immediately. Because our answers confine us to the known, whereas our questions open us up to infinity. I do not believe in anything, I question everything.'

'Sadhus are not only those who wear saffron colour,' said Saarvan Giri. 'You are a sadhu in your way.'

In the depths of our terrace, a trunk adorned with strips of jute pierces the corrugated iron roof. Above, it is a *pipal* with its large leafage. It takes root below, under the concrete floor. It is encircled by a low paved platform which hosts a few effigies and calendar pictures of Gods. Yellow marigolds shine happily on a beloved guru's wooden sandals, next to the painted orange ones of Hanuman.

Mahant Dormendol Puri laid down his *asan* next to this small scale temple, on a board covered with a rug raised on four bricks. He was burning incense and a small oil lamp, offerings to Ganesha whose festival would start the next day.

Thin and small, fortyish, delicate, elegant, almost precious, Dormendol Puri wore his bun to the left, a distinctive sign of the powerful Juna akhara. He had earned his title through personal achievement rather than bureaucratic politics.

One afternoon, after the time of the daily nap, Mr Pivel asked me to translate a conversation he wished to have with him. He ordered chai, offered a piece of *charas* and several *chillums* did the rounds before he questioned him about his family, and then on the day of his departure… Dormendol Puri's father was a *zamindar* (a wealthy landowner). As he had no children, he had asked a sadhu to grant him a son. The sadhu blessed him with the promise: 'You will have five children. Four for you and one for me.' Dormendol Puri was the youngest of five siblings

'As a child, I never missed an opportunity to sit with babas staying over in my village. The neighbours told my father that I acted like them. It is said that those who leave their homes before the age of nine were sadhus in their previous life. I left one morning at dawn. I was seven.'

'Were you scared?' asked the French man.

'No, I was sure *Bhagwan* was with me.'

'Did you ever return home?'

'Never. A sadhu regards all beings as his family. He respects all living creatures. Even plants. He does not eat animals. Some can understand birds. Everyone is me and I am everyone.'

Mr Pivel was writing away in a notebook.

'Everything is an emanation of the divine power,' Dormendol continued. 'This power governs the universe.'

'That is not true,' objected the writer straightening up. 'Millions of people pray to God to grant them a little more wealth and they are still desolate. There is no divine power.'

'If you believe in this misery, you see misery. If you look for the beauty, everything is beautiful. It all depends on your heart. Our way of seeing makes the world. Good and bad are human classifications. The sun shines on everybody.

For God, there are no rich and poor, good and bad.'

'You should teach God how to put an end to suffering, because many people would benefit!' Mr Pivel replied with a disbelieving smile.

'All creatures are created by God, the meat eaters, the vegetarians and those who are eaten. For God, all creatures are the same.'

'But being eaten or not is not the same for the creature.'

'How do you know?'

'You answer as if *dukkha*, suffering and the cause of suffering, did not exist.'

'*Dukkha* exists because of karma and the senses. And also because of "I", "me", "mine", owning, greed... Pain comes from not getting.'

As he was writing, I found it useful to warn Mr Pivel aside, in French:

'You won't find flawless logic in what he says. Logic isn't his priority. He doesn't use words to build an argument but to bring about a kind of awareness. You should observe the effect these words produce in you, and not their absolute relevance or truth,' I exposed, remembering that I had long made the same mistake. 'In any case, you will never hear a formulation of Truth that will satisfy you.'

Nevertheless he continued to resist. He was under the spell of the mental faculty, as they say in the oriental schools of practical philosophy. He wanted to ignore the intuitive access to the reality of unity emphasized in Hindu wisdom and taught by its paths. *The source of the words*, as Ananda Baba would say. Mr Pivel wanted the answer to be complex, articulated and rational.

'There are causes of suffering other than greed,' he retorted.

'You harvest as you sow. If you do good, you receive good in return,' assured the *Mahant*.

'No,' Mr Pivel still objected. 'It's not that simple. There are examples of good deeds producing bad consequences, and of bad ones causing good outcomes. Providing food to hungry people saves lives but it ruins local economies and destroys the means of living of many. And if I sow wheat, a storm can destroy my crops... Basically, you never know what a good deed is.'

'Either you see the *leela* (God's divine play) in everything, or you are in it as a character. As a character, you experience the drama and sometimes suffering. If not, you are a spectator. You cannot do everything, but you can observe. See everything as oneself. God is in oneself.'

'What have you found?'

'Words cannot say. How could you describe *Maha-atman*?'

'The Supreme Self of oneself, the ultimate self-reflexive,' I explained, as a scrupulous translator.

Mr Pivel would not let Dormendol Puri dodge the issue, hiding under the shelter of the unutterable.

'In my tradition,' he answered, 'we don't describe it but we show it: it is said that half or even the tiniest fraction of infinity is infinite. So I am also and already infinite. Words can lead to the threshold of the unutterable. In the beginning was the sound. *Om!* And from the sound arose the word. And words created the world…'

'But silence destroys it,' dropped Dormendol. 'One cannot explain this liberation. You must follow the teaching of a guru step by step.'

'Every baba has followed the teachings of a guru, and several, I am sure, will swear they have found liberation, but I see few who really have destroyed the world in themselves!'

'You cannot know. You may not be seeing all there is to see. The only way is to try. Mind is infinite and omnipotent; when you realize that, you know the secret of life and death.'

'At the moment, what are the questions you are asking yourself?' Mr Pivel went on.

'In normal life, there are questions, but in meditation there are no words, no sounds… It's a light with no words. A yogi sees God and is afraid because he is afraid of death. A *samnyasin* is not afraid of death. He goes beyond God. He sees the light. I can lead you to God. And if you are not afraid of death, you will see the light.'

There was a promise and a challenge in this offer. Surprised and perhaps embarrassed, Mr Pivel remained pensive for a moment. He was an *intellectual* as the French say, a person who toys with thoughts to know the world. He didn't have the embryo of a desire in him to renounce anything, to change his lifestyle, to follow a guru, devote several years of his life to the effort needed to free himself from himself or contemplate the light beyond God. He received the promise in disbelief and found the challenge too risky. He was afraid of wasting his time.

'I am not sure I won't be afraid,' he finally answered.

'We were born naked and we will die naked,' Dormendol Puri reminded him.

'So, you met God,' dodged Mr Pivel. 'How is he?'

'How can I describe the Lord who dwells in the heart of all beings, the essence of breath? One can see him as the four armed manifestation of Vasudev and find in him a great peace of devotion. From this peace, the *samnyasin* seeks the essence of Vasudev and sees Time as the incarnation of Shiva. Then, the light of lights appears to him and he realizes that his own form is Shiva and is thus freed from time and form.'

Incomprehension was, between them, insoluble in translation. They did not speak from the same kind of intelligence, if I dare say it. Mr Pivel articulated concepts; Dormendol drew a map of consciousness using mythological and symbolic markers to indicate a *darshan*, a point of view, the experience of a state of consciousness.

'What do you do when you bless?' the writer began again.

'I was born from a blessing,' recalled the *Mahant*. 'I do it in my own words. Sadhus acquire powers performing their *sadhanas*. Their words are powerful.'

'If you are so powerful, you should bless everyone so that, immediately, there would be no more suffering anywhere!'

'Everyone is not able to receive a blessing. You must bow, you must be humble. Suffering is useful to consciousness.'

Mahant Borot Puri Maharaj, the saint and master of Bang Handi Temple, lived on the second floor of the round pavilion between the kitchen and the temple. A flight of white marble steps led to a small anteroom where Dormendol Puri, Mahobat Giri, Partib Giri and I, squatted and sorted out a mountain of coins: the offerings from one of the donation trunks scattered on a cloth.

Borot Puri received his guests, sitting on a spring mattress on top of his *takhat* situated in the middle of his room, facing the open double doors. It was a shambles all around him with piles of blankets, utensils, dried-fruit baskets, *lungis*, *dhotis*, sandals, rolls of cotton cloth, radios, marble and bronze Gods… all the gifts he had received and had not yet had the time to distribute. He had been living in this room for forty years and seldom went out. He was fifty and had a large round head with a gruff face over a short but heavy body. When Mr Pivel, the Westerner whom he had not failed in hearing about, came to see him, Borot Puri looked at him with a condescending smile and, with an inquiring chin invited him to say something.

'What is your teaching, Guruji?' asked the writer in English, squatting on the visitors' carpet.

I was listening from the anteroom whilst gathering two-rupee coins.

'No message,' said Borot.

'No message is a message,' replied the writer.

Borot Puri did not react.

'What do you do all day?'

'I don't do anything. I only observe,' the *Mahant* consented.

He scraped his throat tilting his head back, and then leaned forward to expectorate a yellowish sputum in the spittoon placed between his bed and the guest. He then straightened and breathed deeply, as if he had resigned himself to speaking less laconically.

'If you seek God, it is an idea, not a reality. God is unknown. How could there be a way? There is no path.'

'What then?'

'If I answered you, there would be a way. However, there is none.'

'I am surprised to meet a saint living in a temple so unconcerned by God,' commented Mr Pivel. 'But so am I.'

'Do you think you have found the answer because you don't believe in a God? Man is quite as confused today as three thousand years ago. The mind is an obstacle. It belongs to the known. To enter inside, one must be free from mental conceptualisations.'

'Inside of what?' Mr Pivel asked.

'Inside of outside, inside of outside inside, or whatever you want,' Borot Puri said ironically. 'Observe outside, observe inside. If your mind is not clear, you do not observe correctly. There is nowhere to search. Just observe outside and inside yourself. Observe. Only observe.'

And he then dismissed him with: 'That's enough.'

Ananda Baba was sitting on his *asan*, close to the low wall surrounding the terrace. Mr Pivel bowed deeply in front of his buoyant benevolence and bore the gaze of his sparkling eyes. My guru asked him some of the *ten standard questions* in English, then...

'It is said that you like questions. What are you looking for, Sir?'

'What is there to look for?' he replied.

'Nothing, possibly. Are you looking for it?'

'Yes,' replied Mr Pivel.

'So you are a serious seeker,' challenged Ananda Baba.

'I would have said demanding,' corrected Mr Pivel.

'Are you sure?'

Mr Pivel hesitated.

'Are you demanding towards others or to yourself?' asked my guru.

Mr Pivel still hesitated.

'An uncertain type of demanding then,' inferred my guru…

'I would rather say I seek wisdom.'

'Wisdom? What is it?'

Mr Pivel deliberated a while and realized:

'I cannot say precisely. It is a mysterious intelligence.'

'Everything is contained in mystery.'

'Are there different ways to be wise, do you think?'

'Certainly.'

'But how do you identify them? How do you envisage a wise man? Is it someone quiet, clever, prudent, intelligent? Is it someone who meditates alone in the high mountains?'

'Perhaps somebody who has all these qualities…'

'At the same time, it is possible to be quiet and narrow-minded, clever and dishonest, prudent and over-cautious, intelligent and devoid of love and compassion… Is this the way you imagine wisdom?'

'It is probably someone who doubts,' considered Mr Pivel aloud.

'How can doubt produce wisdom?' refuted Ananda Baba. 'It paralyses or limits you, or hides the truth which may shine. When you walk, you don't doubt your legs. If you did, you would fall.'

'I would say that a wise man faces facts without emotional or sentimental involvement, with lucidity and pertinence,' attempted Mr Pivel.

'Is it enough? Many people who are not wise would fulfil these conditions,' observed my guru. 'Shouldn't lucidity be accompanied with kindness and pertinence with perspicacity and foresight? And once you have spoken about wisdom in this way, will you be any the wiser?'

'Maybe Guruji will teach me how to recognize a wise man and wisdom.' Mr Pivel finally conceded.

'You must be wise to distinguish wisdom,' said Ananda Baba. 'A wise man is he who recognises wisdom, not only those who produce it. When you can recognise wisdom, you are wise.'

It was a perfect example of my guru's methods. He first invited his interlocutor to fight, then led him to let go, give up, and then with a strange sentence often built to cause what I would call a *tautological effect of truth* or a return of consciousness to itself, he gave him the opportunity to jump from an intellectual standpoint to an intuitive experience of Oneness (unity of subject and object). He then appealed to the consciousness that had become aware in order to expand it even further by suggesting oppositions that would be reabsorbed into non-duality.

'What you seek has always been in you because the whole world is in you. There is nothing outside your self. You are wisdom and the lack of wisdom. You are the illusion and that which creates it. This is why you should not limit anything. Here, right now, what are you perceiving if it isn't an image of yourself through what you perceive? This whole game is played out in consciousness. Now if you include yourself in the image, what do you see?'

'The same thing, but differently,' found Mr Pivel.

'What is the difference?'

'I turn from a horizontal to a vertical point of view. I see things from above.'

'Is this the same "I" then?'

'Not quite, in fact,' agreed Mr Pivel.

'Do you have two "I"s then?'

'I don't know where you are leading me but I agree to go,' said Mr Pivel, amused.

'Consider each of these "I"s.'

'One is in relationship with someone or something: you at this moment. The other is less involved in what is happening. He is a spectator of himself and others.'

'Exactly. Whether you see a difference or if you don't see one between yourself and the world around you, it means that you don't see. Consider everything on this razor's edge of uncertainty. It brings you back to what is really happening to consciousness in this very moment. And finally that's what wisdom is. If you realize this, you are wise.'

'What is the difference between doubt and uncertainty?' I cut in.

'Uncertainty applies to the immediate.'

'*Namah Shivayah!*' I hailed my guru joining my hands together.

Mr Pivel bowed too. And remained there. Silent.

Meanwhile Pramod Giri and Sukumar Giri were discussing the quality of *charas* in Delhi. Sukumar Baba got up and went around collecting some funds.

'Are you going to the seller next to Navdurga *mandir*?' asked Saarvan Giri.

'No, it's too far. I am going to the one close by the *masjid*.'

He left.

Saarvan Giri spoke little since Sukumar Giri had arrived. He said:

'Sukumar Giri speaks too much and always to say *me, me, me*. He is young. He poses. I am his elder.' And he added as if the answer were obvious: 'Earlier, he asked me: *Why doesn't the writer interview me?*'

Looking pale, Lal Giri came in and announced:

'This morning, when I was taking my bath, my bag disappeared. I've got nothing left.'

Gopal Giri pulled a nice wooden bowl out of his bag and gave it to Lal Giri. He threw a box of matches in it as a first offering. Mr Pivel dropped in a one hundred rupee note. Lal Giri left to tell of his misfortune further afield. Saarvan Giri warned Mr Pivel that Lal Giri was not allowed on our terrace. 'He cannot be trusted… He loves heroin.'

Meanwhile, three puppies were exploring the courtyard, sniffing it with a brand new curiosity. An eagle landed on the water tank. The bitch quickly gathered her puppies and led them behind the terraces.

Naga Baba Shubash Giri was wearing a red turban with small printed yellow flowers, wrapped in the Rajasthani style. This beardless and fair skinned 18 year old boy introduced himself as a storyteller. His movements were graceful, delicate, almost effeminate, but he was unaware of them. He travelled with his *gurubhai*, Naga Baba Pramod Giri, a well built, twenty-two year old boy, with a sparse curly beard and a keen gaze who smiled at all times and invited himself for every *chillum*.

Sometimes, after dark, together they sang one or two *bhajans* in *ghazal* style. Pramod Giri was the backing singer.

> And me, Shahid, I ran away
> Only to tell you
> That God cries in my arms…

They were splendid.

'Shubash is a glorious name,' Shubash Giri indicated to Mr Pivel who had just sat down with us. Shubash Chandra Bose raised an army to fight the British. He recruited his freedom fighters saying: "Give me your blood, I'll give you freedom."

He was sitting up very straight, as if his words were official. He showed us pictures of him, a few years earlier, posing nude in front of the Juna akhara building in Varanasi, his penis rolled up around a castration stick.

'Why did you become a sadhu?' asked Mr Pivel.

I translated for him.

Shubash was a poet; he did not answer questions directly...

'In a *ghazal*, we sing:

> I spent time in solitude,
> And I played with my chains.'

He sang it twice, in a low voice, almost to himself. The first time, solitude was tainted with pain and the chains were overburdening; the second time, he brought the yogi's serenity to the solitude and mocked the chains which made them lighter. And he began the long story that would perhaps get his name into a book...

'There are different viewpoints in the world. Here, we believe that the karma of one's previous life is the source of this birth. A *sloka* teaches:

> The 6th day after birth,
> The God of luck comes to tell
> Each one his own future.
> And what he says happens exactly.

'Then one forgets.

'Just like King Baltari.

'Now... (in Hindi we say "now" to introduce the time of a tale,' I interfered scrupulously, 'just like we start with *once upon a time* in English.)'

'Now, King Baltari asks his Raj Pandit, (the palace chief priest):

'"Who were my parents in my previous life, and who was I? Why am I a king? What have I done to deserve it? Answer these questions tomorrow," he orders, "or I'll have you killed with all your family."

'The Raj Pandit cannot answer these questions. And he worries.

'Every day, the *Pandit's* daughter spins the wheel at one of her friends' home and, at the end of the day, she leaves her spinning-wheel there. This day, she took it with her, saying: "I shall not come tomorrow, because tomorrow, the king wants to have me killed."

'When she arrives at her house, the Raj Pandit asks her:

'"Why did you bring back your spinning wheel?"

'"Father, the king wants all of us killed tomorrow. He asked you questions that you cannot answer, but I can."

'"So what should I tell him?"

'"Tell him to go into the forest. Tell him: You will find a small mud hovel with a thatched roof inhabited by an old stinking *Mata*. The dog will bark but don't be afraid, he won't bite you. This mother will answer your questions."

'The following day, the Raj Pandit goes to see King Baltari and tells him what his daughter advised him to say... So then the day after that, the king arrives at the old *Mata*'s place in his coach. The dog barks but doesn't bite him. At the door of the house, he hears the voice of the *Mata*:

'"Come in, Baltari Maharaj!"

'It is such a wretched house and the old dame stinks so much that the king doesn't go in. He asks his questions from the door step.

'"If you want to know the answers, go a little further into the forest, to the village. The usurer has no children, but when you arrive, his wife will have just given birth to a son. This newborn will only live the time it takes to milk a cow. You will ask to see him. He will come back to life and answer your questions."

'"How could a newborn child answer my questions?" wonders the king, but he still goes to the village.

'On the way he sees the *kutir* of a sadhu. He orders his coach to stop. At the door, he hears the voice of a sadhu:

'"Come in, Baltari Maharaj!"

'The king is surprised to be recognized everywhere, but he goes in. It is a *kutir* with rotted wooden-boards and a roof full of holes. The only room is clean but almost empty. His host is very old but he stands up straight and his coil of dreadlocks is high and his eyes are keen. He invites the king to sit down on an old jute sack. The king wants to ask his questions but the sadhu does not give him time. He strikes him vigorously on the back and the king suddenly sees everything differently. This *kutir* and the poverty of the sadhu become images of bliss for him. And he also sees his palace. His government and his servants are for him like the heavenly dwelling of loyalty and order. And he remembers the stinking *Mata*'s house as the abode of love and dedication.

'The sadhu strikes again on the back of the king and asks his host:

'"Did you see?"

'"Yes," says the king.

'He leaves and continues his journey.

'As soon as the king enters the village in the forest, the usurer's wife gives birth to a son. The usurer is delighted and offers a lot of money to share his joy. But a little later, the newborn dies and his father laments.

'The king demands to meet the child alone. The moment the Raja sees him, the baby comes back to life and calls:

'"Come in, Baltari Maharaj!"

'The king sits beside him and asks his questions:

'"Who were my parents in my previous life? And who was I? And why am I a Raja? What have I done to deserve to be a king?"

'"You saw what was to be seen," answers the usurer's son, "but if you want to know what you have seen, the Raj Pandit's daughter can tell you what you saw."'

And Shubash Giri started singing:

> Who will open my eyes?
> What will my heart show me?

Then he resumed his story…

'"If someone can answer my questions, it certainly is her, for she sent me on this trip," deems the king. "And if she can, I vow to become her husband and the father of her children."

'On the way back he stops at the sadhu's *kutir* to see paradise again. The holy man strikes him in the back and the king sees the deprivation of the *kutir* and the poverty of the sadhu as manifestations of hell. And he also sees his palace, his government and his servants… but as a dreadful nest of hypocrites and liars. And he notices a large pot of boiling water on a pit-fire that the clerks of hell keep alive.

'"Why do you boil water?" asks the king.

'"It is for King Baltari! Maybe one day we will put him inside," they answer enthusiastically.

'Seeing that, the king opens his eyes and tells the sadhu with terror:

'"You are a magician."

'Back in the city, the king goes to the Raj Pandit and asks to see his daughter. He tells her his journey and she shows him what he saw:

'"You were poor in your previous life. The old *Mata* was your mother and her dog, your father. Her house was your home. The son of the usurer was your brother in your former life and I have been your sister once. The sadhu who showed you heaven and hell came to our house, one evening, when we had only five *chapatis* to eat. And he begged for alms. We all had already eaten our bread, but not you. You offered yours. It is because of this *chapati* that you are a Raja!"

'This is the story of King Baltari.

'He didn't have anyone killed. The *Pandit's* daughter married another man, but the Raja showered her with gifts as if she was his sister. And he brought the *Mata* to live in the palace.

'Sadhus' blessings are powerful. We don't know, when and how our actions will bear their fruits. When all is well, days slip by quickly and pleasantly, and when difficult times come, days pass slowly. May everything good come to you. It is the prayer that I make,' the storyteller concluded.

And he sang again:

> Who will open my eyes?
> What will my heart show me?
>
> Who will teach my eyes to see?
> My heart, O my heart, will open my eyes…

Mr Pivel wanted to interview me as well but I refused to talk to him about myself: 'I adopted a lifestyle which is also a philosophical practice. There is a difference between knowing the concept of non-duality intellectually and making it possible for your brain to experience *non-difference*,' I told him.

'What did you see or understand?'

'In the beginning was the *logos*, the word, but before the beginning, was silence. The monotheists seek the creator of *logos*. Hindus seek the silence that precedes this creator. In other words you could say: they seek the one who speaks.

'The dual principle is a reflection. This reflection produces another which is none other than oneself. It is in this reflection that space, differentiation, forms, Gods, the world, perceptions, life, human beings, names are all generated… and the individual who sometimes sees himself as pertaining to the mirror rather than the reflection, to light rather than a particular image, belonging to consciousness rather than to knowledge, to Being rather than to a single existence, immutable rather than restless.'

One day Mr Pivel bade farewell. He touched the feet of everyone with sincerity and slid offerings under every blanket. 'A door has opened after seeing you.' 'You are the lake where sadhus quench their thirst.' 'You are the God who spreads kindness. Everyone loves you.' 'You are an aspect of myself,' I told him, stopping him from bowing.

There were a dozen of us babas seated in a circle on the terrace wearing different shades of saffron. Pramod Giri was preparing a *chillum*. A *grihastha* entered and touched each *asan*. Ananda Baba returned from his bath and took seat. Another benefactor arrived. *Hari Om! Ram Ram!*

I don't remember how it was that Kaushal Giri ended up telling me:

'Prahlada* was a demon before he became a great ascetic.'

'I don't know Prahlada, Guruji,' I confessed.

'His story is told in the *Puranas*. He immersed himself in *samadhi* and remained there one thousand years,' said Kaushal Giri, 'and during that time, the other demons kept calm. Karma was appeased. "What use are the Gods now?" Vishnu wondered. "Creation stays motionless. There are no more trials and tribulations, no more ordeals or even rituals." He awoke Prahlada and the world took its natural course again.'

Hari Hari! a few babas exclaimed.

'What should we understand from this story?' I asked.

'The demons represent the five senses and the mind,' explained Partib Baba, Kaushal Giri's disciple. 'When they are under control, there are no more changes.'

'Thoughts actually arise out of Oneself,' said Ananda Baba. 'Prahlada immobilised his thoughts. He had attained the Self.'

'Atchaaa!' Bala Baba wondered.

'But why did Vishnu wake Prahlada up? Why didn't he accept that karma was appeased?' I said, surprised.

'Because he wants creation to be buzzing with life,' said Ayayah Baba, *the one who does not age*, the oldest of the circle, with enthusiasm.

Muni Baba was listening in the distance, smiling.

'There were no more rituals,' recalled Kaushal Giri.

'The Gods had no more reason to exist on Earth,' added Partib Baba.

'If there is no friction, there is no world and if there is no world, there is no myth, and without myth no Gods,' Ananda Baba pointed out.

'Vishnu wants it to *Rock n Roll*,' I summarized using my reference points. 'We must dance; we don't have a choice. So why inflict oneself one thousand years of *tapasya* to free oneself from the world since we already know the end of the story: Vishnu will wake us up!'

Ananda Baba burst out laughing. Digging in his coil, he replied:

'Vishnu dreams that he creates worlds and in one world he creates Prahlada, but in this dream Prahlada brings the worlds to a halt. Vishnu awakens Prahlada to awaken himself and continue dreaming.'

'Hare Hare Babaji!' I exclaimed.

'Haaa!!' sighted Bala Baba with pleasure as if he congratulated himself. *Bom Bom Bholenath! Allak.* The *chillum* was passed around.

'The world is God's trick,' Mister Preacher went on. 'What's important is to understand how to get out of it.'

'There are so many paths!' said the old wise man, calmly this time.

A few minutes later he seemed to have escaped in a delightfully soporific way.

'Shiva is the greatest of Gods!' asserted Sukumar Baba, an ardent Shivaist, and a living icon of Yogiraj Shiva in his eternal youth, who seemed to challenge everyone. 'One day, Brahma defied Vishnu and Shiva: *Which one of you can go round my universe?* Vishnu rushed in one direction. Shiva turned around himself once.'

Everyone already knew the story, but it made everyone laugh.

'Remember the story of Bhasmasura, Maharaj,' countered Partib Baba who was a Shivaist himself through Kaushal Giri, his Guru, but a fine disciple of a *political baba.* 'Bhasmasura, this demon, made severe penances to get Shiva to grant him a wish. He kept his mind focused single pointedly for one thousand years. Finally Shivaji appeared to him:– What is your wish? – The power to reduce everything that passes under my hand to ashes. Shivaji granted him this. Bhasmasura then wanted to put his hand over Shiva and reduce him to ashes and Shiva had to flee. But the roar this race made through the universe, alerted Vishnu who took the form of Mohini and appeared to Bhasmasura, and Bhasmasura forgot Shivaji, he fell under the charm of this very beautiful woman dancing in front of him, inviting him to join her. During this ballet, the enchantress placed her hand over her head and Bhasmasura, imitating her, also placed his hand over his head and was instantly reduced to ashes. However great Shivaji is, Vishnu saved him,' Partib Baba pointed out.

Atchaaa! Hare! Every one exclaimed.

'What does Bhasmasura represent?' I asked Partib Giri.

Kaushal Giri gave the answer:

'Bhasmasura symbolizes *manas*, the mind. This *Purana* teaches that you should never think of it as a friend because it is what chains man to karma. Shiva – even Shiva! – lost an aeon of merits because after having been saved by Mohini, his mind misled him and he fell in love with her.

'A man who trusts his mind is the prey of lust, pride and deceits,' stated Mister Preacher expectedly.

'Each power has its own limit,' explained Ananda Baba. 'You have the power to speak but also to remain silent, you have the power to move and to stay still. Bhasmasura possessed such powers as to be able to reduce the universe to immobility in a single point. When he conquered the power to destroy, he wanted to destroy Shiva, the destroyer, but Vishnu showed him the shortest way. Bhasmasura destroyed himself.'

'Hare Hare Panditji!' Some exclaimed.

'Let us recapitulate Babaji,' I tried. 'Bhasmasura, a demon but still a formidable ascetic, and a powerful saint in his kind, focused his mind single pointedly for one thousand years, and thus reduced his being and the universe to nothing. He asked Shiva, the God of destruction – and of what else but illusion, because that's all there is – the power to destroy. But he had already acquired this power through his *tapasya*.'

'He who has destroyed everything wants to destroy the destroyer. Which can only be him,' added my master. 'This is what Vishnu, in the form of Mohini, showed him. But Shiva also fell in love with Mohini: the destroyer of illusion, the master of maya, was deceived by appearances as well. Even Gods fall prey to charms. But since Shiva is everything, it's in him that Bhasmasura and Vishnu and Mohini and the *rishis* who told this story, talk about Shiva. And so, this world is his *leela*, his play,' concluded Ananda Baba guffawing.

'Hare Hare Panditji!' shouted those who had followed.

'Anything that Brahma creates, Shiva will destroy,' Sukumar Giri prophesied.

'But it seems that after one thousand years of *tapasya*, one can still have understood nothing,' I grumbled. 'Take heart!'

That made everyone laugh, even Mister Preacher.

Ayayah Baba awoke and proclaimed in the most learned and toothless voice: "*Sa Brahma, sa Shiva, sa Vishnu*" (Shiva is one of the names of Vishnu and vice versa). Bala Baba moved to massage his back. A sadhu sang a soporific litany of adoration at the end of which Pinaka Baba boasted having been several times around the universe.

'Is the universe finite or infinite finally?' I questioned to be informed.

'It is infinite and one can go on a tour around it,' answered this poet.

I stood up, took small steps around him and sat down again.

Everybody burst out laughing. The Muni Baba smiled at me, probably because I had found a mute answer.[1]

Mahavathar Babaji, a legendary and immortal Baba, turned up in conversations several times throughout the days. He has actually been famous for several centuries, for this baba never dies. He appears, then disappears, and sometimes without going through birth. He was claimed to be back as a young man in the Himalayas. But also as an old baba in the Narmada valley. Occasionally, a baba would tell of having seen him. The time element was fuzzy in their stories. Present-days crossed with mythology which stimulated imagination transforming facts into a modelling clay of reality. One evening Ramji Baba told us how he died:

'I was there. It was above Gangotri in the Himalayas. Babaji then had a thirty-five year old body. He was with his seven disciples and some other babas. A Western sadhu arrived and took seat in the circle. A little later, he gave Babaji a book on Hiroshima. Babaji flipped through the pages, looked at some photographs, read the comments here and there… He spoke a few words and then, ten minutes later, he left his body.'

'What did he say, tell us, Ramji?' I asked, impatiently.

'He said: "A revolution is necessary." Then "One is responsible for everything; one is responsible to his true nature."'

'And did he really die?'

'We have burnt his body.'

But this was just an episode of a longer adventure. 'He came back,' said Sukumar baba. 'He is in the Himalayas with his seven disciples. In Rishikesh, I met a baba who saw him in August.'

'Mahavathar Babaji is immortal,' confirmed Shubash Giri, the storyteller.

---

1 Without knowing it, Pinaka Baba was giving Poincare's answer: 'We will never find the end of the universe but we will be able to go on a tour around it.'

And one day, one takes one's leave and roams the roads again, just to go and see elsewhere whether he would be there as well. And although tomorrow is a great adventure, it is nevertheless a heartbreak.

'I considered myself lucky to have met you.'

'I will dream of you every day of my life.'

'You are the pearl of the universe.'

One says goodbye, turns around and goes away. And we don't know if we will ever meet again.

What will the *Astavakra* tell me today?

> As I alone reveal this body,
> Even so do I reveal this universe.
> Therefore mine is all this universe,
> Or verily nothing is mine.
> [*Astavakra Samhita* 2, 2]

Connor

As we were going through Jaunpur, I noticed a young Westerner, sitting in the street, alone, indifferent to the commotion of the town surrounding him, hanging his head, dirty. I let Ananda Baba go ahead of me, and I squatted down in front of him.

'What's going on, little brother?'

The young man looked up with a start and took a moment to decide before giving me an answer.

'I have lost everything,' he said in a quivering voice. 'I don't even have my passport, not one rupee, nothing.'

He seemed to be endlessly ruminating over this nightmare that anyone on a journey to a distant country tries hard to avoid. Without money one doesn't eat, and without ID one doesn't go far… What could he do? He urgently needed a friend. And that's all I had to offer.

'Come with me,' I decided. 'We will take a bath, have a meal and we will think about it.'

I helped him stand up. Vertically, Connor had a nice build, a pleasant face, blond hair and hazel eyes.

We found Ananda Baba on the riverbank and took our bath.

'Wear this *lungi* rather than your jeans,' I suggested, giving him one of mine.

Connor was doing his big year of post graduation travelling. He was an Australian, twenty-three and had a degree in sociology. A few days earlier, during one of the countless stops in the countryside, in the middle of nowhere, he had stepped out of his train to relax. The train had left without him. He had taken a bus to Jaunpur and survived a few days on his last rupees.

We ate in a *dharamsala,* and then settled for the night in a small *lingam mandir* on the banks of the Gomti.

'… at first I thought I would be able retrieve my jacket and my backpack. I went to the station and filled out lots of forms. When I found out that this wasn't going to happen, I didn't even have enough to pay for a phone call.'

'And he waited to die of hunger in the street!' Ananda Baba exclaimed.

'If you had asked nicely, a cybercafe would have let you send an email for free,' I assured him.

'The best is to now accept what is,' my guru advised.

But I was more specific:

'You can go to your embassy in Delhi and get repatriated. Or ask for help from your parents or friends, by email or phone. We have enough money for this and for the bus to Delhi as well.'

I shared my blankets with him that night.

The next day, Connor said he preferred to send an email. I gave him twenty rupees to spend an hour in a cybercafe, but he didn't go. He spent the day strolling around on the *ghats*.

He joined me while I was sitting apart contemplating the dozen *dhobis* who were grunting like Serena Williams when serving, as they beat the wet laundry on the large flat stones by the riverside. The echo reverberated the off-beat chant of the groans, immediately followed by the detonation of beaten laundry which composed a minimalist and repetitive rhythm in Steve Reich style, regularly adorned with the choir of a funeral procession which came to a crescendo as they approached and then faded into the distance towards the cremation ghat: *Ram Naam Satthya Hai!*

He loved India, her slowness, her languor, her magic and even her dins. I told him my story about the crows and their scam. We talked about pollution – *two hundred million wood, coal, dung and plastic bag cooking-fires every single morning and evening… but natural gas buses in Delhi!* –, and about overpopulation – *89 girls for 100 boys*, about terrorism and globalisation's inherent violence – *Free trade and neo-liberalism means Law without Justice!* –, Materialism is killing the Planet. The philosophy of non-action can save it –, about U2 – *The more you have, the more it takes today.* And Bob Marley – *The Human race is in a rat race.* He was a vegetarian due to ecological sincerity rather than from a love and mercy for life: – *Cattle-rearing produces methane responsible for twenty per cent of greenhouse gases. It's more difficult to do without oil than to give up eating meat.* We often agreed and shared an overall contempt for politicians.

'Liars.'

'Over-ambitious pompous clowns!'

'It's not the job they hanker after, it's the role and image they're seeking.'

'The world is run by lobbyists actually. Australia is contaminated with American Puritanism.'

'It's the same in France on a secular level. And India has always been prudish.'

But he felt he had a duty to be loyal to a religious faith. He was…

'A grandson of Irish immigrants, a Presbyterian, but practicing half-heartedly…'

'Which is already a lot…' I slipped in.

'…Because my parents are. I believe there is a God.'

'The God you believe in drowned humanity and all living creatures in a flood – except for a few – and you don't feel outraged by this? The God of Israel let half his people be murdered in gas chambers and you still want to give him a chance! Epicurus said:

> If God wants to prevent evil and never can, he is powerless;
> If he can and does not want to, he is perverse;
> If he neither can nor wants to, he is powerless and perverse;
> If he wants to and can, why doesn't he do it?

'It is to this implacable logic that we must bow!'

But for Connor, God-the-Father, Jesus-Christ and the prophets of Israel fashioned a sacred space inscrutable by reason and amnestied of any critical inquiry.

'What did you do before?'

'A sadhu does not talk about his past. Not saying anything about what you have been exempts you from regenerating from it,' I replied.

He had sat in circles of sadhus during his trip. He was succumbing to the *miracle babas* myth. He imagined them to be wizards and miracle workers endowed with psychic powers.

'The miracle is that we can live this way,' I said, giving a different slant.

'People here accept that some men live exempted from work,' Connor thought aloud. 'It's an amazing society.'

'That filled me with wonder as well. But it's not stupid. Hindus believe the world is a prison. Sadhus are explorers who search for the path out. If they find it, they show the route to the others and if possible the shortcuts as well.'

'Did you convert?'

'I'm interested in the route.'

The river was flowing at our feet like liquid time pleated with fleeting wavelets scattering moments of vivid light. *Ram Naam Satthya Hai!*

'Don't worry about conversion and faith!' I lectured him. 'A very long time ago, one of your Celtic ancestors changed his religion to embrace Christianity; then, centuries later, another one of your ancestors became Presbyterian. Which one of your forefathers should you be loyal to? Why should you have to be faithful in that matter? Fidelity is not positive in every circumstance. What innovation will you introduce to your lineage? The metaphysical assumptions upon which you want to build your life cannot be an inherited duty... Everything that belongs to humanity is mine,' a French man who is writing a book on sadhus told me.

'What about girls?'

'*Yeh to manogay ki sare log apas main bhai behan ya ma baap hain:* you will regard all beings as your brothers and sisters, fathers and mothers.'

'And you agreed to it?'

'I don't know. A little... It doesn't happen.'

'Is it a hard life?'

'Whole days doing nothing... Satisfaction, confidence and nonchalance are the three qualities of a sadhu. Agreeing with whatever turns up is the key to well-being; learning to keep quiet is the secret of bliss. *Vairagya*, the Sanskrit word for renunciation, means "absence of passion". It's not the contrary of happiness; it is the opposite of desiring, acquiring and keeping. Nowhere close to the idea of refusing something. We just don't seek anything. We don't choose. Possessing, which is both oppressive and delicious, no longer exists. And that's also delightful.

'But if one approaches renunciation with a fundamentalist attitude, it would then still be an attachment to something: principles, regulations and obligations. I say to those who are too strict: "If you still follow rules, you are not liberated, Babaji." But some have also renounced so much that they also renounced renunciation... The illusion is everywhere. To rise above it requires a kind of derision towards everything, including the principles which are supposed to result in denouncing it...'

Ram Naam Satthya Hai! the chorus punctuated.

The *dhobis* were helping each other fold the laundry that had been laid to dry on the steps; others loaded it, in heavy bundles, on the backs of their donkeys.

The next day, Connor had his head shaved but did not go to the cybercafe. His skull rapidly changed from white to red. Ananda Baba gave him a *gomcha* to tie on his head.

Three days passed. Then two more.

'What do you intend to do, Connor babu?' Ananda Baba asked him at night in our *mandir.* 'Anand wants to go.'

The *puja* broadcast via loudspeakers from a distant temple reached us as a crackling moan. *Shri Ram!* shouted a man, rowing, from his boat. Ananda Baba raised his head and blessed him: *Jay Ram! Sarvam khalvidam Brahman Om.*

'Actually, Babaji, I want to stay with you,' Connor said after some hesitation.

'You are not a sadhu, Connor babu,' said Ananda Baba, frowning at him.

'Yes, yes I am! I have nothing left,' opposed Connor.

'That makes you a beggar, not a renunciant,' qualified Ananda Baba.

'It's because I've nothing left that I can dare to do it,' admitted Connor whilst his gaze sought support in my friendship.

I was delighted that Connor wanted to join us. He didn't disturb quietude and he knew how to live with little. His presence was light, friendly, and he wasn't over-talkative. He brought a cheeriness to the days. But this seemed to me the sort of thing that Ananda Baba alone had to settle.

'Having lost everything to then meet you – for me this is like a sign from God,' Connor insisted, turning mystico-spiritual.

'You are not a renunciant, Connor babu.'

'I do renounce!' Connor swore with temerity.

'It's not true,' retorted Ananda Baba both severe and smiling. 'Look deep down in your heart; you will discover that you don't want to give up the world. What is it you really want?'

'I want to live like you, to take you as a teacher,' answered Connor with sincerity.

'Teacher…' contemplated Ananda Baba out loud.

'Yes, Babaji, a Professor. Like in university,' Connor said hopefully.

'Professor…' repeated Ananda Baba. 'But of what? Do you want to be freed from the hypnosis of the world? Do you want to give up the idea of there being a "me" that exists? Can you love a God to the point of craving to dissolve into him?'

Connor did not answer. He would not put the problem that way.

'Do you have a religion?'

'Yes. I am a Presbyterian. But I know that God has several names and various forms…' he hastened to add in a politically irreproachable religious tolerance waffle.

'What do you want to learn?' asked Ananda Baba.

Connor hesitated, then turned to me: 'How did you answer this question?'

'Be yourself. Don't use tricks,' I advised him. 'Babaji knows everything…' And I held my hands out towards the feet of my guru before joining them and bending low with love and gratitude.

'I want to know you, understand you, learn to travel with nothing, see how it happens. Live it. And seek God doing it.'

'*Atcha!* You want to be poor to see God!' summarized Ananda Baba filled with wonder. 'To seek God… What kind of Gods would you be looking for?'

'Any,' ventured Connor recklessly.

Surprisingly, this answer made the deal.

Ananda Baba rummaged about his bun and withdrew his pack of *bidis*. He put many questions to Connor, whether he was married or attached by love, responsible for his parents, had a job, debts, responsibilities… Connor was free. He had good manners and a kind of Anglo-Saxon college candour, a little clumsy but full of goodwill.

'You will have to serve Babaji and obey him. Are you willing to do that?' Ananda Baba asked him, lighting his *bidi* in his hand.

'Yes I'll do it,' promised Connor in the joy of victory.

'If Anand orders you to jump into empty space, you will jump. If he says "leave your meal", you will leave it. When Anand orders you to remain seated for days, you will do it. Will you do it?'

Jumping into empty space… Babaji was not that type of a guru. But missing a meal often happened. And remaining seated can be a torture. Non-action is not a conditioned reflex of the *homo-liberal* globalisation contemporary. Neither is it one of his virtues.

'I have confidence. You will not ask me anything I can't do,' Connor agreed diplomatically.

'*Samnyasa* is not a game,' Ananda Baba replied incredulous and worried.

'But the world is one, Babaji,' I cut in.

'At first Prassad got attached to him, and now there is another one!' grumbled our guru. And he burst out laughing.

He welcomed whatever happened.

Connor took *brahmacharya** vows.

With the *dakshinas* and offerings of the following days we bought him two white *lungis*, the colour of chaste students. He sold his jeans and bought a blanket. A shopkeeper offered him a *komandalu*, another one a bag. *Om Namah Shivayah!*

And we took to the road again.

An immense bale of hay overflowed from a cart pulled by two white buffaloes… 'Sadhujis, do you want to come up?' shouted the driver. Our afternoon finished at altitude, on this travelling mattress. Then, we crossed a market on foot: snake-charmers, medicine men, coupon hawkers, itinerant shoe-repairers… The headlines of *The Hindustan*:

Missile "Agni IV": Successful Testing
A range of five thousand kilometres

Ananda Baba had suggested that, as we were walking, I teach Connor some Hindi basics and a few of the customs and various sections of the code of good manners in the company of shaggy ascetics. I remembered from time to time… 'Don't throw anything in the *dhooni*. It would be an error of taste. The holy hearth is *Agni's* dwelling place. It manifests the messenger God; it's not a dustbin. Also avoid turning your feet towards it…

'When the *chillum* dies out, the privilege of matches is given to the nearest who hasn't smoked yet, unless he is someone important. If there is a *dhooni*, an ember replaces matches. Ananda Baba prefers that nobody talks when the *chillum* goes around and for a while after. But some babas overlook this practice.

'Even if invited to, you should not sit on somebody else's *asan*. Our blanket is our home and our temple… Sit on your own blanket.

'We accept a gift turning palms upward. To refuse, turn them down. To give, you don't offer presenting, you put down in front. The recipient has no choice. *Would Babaji do him the favour of obliging him…* The confusion of the third person singular is a summons to union – the spiritual obsession, the metaphysical horizon – but it does not remove the rules of precedence, privileges and good conduct. It's extremely complex and I have given up trying to figure it out. The ego of men who have renounced ego is sometimes much larger than the ego of those who have had the modesty and prudence not to renounce anything.'

'But think about what it would be like if they had not had the courage to try giving it up,' said Connor.

'Ah, I see you're already a wise man!' I noted with pleasure.

'Why are we going from temple to temple?' asked Connor on his tenth day of walking.

He was not in any way suggesting we stay in one place. He loved our slow penetration of India by foot and by bus. He had fun sleeping on straw, in a beaten-earth courtyard or under a shed in a baba-ashram. He would tease children, help a man pull his cart, played the jester making a pretence of not watching girls, joked with everyone on buses... He appreciated the never-ending encounters we made. But he also loved to ask questions. It was his way of integrating himself into this world. He did not inquire about metaphysics, like me; he had a religion. Conciliatory, he gently bowed to the idols and saints that we met. He hoped to discover the meaning of the customs, but most of all witness holiness *live and direct*, with miracles and magic spells. He was from the Harry Potter's and NUMB3RS' generation. 'Can you levitate Babaji? Is it true that some yogis can create anything they want?'

Ananda Baba did not speak of *siddhis*, the psychic powers of legendary yogis. He lived, it seemed to me, at the limit of two worlds, a world of wisdom and one in which his consciousness bathed in the colours of bliss. He would answer Connor asking him strange or absurd questions: 'In our dreams, how is it that the characters don't sleep? Can a bald man also have horns and find happiness? How many girls can a barren woman give birth to before she stops being the daughter of her mother? What are the characteristics of a square circle full of holes?'

He prescribed him to repeat the *Om mantra*. 'Mental modifications will gradually be fewer, then will stop,' his guru promised him.

'What power do you get repeating a *mantra*?'

'The power to think of nothing else. *Om* is the closest sound to Brahman.'

But the questions continued to burst forth: 'Is God in this idol? Shouldn't we see him outside temples?' Connor took the Hindu religion as he had been taught Christianity, through compulsory faith. He knew little of it but accepted with no effort that one differs on details, considering that Jesus, Krishna, Ram,

Shiva and the others, indicated the same thing in different ways. All in all he believed himself to be tolerant but was nevertheless afraid to say or think something that would displease the *one-and-only* God of whom he still had a very precise idea.

At nightfall, Ananda Baba would teach his disciple: 'Shrines, temples and holy sites are holy because devotees make them holy.' 'There is no goal, explore the link between present and future.' 'God is not a reward for good behaviour. Everything is because you are.' 'Seek the one who asks the questions. That's where you'll find atman, the unalterable Self.' It was too quick and too esoteric for Connor.

Connor sought God with a Christian desperation. He did not really expect to meet him and even less to become him, (for him, God was radically different, by definition), but he also had the Christian simplicity which accepts supernatural feats. His *one-and-only* God who had had a son, blind men recovering sight, cripples walking again, the multiplication of bread, resurrection… opened him to faith in levitation, ubiquity and many other miracles. But Ananda Baba offered gazes, enigmas, the ambition to be *That*, the obvious and the mysterious aspect of all things. Connor was craving for miracles. He was living an adventure.

And he liked to classify things.

'How do you recognize a realized man?'

'He lives in multiplicity like the others and yet he remains in Oneness where the stream of events acts without him having to act,' Ananda Baba answered him.

Thus he lived.

For Connor, the world was populated by believers and non-believers. Not only did he have a difficult time understanding that I was a sadhu with very little concern for religious practice, but he resisted integrating a third category, that Babaji made him discover: 'He who seeks the refuge of Gods, in honouring them, receives the refuge of Gods, but he who performs rites with no desire becomes the creator of Gods.'

There was something beyond God if we spoke of consciousness rather than power. And it tickled Connor. He considered these sentences almost blasphemous. He was not uptight when it came to religion. But he was not free either. He believed in God without wondering what God could mean other than what he thought.

'Brahman is *Ishwar* (God) in the process of creation and maintenance of this world,' Ananda Baba said. '*Ishwar* transforms the power of maya by assigning objects with their determinants. He creates differences. He organizes a universe. The objective world is God.'

We were sitting next to each other on a bus which would bring us to Bilrayaganj if Ananda Baba, sitting near the driver, did not decide to get off sooner.

'What is Babaji's teaching?' Connor asked me, looking for the Western's shared keenness of reason and rationality.

'He says that the world we live in is made by the mind and that thoughts are shaped by prejudices, habits, conditioning, references, names, layers of filters… determinants also, said the Stoics. Babaji sometimes spots them and shows them.

'In his philosophy, life in the realm of names and forms is subject to creation and destruction, in the same way that dreams are. They are imposed by the intellect on to Brahman, or they are Brahman's creation, like waves on an ocean. The secret is being able to look at the waves from the perspective of the ocean, and then from that of the water… and then without any perspective at all.

'He teaches about the appearing of a world to consciousness and about the possibility that this world is nothing more than an appearance. He gives invisible reference points for a boundless world.

'Mind has split the world into two parts: me and everything else. This separation between me and what I perceive is also seen to be illusory, false. There is no outside. *I* and *you* do not exist. There is only a *he* who is talking to himself, as if in a dream. That which makes it possible to observe the transient nature of things has to be relatively stable, non-determined. That is the state of consciousness we're talking about.

'The Kena Upanishad says:

> That which cannot be thought by the mind, but by which, the mind is able to think,
> That which is not seen by the eye, but by which the eye is able to see,
> That which cannot be heard by the ear, but by which the ear is able to hear;
> Know that alone to be Brahman, not this which people worship here.
> [Kena Upanishad I 5-7]'

'And is there God in all this?'

'Babaji is not interested in God. Not with me in any case. But he is open-minded and ready to swear that all the Gods exist and are happy, because he thinks that, in these matters, no point of view is closer to truth than another.

I would say that for him, the Whole, as a whole and in pieces, is divine and unreal. The divine for him is a sun-lit view of things, an underlying feeling of harmony or peace.

'You can try to become impersonal, like Brahman, the most abstract of supreme Beings. In practice, some adopt a Godly figure like Yogiraj, the God gone mad or God in the image of an ascetic absorbed in *dhyana*, consciousness focused on itself in a single point. You can aim at the metaphysical union of Shiva and Parvati, *Purush** and *Prakriti* (consciousness and its manifestation, nature). Uniting the seer and the seen, giving up the one who sees is a perfect non-action. And a way to know bliss.'

'Do you think it works?'

'What do you expect? There are no miracles. It's either *now* or it is not.'

But Connor kept on asking questions.

'You said that what we think happens, Babaji, but it is not true. Many people are obsessed with money and remain poor.'

It was an afternoon in the shade of a kapok tree, in the courtyard of a village baba-ashram.

'Anand has said that you become what you think; it's not the same. Whoever identifies with his thoughts becomes his thoughts. Someone who only thinks about money does not necessarily become rich; he might discover himself to be greedy. Similarly, if you continuously absorb your mind in *That*, you embody *That*. Everything.'

'What does it mean to absorb the mind in *That*?'

Ananda Baba smiled:

'Consciousness can be limited to a "me", but it can also extend to all. *That* is all.'

Connor started practising meditation. Sometimes, there was nothing else to do. He discovered the torments of being face-to-face with oneself, the struggle between urges to avoid it and willingness to persevere, and he went through these stages which seem to be necessary and unavoidable.

'It makes me yawn,' he told me.

'It's purgatory,' I said to encourage him. 'A sadhu who has practised meditation twelve hours a day for a year told me that patience is the only way to endure meditation. Seek patience.'

'Why do some babas practice *sadhanas* whilst others don't? Why do some travel and others remain totally motionless?' he wanted to know another day.

His guru replied:

'Some think that one should go through all kinds of efforts (*tapasya*) to understand that there is no effort to produce. Anand's teaching is direct. Observe. Observe, being careful not to filter observation through a "me".'

'And God, Babaji, where is he?'

'Precisely. He is here.'

And he began laughing.

'Is living without an ego more pleasing than to endure the vicissitudes inherent in the persistence of an ego?' my guru asked me.

'Is the effort it takes to root out that ego less painful than to endure the vicissitudes, etc.?' I replied.

That made him laugh; I expected it.

'Stop haggling over words! No effort is required to remain motionless. This shows you that it is not an effort which must be deployed. Effort should be reduced and it is not painful. When ego disappears, inherent bliss appears.

'It is possible to understand Brahman through three different paths: *sat*, *cit* and *ananda*,' Ananda Baba finally explained to Connor.

'When a pot is broken, clay is still there. When the body is burned, ashes remain. There is nothing left when names and forms disappear, but this "nothing" is still consciousness knowing the destruction of names and forms.

'This is called looking for the nature of Brahman through the path of consciousness (*cit*).

'There is no outside of consciousness. Through its energy, the universe is known. Through its light, it appears in every act of knowing. Consciousness is knowledge. Without knowledge, you cannot even say that you don't know. Consciousness is neither the known nor the unknown. It knows everything that is knowable: the object and subject.'

Thus spoke Ananda Baba.

The focus of his teaching was consciousness. He tackled it and spoke to it about it, and thus revealed it to itself. 'How may that by which all is known, be known by another? The content cannot contain the container. If the object of attention is abandoned, what's left is pure consciousness (without object), attention alone without anyone to know. There is no experience of Brahman more fundamental and direct.'

I let the way find itself, and consciousness discover itself as being the ground of the entire universe, and in this way it knew itself to be bliss.

Connor was enthusiastic. He loved his adventure and had confidence. I had saved his life, I would always save him, he seemed to believe.

He often went bare-chested on the roads, only wearing a white *lungi* and his Nikes, showing off his ideal surfer's hairless six-pack of abdominals. An idyllic icon of the begging monk in Bollywood glamour style. When they are so sexy, renunciants turn people's heads. And not only the girls'. Seeing him, one would wonder what treasure is found in abstinence for one who has so many assets in a world of charm and pleasures.

In the nightly promiscuity of *dharamsalas*, he sometimes happened to receive sexual advances from very liberated, or rather libertine monks. And he was offended without end by this breach of morality and vows. And of his prejudices. Sadhus are men like any others. One does not enter wandering with a certificate of virtue.

Brought up with *Mister Clean* (i.e. in a heinous aversion to bacteria and germs), at night, before lying down, Connor wrapped his face in a light cloth which protected him from mosquitoes, cockroaches, lice, spiders, scorpions, snakes and, he also hoped, from the innumerable invisible threatening beings. He liked to make up dreams with spring mattresses, fresh linen and private bathrooms. As a joke.

I was less obsessed with chlorinated cleanliness but I have long had the dreadful imagining of becoming ill and penniless in the hands of hairy healers and sorcerers. I had more faith in the effectiveness of chemical medicine. My first bronchial infection made me discover a network of free clinics where a competent doctor listens carefully and also provides his patient with the appropriate drugs. If there is none, a sadhu can go to almost any doctor for a free consultation. If there is none, then a pinch of ashes from the *dhooni* heals everything, so they say...

I liked to sleep under a tree or beside a buffalo. I made a sarcophagus of my blanket. Eyes open, in that atmosphere, I was home.

'Talk to me about bliss, Babaji.'

'To rejoice about everything.'

'Atchaaa!!!'

Pushkar, on the Ghats

We spent three weeks on Pushkar's ghats in front of a small blue lake surrounded by about fifty white temples which were reflected in it. Pushkar is a holy city. Here the Earth is friends with the Heavens whose features are reflected in this mirror.

A very very long time ago, looking for a place to perform a *yagna**, Brahma dropped a lotus flower on Earth. From this, a spring gushed forth and a lake formed – Pushkar. Brahma carried out his fire sacrifice in honour of the Gods on its banks. Bathing in this lake washes away all sins and ensures the achievement of liberation from the cycle of life in this very life.

People come here on pilgrimage; tour organisers make it a stopover town; backpackers spend the winter, and sadhus, staying here, bless it. Every day, the temple of Brahma provided us with a meal which we took to Andreswar ghat where other *samnyasins* joined us. Along with them, at various hours of the day, cows, dogs, ravens, hanuman *langurs** and organized tourists would come. The latter were led by their guide (their guru!), caps over their eyes, small backpacks on shoulders, bottle of water in one hand, camera in the other, capturing multiple images of the ancient, sacred, mysterious, pathetic, elusive India… They also came over to take our picture… But an old man returned from the temple holding a small cup of holy water, his *tilak* still wet on his forehead and suddenly they were much more fascinated by him. Flashes twinkled. Some felt they had to pay for the digital *darshan* and awkwardly left alms at our feet. It was not inappropriate to give us money, but not as a fee.

Backpackers, who looked a little more like us, came to smoke a *chillum* or two, passing by, or staying. And became friends if they found a way to enter the harmonious stream of the moment or practised blissful laziness. And soon we formed a circle, although scattered at various levels of the wide stone steps descending into the clouds.

One afternoon, ravens cawed nervously and then a powerful wind suddenly lifted dust all around the *ghats*, the sky darkened, rumbled, cracked, thundered; bolts of lightning scraped across it violently. We ran up to the nearby temple and finally heavy grey clouds poured a torrent onto the town. The warm water immediately started evaporating from the hot stone pavement. Heavens and earth had joined. We were in a steam bath.

Hans Garfeld, a German chap in his thirties, was touring around India very slowly on a bicycle with a small digital camera fixed on his shoulder. In the evening, he edited and downloaded some footage of his day onto his *blog*. He usually came to Andreswar ghat at around eleven o'clock.

'Did you notice,' I asked him, 'the way you bowed with grace before the other babas and how your joints creaked when, after some hesitation, you granted me a *pranam*? Yet, I am also a sadhu.'

'You look too much like me,' was his justification.

'Bow to yourself then.'

'How many people will watch us smoking this *chillum*?' Jawahar Baba asked him.

Hans turned his camera towards the baba.

'Between two and twenty thousand. What would you like to tell them?'

Jawahar Baba straightened up, looked into the eyes of all those who were in the lens, focused and with full lungs proclaimed his victory cry: *Jay Shiva!*

Manavendra Baba spent two or three hours every day at Andreswar ghat, then he went on to visit other circles. His oiled black hair fell in a ponytail on his shoulder. He was about forty. Thick beard, long face, black bright eyes, intense gaze, muscular, wearing earrings, an amulet knotted at his bicep. This Shiva baba carried a sword. Watching the camera, whilst I did the subtitling, he told the world:

'Jesus Christ didn't have the power to save his life. A real sadhu changes according to the circumstances. If everything is calm, he is nice, but if there is a problem, he solves it with a magic *mantra* or becoming invisible, smaller than the atom, larger than the sky. He can materialize objects or enter the body of other living beings… He is entitled to fight, injure and even to kill if necessary.'

Once this propaganda had been announced, he untied a small purse, plunged his index finger in and then marked Hans's forehead with a vertical line of ash. He carried immortality with him.

'Can you become invisible, Sadhuji?' asked Connor.

'Of course,' he replied.

And he got up and walked away.

'Babaji, would you say something for the viewers on the net? I am sure they will be grateful.'

'If you are sure of anything, you are sure to be right, but actually, you just hope you are right, and you want to forget it is a hope, so being sure of anything is anything but sure,' Ananda Baba answered.

Hans pointed the camera on himself and addressed the net viewers:

'Paradox and the union of opposites are liberating paths for *Jnana* Babas.'

'Because they short-circuit the mind…' I added.

'They open non-duality like space,' said my guru.

'There is no certainty! Is that sure?' asked Jawahar Baba giggling.

'There is no certainty and even that is not sure,' corrected Connor.

'"Though the visible Whole has come out from the Invisible Whole, the Whole still remains unaltered,"' I quoted. 'This is one of the most prestigious paradoxes of Hindu literature.'

'The opposite of the Whole is not nothing, it starts from Whole less one,' observed Connor.

'Very good!' approved Ananda Baba. 'Is the Whole plus one included in the Whole?' he asked.

'That's a variant of the heap paradox,' answered Connor. 'How many grains of sand are necessary to make a heap? And then how many grains should be removed from it so that it is no longer a heap?'

'None!' answered Indralok Baba after I had explained the *paradox* to him. 'The atman dwelling in our heart is smaller than one single grain of mustard and nevertheless it contains the earth and all the worlds together.'

'And if you remove everything from the Whole, what is left?' asked Jawahar Baba very seriously, as if struck with wonder in an abyss.

'Dispel the mist of illusions that makes you believe that there is no mist,' proposed Santosh Yogi.

'Or that there is one!' added Jawahar Baba.

And we all forgot this camera.

A nimble and suspicious hefty grey Hanuman *langur* with a long tail and a black head climbed down the temple gate and examined us from afar. Hanuman *langurs* have the austere and anxious look of an old man with their n-shaped thin lips, crushed nose and prominent arch of the eyebrows which intensify their sharp gaze. Ananda Baba drew one of the two *chapatis* he keeps for this kind of encounter out from his bag and offered it to him. The *langur* had no choice but to approach. My guru encouraged him looking away. The primate came closer without haste, stretched out his arm and seized the *chapati*, ready to jump back. Ananda Baba held on to it a little more and then let it go, seeking his eyes. The man and the *langur* looked at one another for a moment. And for a moment, these two consciousnesses became only one consciousness in the same story, the *darshan*, a vision of Being.

The others in the group were watching from a distance. Shortly after, we shared with these furry Gods a second *chapati* and the shade, for a few minutes.

One day, Sitaram Baba, a sadhu whom I had met in Varanasi five years earlier, joined us in Andreswar ghat.

'You are the same!' I told him.

'You too,' he said to me.

I believed I had changed a little. The last time we had met, I was... I belonged to the economic order of the world, to the promises of work, to the materialistic illusions and to the realities of the market. He was pursuing his eternal four years pilgrimage which was taking him across all the states of India. 'When he has completed it, he will start again,' he said peacefully.

He was a very quiet man. He had taken a vow not to hold out his hand. His gentleness soothed everybody around him.

With a heavy and swaying step, a tall grey female buffalo came to examine the public garbage-bin. Her protruding ribs clinging to her oversized coat hanging in folds contrasted with her haughty horns, noble bump and sulky muffle. Her long pointed ears made eye-shades and flyswatters for the nonchalant gaze, a little above it all, of her ringed black almond eyes. *Namah Shivayah*, whispered Sitaram Baba when she arrived close. He gave her a *ladu* which she swallowed as if it was her due. I love these ruminants. Their short-sightedness confines them to what is immediately around them, and their paunch seems to grant them the bliss of a never-ending feast. Like us, they understand stillness, and they belong in the realm of holiness.

Mujhe Baba was always delighted about everything happening to him and to others. *Mujhe Mujhe!* Me me, he would say designating himself proudly. The sun and the shade, the benefactor who came and the fruit he offered as well as the *langurs* trying to steal it and whose tense and delightful *darshan* we took, the cause was *Me me*. I. Him. Him and his charming grin. And if an unpleasant event arose, he looked downcast but persevered, *Me me*. He was admirable in his straightforward sincerity, assuming the totality of everything.

'It's now three days I haven't smoked anything!' announced a Naga baba with dismay who had just arrived. His biceps were marked with three lines of ash and his face, plastered with crumbling red paste, gave him the air of an old fresco whose excitement was unexpected. We didn't have anything of this kind for him at that time, but Ananda Baba assured him that it would happen without delay. Sceptical, the sadhu let his bitterness overflow:

'*Atcha*, irresponsible Mother!' he went grumbling, 'you don't deserve my devotion. Another day, I'll go back on you, Kali-the-bitch! How dare you deprive me of *ganja*. Vixen! I'll catch you by the hair and I'll beat you and you'll understand…'

He was carrying on with this vituperation when a Westerner passed by.

'Hey, Babu, do you have some *charas* on you? Maybe God sent you!' the Naga baba called out to him.

'Yes Baba,' nodded the foreigner.

He came close, sat down with us and offered a nice piece of hashish. 'This is how I must talk to you so you look after your son?' scolded the sadhu, going on with his conversation with Kali and preparing a strong *chillum* at the same time.

Having smoked, he was moved to tears: 'How rough I was with you, my poor Mother. What a despicable son I am: you get me all that I need, and me… Shame! Indignity!' He pinched his ear lobes to humble himself. 'Tomorrow, I'll stop this *ganja* that makes me wicked,' he promised. But the half-smile that came across his lips testified he did not really believe it.

Berardo, our benefactor of the day, was Italian, about fifty years old, a little plump with shiny baldness.

'Would Babaji tell me something?' he asked Ananda Baba.

My guru observed him with his consent. His appearance suggested an educated man and a *bon vivant*, but Berardo displayed respect that was over formal, an exaggerated humility; a duller recess of his eyes and his way of clenching his fists for no reason also revealed an anxious man.

'From this body, you experience sensations, feelings, emotions, moods,' replied our guru. 'Move the centre of gravity of your being. Go from feeling to perceiving. Make of your feelings impersonal physical and psychological events. Become a witness rather than an actor. And you will know that you are the author of all this. Individuality is identification with non-self.'

'*Shukran Shukran* Babaji,' thanked the Italian, pensive and doing *pranams*.

He put down two one-hundred-rupee bills at Ananda Baba's feet before being blessed and left.

Ananda Baba handed me the bills:

'Go buy *charas* for the Kali *bhakta** so he knows that his mother takes good care of him.'

Westerners were naturally interested in me. The magic formula *a sadhu has no past* allowed me to avoid returning to a person I no longer was. 'I have not embraced a faith; I'm trying a lifestyle, a way to experience a freedom which, if it is also an inner one, is called liberation. But what does freedom mean? Everyone has his own answers…' I explained to those who tried to pretend they envied me.

'Memories of your previous lives will only lead you to this life, and you're already there,' I told a Canadian woman who did not speak about anything else. 'Drop karma and past lives. These concepts keep your consciousness in a subservience to the unknown. There is no posthumous future in liberation. Nor past other than dead. Give up karma, abandon even the idea that there could be traces of anything. And that anything could leave a trace. And try to be content with this freedom that lightens the present moment from everything that made it happen. Liberation is not a future merit.' I played the apprentice guru.

A buffalo awoke me from my nap, sniffing at me. Kanaya Das Baba was still asleep. He slept almost all the time. Offerings of banana, orange and biscuits piled up on his blanket. A grey *langur* came down on a raid and swept up everything. He didn't care.

His usual place was a cremation ground in Bikaner, but he often was on the go for several weeks from one Rajasthani holy city to another. He wore a yellow turban and a small black stone as an earring. He was twenty-five, had high cheekbones, a thin moustache and eyes, sometimes anxious, sometimes immensely sad. He spoke very little. He was a bit crazy: a fire would sometimes come across him and if he had had the power, he could have destroyed the entire universe, and then he would turn this anger against himself. Sitaram Baba pacified him, tenderly taking his head between his hands and forcing him to look directly into his eyes. And Kanaya Das calmed down.

He had a transistor radio he switched on from time to time, not too high, but he sometimes suddenly raised the volume to sing along with the broadcast voice, mimicking the impish energy of a Bollywood star.

One day, Ganga Das Baba asked Kanaya Das for the one hundred and fifty rupees that he owed for the radio. Kanaya Das fetched the transistor and threw it, crashing down at the feet of Ganga Das.

'No more radio. *Fuuuift*,' he then stated with no sign of remorse and with these words, he made a swift gesture of his hand as if he had got rid of junk.

Who can you get angry with if you are a renunciant? Ten seconds of silence followed the emotion of surprise and the conversation resumed as if nothing had happened.

'I also had a radio,' Kaliam Baba said later. '*Fuuift*. One day someone took it.'

And we stopped talking about what is no more.

When a surge of madness came over him, Kanaya Das embodied Shiva in one his wrathful aspects, and we respected him for that.

It was an evening, in front of the temple of Brahma, in the veranda of a closed store where we slept. Ananda Baba made us sit in front of him and explained *ananda marga*, the path of bliss.

'In deep sleep, the mind is absorbed in its cause, undifferentiated ignorance, and everything is calm. During *samadhi*, consciousness is focused on the atman (self) as an object and is subjected to no subjective knowledge from *manas* (the mental function). In deep sleep and *samadhi*, free from mental activity, *jiva* (man, individuality) has direct knowledge of the *ananda* (bliss) of *SatCitAnanda* Brahman (the unchanging consciousness).'

'Can we call "knowledge" deep sleep even though consciousness is absent?' Connor objected.

'Everyone knows what deep sleep is, although consciousness is absent. One has a positive memory of it. Memory presupposes experience. We love deep sleep. When we wake up, we still feel how nice it was! We remember it as bliss.

'Just as happiness and sorrow are knowledge, their absence is knowledge as well.

'In deep sleep, a blind man is not blind; a wounded man is not hurt. Consciousness has an immediate experience of knowing the absence of grief. And as grief is the opposite of bliss, its absence is bliss.'

'If, when I feel nothing, neither pain nor pleasure, that is bliss, this stone must also be in bliss,' he still objected.

'Objects know neither sorrow nor joy. They do not know their absence,' refuted my guru. 'When the knower disappears, bliss is revealed. The Self is known by the Self.'

'Tell me more about bliss…'

'A king at the height of his glory, receiving maximum human happiness, personifies happiness. A child in open-eyed wonder enjoying his own nature. The *Jnana baba* (knower of the Brahman), who has gone to the extreme limits of knowledge, has spread its bliss, has achieved what should be done and remains established in this state. All this is bliss.'

And we left Pushkar.

The divine is polymorphous and its maya works wonders. A God sometimes incarnates as a man, but men can become Gods as well. One can take on this role, or one can have this function allotted by others. This is what was posthumously happening to Shanta Puri Yogi.

We made a short stay in his ashram on the outskirts of Kulu.

Mataji, his widow, told us that the master had gone to the Kumbh Mela of Ujjain to die there, but the yogi changed his mind and returned home where he finally left his body, a little more than a year earlier.

She was of British origin. They had had a son and a daughter, now 22 and 18 years old. This family had erected a *samadhi* in the garden: a white and pink marble kiosk protecting the holy man's body underground in a salt sarcophagus, and above it giving shelter to a naturalistic statue showing him in meditation, motionless, blissful and kind-hearted, forever. At a par with the Gods.

This *samadhi* had changed the ashram into a pilgrimage. Pilgrims came to take the *darshan* and blessings from Mataji and left an offering if they could afford it. The ashram was made up of a few rooms, a marble *dhooni* under a shade and a large room, set up around a courtyard enclosed by an iron gate; a beautiful kitchen-garden, paddy fields, barley fields and six cows.

Connor made friends with the guru's son. Gursharan Puri wanted to become an airline pilot. He told him in confidence that he had not liked his father. He painted a picture of a quick-tempered man who was not always fair, rather macho and who beat his mother. We also learnt that Shanta Puri had been excluded from the Puri Sampradaya because he had married, but was then reinstated because he owned an ashram and lands now worth a fortune. They had created a lineage of married Puris for him.

We had visited many *samadhis* on the roads, but we had only ever heard the official stories of the saint resting there. Hagiographies and panegyrics. The flip side of praises could be ugly. Can a man who does not control his anger be considered a perfection of being, intelligence and bliss?

'Is this the way one becomes God, Babaji?' asked Connor in the room where we had withdrawn to.

'Husband is God, wife is God, son is God and you are God,' his guru answered in a perfect Hindu mystics' waffle.

Thus also spoke Ananda Baba. He never let himself carry judgement upon anyone.

'Catholics also have their saints, who are always dead, and who were certainly not all as shiny as they were later made out to be,' observed Connor realistically.

'India accumulates Gods,' I added. 'She has so many that some only possess a few hundred believers. For polytheists, believing is not synonymous with exclusivity.'

Mataji served us with devotion beyond reproach at all times during our stay. The cows went alone to the forest in the morning and returned by night. We spent our time with other sadhus between the *dhooni* and the riverbank.

Swami Dharmesh, who had just arrived, told us the tale of his life. He had been a bad pupil. His father, a store owner in Lucknow, plagued him so much to study that one day, he ran away from home.

'So sudden was my decision that I took neither clothes nor money,' he said. 'I was fifteen then. It was in June 1980. It was very hot. People were awaiting the arrival of the monsoon with impatience and anxiety. I took a bus and travelled a good distance before the controller asked me for the fare. As I couldn't give him anything, he threw me out, on the road, leaving me in a forest in Orissa. A tribe of Aborigines captured me. They wanted to offer me in sacrifice to their God to bring rain.

'I had to do something to save my life... I had an idea. I told them: "Tomorrow, I shall perform a *yagna* (a ceremony of propitiation). If it does not rain by tomorrow evening, then I shall accept being sacrificed."

'The villagers consented to wait until then. They offered to get me anything I needed to perform this ritual. But I did not know the Sanskrit incantations and I did not know what to do. I came up with the idea to write down the name of each of the villagers. Then I built up a fire and I poured spoonfuls of *ghee** chanting their names.

'At night, it rained. A little rain, but nevertheless rain. The villagers praised me and wanted to keep me for their permanent priest. But I returned home and I studied rituals in a brahmin's school. Later, I went back to Orissa and I became the *pujari* and the guru of this tribe. I earned a lot of money. Much more than my father.'

'But if the monsoon is poor two years in a row, you may become a sacrifice again!' I suggested.

'No! If it does not rain enough and when needed, it's never the priest's fault, but always the villagers' who have not offered all the *pujas* Gods want! But I left them, and now I am a *samnyasin*.'

'In the end, they held him captive longer than he thought,' said Ananda Baba.

This ashram was equipped with a bathroom with door and mirror. I had rapidly stopped bending over my reflection in water. I had not seen my face for long enough to be amazed to belong to the image I saw. I had almost forgotten it. I had never had a beard. It was curly. My hair had grown again but, all of the same length and never combed, they stretched outwards as if I had put my fingers in a comic strip power socket.

I tied my turban; then made a face to my face before contemplating for a moment in the eyes the *him* I had become from the point of view of the *him* I had been; and then the *him* I had been from the point of view of the *him* I had become. Where was the difference? It was scary if I compared it to my clean and proper self of my previous life. Unusual. 'I am a wandering monk, a mystical bum, heir to the *rishis*,' I said to myself. 'I am freed from the economic society and its sordid ideals based on competition and unscrupulous, pitiless and unrestrained lifestyles. Hard to believe this could happen to me.' There was still a "me". But I could tell my story knowing that I would never completely buy into what I was saying. And in that also I was still me. And yet I was changing in small, unfelt and unconscious ways. I could now find pleasure in meditation. My practice helped me to know myself and change at the same time. And to love myself. Who is it that one loves when one loves himself? A state without demands, obligations or requirements. A state of peace. The desire or the fear of being someone else, suspended.

A Sadhu at Work

G uru means *darkness-light*. Is *gu-ru*, the one who *dispels the darkness of ignorance with the light of knowledge*? One can read this in books. So is he a *Deva*, a celestial being. He is looked upon as God, but he does not pretend to be God in the *monolatrous* sense of the word – the all-powerful, exclusive, jealous and temperamental despot. He is God in a metaphysical way, for he speaks of and shows a founding point of view on reality and embodies it. Guru has a second meaning: *heavy,* thus *he who has weight*, the weight of the respect he is given. *He overcame rain, heat and cold, he conquered joy and forsook grief*, one can still read such phrases over and over again, *completely detached and passionless, discreet; his meditation must be perfect...* Books are full of this jargon and such garlands of perfections. But the actual practice is different.

When we went through a village or if we stayed somewhere under a tree, people flocked around to see us, and they would announce, with modesty and cheerfully: '*Maharaj*, we have come to take your *darshan*. Only a blessing would make us happy.' Ananda Baba gave blessings. *Sarvam khalvidam Brahman*, everything is Brahman. Joy shone in him constantly. Everything brightened under his gaze. He joked, laughed, appeased, taught, guided, and greeted whatever happened. He showed a lucid point of view on events inhabiting it. One is guru in the here and now, but it requires a long apprenticeship. And talent. Wisdom is an art...

One evening, in a village of Uttar Pradesh, we saw a teenage girl fleeing from a pack of angry men whose dignity was holding them back from running. But their steps were long. The girl was eluding them but wasn't running away. She kept within earshot as if she and her pursuers knew that her escape was vain. What's happening? The girl is a *Panchalas**. She loves a *Palla** boy. *Atcha!*

Against caste love carries no weight. And since they don't mix, where could she go outside of her community which was condemning her? Love is stronger than death, it is said, but Romeo and Juliet ends in tragedy.

Ananda Baba called out to the leader of the group with an energy I had never seen him use.

'Stop!'

The man obeyed and came to him with his same resolute walk. Connor tried to protect Ananda Baba but his guru pushed him aside. In the arsenal available to a sadhu, a curse is a serious enough threat to calm a hot head. He does not even need to wield it; he is believed to be endowed with powerful secret *mantras*. And as he moves within the realm in which events take shape, the vacuity from which it may be possible to help fate, and since he is an outsider, he can act as an arbitrator or a judge and is easily granted the right to interfere with anything.

'Don't chase her. Where can we talk?'

'In my house.'

We went with him, three streets away, to a concrete two-room house under a roof of interlocking tiles. The walls held on to a distant memory of a coat of green paint. A scooter was parked in front of a window. Ananda Baba followed the man into the first room but stopped the others from coming in. Connor and I also waited outside. We watched in turn through the window. Within twenty minutes the angry man was calm, but Ananda Baba talked to him all night. We learned from his friends that he was the elder brother and the girl's guardian, for their parents had died. He was trying to protect her against a misalliance and defend the reputation of the name he had inherited. The girl came back and waited with us. At dawn, our guru finally stepped out with the brother; he blessed him and his sister in front of what was left of the group of henchmen, bade farewell and we left.

'So, Babaji?' I asked him when we had stopped for the first well deserved chai.

'A caste problem,' he answered.

'Yes, we understood that, Babaji,' I said impatiently.

'What did you say?' Connor insisted.

'Anand advised him not to hinder the action of karma.'

'And he accepted that without balking?'

'He balked all night!' Ananda Baba rectified.

I took over:

'What argument won him over?'

'Anand told him that the child who will be born from the marriage of his sister with the boy she loves will be father to a man who will do great things. Anand advised him to accept the karma that will have allowed this man to be born.'

'But you don't believe in this fairy tale, Babaji?' I jumped.

'Except for impermanence, if there is a single permanent phenomenon in the universe, it is the fright that seizes Prassad Baba when he might venture into the flow of things,' said Ananda Baba laughing. 'He always raises his own criteria of right and true in front of him. For this, Prassadji is always attentive.'

I bowed.

If circumstances required, Ananda Baba got involved. He played in the illusion with lucidity and love. In Shakespeare's place, he would have no doubt reconciled Montaigues and Capulets. That night, he sowed blessings over three generations, offering a destiny to a family threatened by tragedy.

> Done, nothing can be. When one understands this deeply,
> one is in peace to do whatever presents itself to be done.
> [*Astavakra Samhita* 13 3]

'How long have you been a sadhu, Babaji?' Connor asked, one afternoon, in the shade of a large banyan we shared with a cow, three drowsy dogs, a rhesus monkey and its young, perched on the branches, nibbling on shoots and threatening to urinate on us.

'A sadhu doesn't have a past,' answered Ananda Baba.

Non-negotiable. He was not making his past a secret; he was making of secrecy a principle, a principle of liberation. The experience had been acquired. No identification. But Connor would not be intimidated.

'How old are you, Babaji?'

Ananda Baba would always find something to make him think for a while:

'Anand is younger than you are, because the world in which his body was born was younger than the world in which your body was born.'

Connor eventually bypassed the obstacle.

'And how old was the world then?'

'Better yet, consider that you were never born. You're existence itself.

'Here is a way to find the nature of Brahman through the path of existence (*sat*):

'The first change on the immutable *SatCitAnanda* Brahman is space (*akasa*). The existence of space, distinct from Brahman, is possible because of its properties in the realm of name and form. The properties of space are to give volume, to allow movement and in some cases carry sound. Space exists in its properties; it is its *dharma*.

'But in space, as in all things, it is being or existence (*sat*) which appears first and foremost. If you remove existence from space, space disappears. But if we remove space from existence, existence remains.

'This is immediate knowledge of Brahman.

'The water of a mirage does not quench thirst. This world of appearances does not affect the oneness of reality. The mutual deceptive identification of duality and *sat* Brahman (one-without-a-second Being) is destroyed when they are differentiated. Being is not two.

'It is existence (*sat*) which exists (or is manifested) through all things. These things have no separate existence from existence. That is why existence is One without a Second.

'See that!'

Palm huts. Half-built houses already occupied, but expanding at the speed of people's savings: five hundred bricks and a bag of cement per month. The silvery song of the wind in the sugar cane plots. Intense and brief uproars in banana plantations raided by monkeys. We pass through a flock of shorn sheep, backs marked with red powder. Before hitting the road, a bus driver smokes a *chillum* with us, in front of the Durga shrine at his windscreen. Squatting in the litter, two women search and sort through their finds.

We walked…

From afar, the temple appeared like a succession of terraces scattered with chapels, sanctuaries and porticos, descending in levels and flowing into the smooth emerald waters of the sacred reservoir. Like an open-air palace facing its jade mirror. A procession of women walking alongside in their multicoloured saris reflected in it, at the edge of earth with the heavens turned upside down… but suddenly they gathered pace. Four men came out of the reservoir with a corpse. A woman made a deathly scream. The dogs were already joining in. People started running from all sides. We reached them.

'*Woh kab se paani mein padaa hai?* How long has he been in the water?' I asked casting down bag and blankets.

The men put down a wet skinny teenager in brown underwear on the paving stones and did not answer. I pushed them aside and stuck my ear on his cold chest. I stuck two fingers in his throat. Nothing. I tilted his head backwards, pinched his nostrils and blew twice forcefully in his mouth. Connor crouched in front of me.

'I push thirty times; you breathe in once with force,' I said. 'Pinch the nostrils, but only when you do it.'

Ananda Baba held the mother back: '*Wait Amma. And hope.*'

I placed my palms one on the other on the sternum and pushed every second counting aloud… twenty-two, twenty-three… twelve, thirteen, fourteen… five, six, seven…

'He's moving!' said Ananda Baba.

He moved. I turned the boy on the side. A spasm. Water came out of his lungs. He coughed.

Om Namah Shivayah.

The whole village had seen the young man return to life, being reborn… Nothing more was needed to call it a miracle. And it was one. Three sadhus had appeared in a moment of the depths of adversity and had turned time back. It was a dawn. God is whoever arrives in a timely manner, just like Zorro. Women ran bringing flowers, coconut, cups of milk, sweets… A girl poured water on our hands. Other kissed the ground at our feet. In the evening, the village held a *bhajan* in honour of the *avatars* we had suddenly become. *Sankara Shivai, Sankara Shivai…*

'In your country, do they teach you in school how to bring the dead back to life?' Ananda Baba asked me, shouting over the voices and cymbals.

'Not in school, but whoever wants can easily acquire this skill.'

I added: 'Shiva's *leela* (game) can be deathly at times.'

'He who knows it is a game does not see anything deathly. Prassadji is Shiva!'

'But Shiva is still not quite as good as Zorro.'

Ananda Baba started laughing and said:

'What does someone who has transcended thoughts think about, as he sees no other?'

'*Hare!*' I praised, bowing.

The next day, while I was meditating with him on the steps on the reservoir and Connor was swimming in it, Patel, the *risen-from-the-dead* miracle, came up to me, pulled his earlobes, did an *omkar* forehead to the ground, and then got up to tell me:

'My life belongs to you now, Babaji. You saved me.'

'Your life is yours, little Brother,' I appeased him.

There was a matter more urgent. Patel had a fever and was shivering. We sent him to the clinic in rickshaw with an elder brother.

Swimming in the holy reservoir, Connor had been a sensation: the young crowd had watched him with envy and the *pujari* rebuked him firmly. However, he made a quick survey and presented his findings to Ananda Baba:

'In this village, built on a narrow strip of land between the reservoir and the river,' he explained, 'nobody knows how to swim. If we stay here five days, I could teach them breast-stroke.'

Things were happening that way. Ananda Baba consented. He undertook the task of negotiating with the *pujari*.

Connor organized two daily swimming lessons for boys. He had soon spotted and grouped together the weak and the gifted, and he dedicated his afternoons to those he planned to promote as instructors for the others. As for me, inspired by Connor, I tried to teach artificial respiration and cardiopulmonary resuscitation to the mothers. As they refused to touch with their lips to the mouth of another person, Ananda Baba advised me to present this method as *mrit-sanjiwari*, a *tantric* technique to obtain the power to bring the dead back to life.

In the evening, having us sit for a moment with him alone, Ananda Baba brought us, through a passageway made out of words, to pay attention to consciousness.

'Maya means *that which is not* (*ma*, "no", and *ya*, "me" or "that which is"). It neither exists nor does not exist. It is inferred. Its power to make reality appear must exist because it is experienced. It exists in the realm of dreams and the waking state, but disappears during deep sleep, fainting and *samadhi*. Therefore, it does not exist in all states of consciousness. The realm of name and form arise from it; but that from which names and forms arise, that which is before name and form, has neither a name nor a form. And does not exist. Yet, it has a name! This is why maya exists and does not exist. Maya makes the immutable capable of imagining changes.'

The day before our departure, Ananda Baba gathered the new swimming instructors and made them promise to tell the boys from the surrounding villages the story of Patel's rescue by Prassad Baba with the breast-stroke instructions of Connor Babu. For free. And they also had to obtain the pledge from them to spread this even farther. Mothers had to teach the latest *mrit-sanjiwari* to the daughters and mothers of surrounding villages. He told the elders; then threw a heavy stone in the reservoir, thus transgressing a taboo so as to strike their minds and mark the oath.

'The wave of these teachings begins here. May it spread far for the good of all the beings. *Om Namah Shivayah.*'

Thus Ananda Baba acted.

Every year, before the rainy season, when they clean up the reservoir, the stone will reappear, and their oath, will be remembered.

We left accompanied by drums and trumpets the next morning.

'*Maharaj Sadhu!*' roared the man. 'Come in my house, *Maharaj*! My daughter has not spoken for months. A strange disease has caught her.'

His voice was harsh. He was tall, large, raw and sour. The expression of his face bore a natural pout of distrust. Lips pinched forwards, a grim gaze, he was having a bad time on earth and contaminated bitterness around him. 'How will I marry a mute? How difficult it is to father a girl? She is good for nothing,' he cursed to himself like an old woman, but in a roaring voice.

We followed him into the first room of his house. It was covered with a large straw mat and was only furnished with a sofa. Ananda Baba sat there alone. In a corner, a family shrine had a collection of a few earthen Gods. The man called up in a hoarse and already impatient voice 'Kamala! Kamala!'

'No, Babu, she is not needed,' said Ananda Baba.

He was not smiling. He was ordering.

A girl about twelve appeared at the door, puny and frightened. Neck sunken, head low, back arched, hips disjointed, knees bent, she cowered and withdrew in every direction.

'Chai for my guests!' shouted our host to his daughter, as if threatening to bite her.

'Take your sister to the porch,' whispered Ananda Baba to Connor, 'and give her a swimming lesson.'

Connor executed this order before the Babu had had the time to be surprised, the master was already asking:

'Is there a mother to this girl?'

'The mother died three years ago.'

'What is your name?'

'Kumar Chand.'

'*Kya tumhare aur bhi bachche hai?*' (Do 'you' have other children?)

This use of the informal '*tum*' was dissonant.[1] It established his control over him. Ananda Baba amplified it with a stern gaze. In order to help him, he had to impose his authority over this man who had been clear-minded and courageous enough to ask for assistance.

'No. Just this girl,' he answered back.

'The girl is sick, Babu,' confirmed Ananda Baba calmly, 'she should be treated. And you will give something to Babaji to help her heal.'

'Do you want money? I don't have much!' he grumbled.

'No, Babu, the vows Babaji took forbid him to ever accept a salary.'

'So what do you want, *Maharaj*?' said Kumar Chand, waiting impatiently.

'For Anand, nothing,' answered Ananda Baba very slowly. 'But you have to give something to get her cured. Your daughter is an appearance of Lakshmi[2]. Her karma is to be gentle. But you, Babuji, deny her grace. You prevent her from being what she is. This is her disease. The cause of her illness is you, Babuji.'

'*Atchaaa!*' said the man, amazed.

'*Atcha,*' confirmed Ananda Baba.

'What should I do?'

'You have to give your anger to Babaji, Babuji.'

'My anger!' Kumar Chand thundered furiously. 'I am not angry.'

'Anger is the first of the three poisons,' explained Ananda Baba. 'It flows into your blood when you say "I". When you say "I want", it already invades your mind and makes you impatient. Anger rules your life.'

'*Atcha! Atcha…*' said the man waiting to see what was coming.

'You will not speak to your daughter until she speaks again,' ordered Ananda Baba. 'Not a word. You will buy her a new sari and you will serve her the dishes she likes. Because tomorrow will not be like yesterday.'

'I should serve her food!' stormed Kumar Chand, stunned and incredulous.

---

1 As in French and Spanish, the second person singular in Hindi has both a polite, formal form and a familiar, informal form, which Ananda Baba uses here.

2 Lakshmi: Deity of fortune in her enchanting quality. Kamala – red lotus, that is to say the heart, is one of Lakshmi's names.

'*Haan*,' confirmed Ananda Baba, coolly. 'You will look at her the same way you look at *Iswhar* in a *mandir*, you hear! And when she starts talking again, you will talk to her as she talks to you, with the same voice. You will never beat her again. And you will add the image of Lakshmi to your family altar. And you will give a day's pay to a sadhu baba. Go take a bath. Then you will prepare chai and Anand will receive your vows. And Anand will bless you.'

When tea was ready, Ananda Baba sent me to get Connor and Kamala back. The girl had her share of the offering prepared and served by her father. Ananda Baba received the vows of Kumar Chand on behalf of Shiva and Lakshmi and blessed him, saying: 'Without concern for his own greatness, he no longer distinguishes between what is "me" and what is "not me". Putting everything together, he bows before everything with the same humility as if God himself.' He made him repeat this until he knew it by heart. 'You will say it at least three times before Lakshmi every morning to end your *puja*. And you will say it once to Kamala. You will become prosperous. Anand and his *shishyas* will stay with you two or three days so that you don't forget the vows you took.'

Thus spoke Ananda Baba.

He forced him to sit with us three full days in his living room doing nothing. 'When you go home after your work, sit down and breathe, sing a hymn, change rhythm.' He had him smoke *chillums*, made him laugh and slowly drew him into the pace of patience. As if taming a wildcat. And he did tame this tiger of a man. He also spent time every day playing with Kamala. He taught her to look into his eyes. At night, he meditated on the couch as we slept at his feet.

Ananda Baba turned both a penetrating and friendly glance on beings and events which stirred him up. And if he could, he showed a way to get them out of their chains. He was a virtuoso in his art.

Upon leaving, he promised Kumar he would come back, one day. He blessed him again, and Kamala. And we took the road again to stop, five hundred meters away, in a *dharamsala* where another story began.

'What did you do every night, Babaji?' Connor asked with my support.

'Anand was straightening Kamala.'

'*Atcha!*' said Connor.

'But how did Babaji do it?' I asked.

'How to say this… Anand bathed her with love.'

'*Atchaaa!*'

One day, an old Muslim came with one of our benefactors and joined the conversation as we were having a chai in Sultanpur.

'Your idols, we can break them. None of them are God,' he told Ananda Baba, almost contemptuously.

The other clients were listening. Among them, some Muslims were showing that they did not approve of this provocation, frowning eyebrows and shaking heads.

'Don't do such a thing, *Sahib Babu*,' begged Ananda Baba in a caressing voice and joining his hands as if gently exorcising a disastrous prospect, 'Anand knows that idols indicate something about God but are not God. They are his recitation, just like your Koran[3].'

'Allah is a unique God, and Shiva also is a unique God,' he explained further, 'and Vishnu besides, and Krishna as well... The difference? Shiva is not offended to be worshipped and loved with others because, being the only one, he is all the others as well in different figures and receives worship wherever and to whoever it is addressed. The same applies to Vishnu and to Krishna, and many others.'

This answer convinced those who were already convinced, but the *Sahib* continued as if making a list of his resentments:

'Are not all men brothers? So why are there castes?'

Indian Muslims are mostly descendants of *dalits*, *pariahs* or untouchables converted to a religion which abhors idols, and so they in turn can demote Hindus to a kind of Islamic untouchability. The *pariah* is to a Hindu what a *kafir* is to a Muslim. Untouchable or monstrous. A mirror effect. An acquitting of contempt.

'Ignorant Muslims distinguish between faithful and infidel,' Ananda Baba answered, 'don't they know that *Allah* rules over all things? Ignorant Hindus segregate into castes. Anand says there is only one Being. How can there be faithful and infidel, Brahmin, Kshatriya, Shudra and Vaishya? These distinctions belong to ignorance. Anand will take food from his hand as if it were his own to prove that he does not discriminate. Anand will go to the mosque if he is asked and he will tell his brothers what he knows about *Bhagwan*.'

Maulvi Mohammad Haji introduced himself and then invited Ananda Baba to come speak to his brothers in the mosque of his neighbourhood. And so we

---

3 Koran means recitation.

went, readily, in a rickshaw. After the prayer of *Asr*, Haji Maulvi asked Ananda Baba to address a crowd of around thirty men:

'The path of Islam is peace,' said my guru. 'This peace is manifested through brotherhood, which means love of all creatures. All of them,' my guru insisted, 'even those that *Allah* does not command you to spare, like cows and goats. The path of peace is submission to whatever happens and this submission begins with renunciation of "it must" and "I want". The knowledge of God is none other than feeling his being there within yourselves and everywhere else at once. Because God is outside and inside, the first and the last, the faithful and the unfaithful. He does not ever punish anyone because he is in everyone and everything.'

Having consulted each other, these men of goodwill approved the words of Ananda Baba and Haji Maulvi invited us to have dinner with him.

He received us in a rather empty room, covered with beautiful carpets and pillows wrapped in unbleached cotton pillowcases. On the wall, a verse from the Koran, forged in iron calligraphy, hung on a chain as if convicted.

Haji Maulvi had two Western guests; he told them of his grievances with reference to the West. For him, television, movies, music and advertising were means used by the white people to spread their materialist ideology. The white people continued their attempts to invade the world using methods other than colonization and Christianity...

'The British split our country in three parts and left a situation which could only bring war. Why did they do this?' he asked us as if we knew more than him about it.

'So that you made war with each other,' I confirmed. 'And bought their weapons, and continued to remain in their dependency.'

He looked at me in an exasperated astonishment, as if he never thought it possible for a human mind to conceive such vile intentions.

'*Bharat*[4] became three countries,' Ananda Baba cut in. 'So what? She was divided in many more *rajyas** and *sultanates* (kingdoms) before the British came. How can we free ourselves from these frontiers? How can we become and remain brothers? What has to be spread, Haji, is brotherhood consciousness and Oneness more than the names of God and his prophet.'

---

4 India is also known as *Bharat* in Hindi.

When we arrived at Harauni, near Banthara, a village of one thousand inhabitants surrounded with paddy fields, we found the doors were all closed, the streets deserted and the square empty. Tied to their stakes, buffaloes were lying in their dung and were plaintively mooing that it was past milking time. A few shops had their metal shutters only half lifted.

'A tragedy befell here,' figured Ananda Baba.

He spoke to the cereals retailer who invited us inside his shop where we were sitting on his stock of rice bags.

'I cannot even offer you a glass of chai, *Maharaj*!' he apologized. 'The *chaiwalla** doesn't work.'

'What is going on here, Babuji?'

'A disaster!' he confirmed. 'Madness!'

'Alopa, a seven year old girl who lived with her grandparents had disappeared for several weeks now. The police have discovered that Shiv Pal was an adept of *tantrism* and had sacrificed this little girl to the goddess Kumari. In a dream, his wife had seen Kumari pledging that they would find a treasure in their courtyard if they buried there the hands of a girl under the age of nine, the first child of her parents. In return, later, there would be a treasure in that place. Later, Shiv Pal turned over his courtyard and found out that the treasure was only a dream!'

'*Om Namah Shivayah!*' Ananda Baba proclaimed as if exorcising something. 'Maya can be appalling!' he pointed out.

'Kumari played a dreadful trick on them!' the retailer figured.

They were both talking about the divine, but not in the same way. The shopkeeper thought the goddess had deliberately deceived Shiv Pal. If one starts believing God is cheating, one cannot rely on anything anymore. The world of these villagers was wavering. Ananda Baba was considering the dreadfulness of maya and her *avatar*, greed. But neither of them was concerned about the murder and the murderers. Unlike me they had not been fed on American TV series, and I reflected sorrowfully about the many years these two idiots would spend in prison. And I lamented over the last moments of this little girl who was deprived of her life and robbed of her hands. I saw the horror.

'Why are all the doors closed?' asked my guru.

'Kumari is angry,' said the merchant. 'Everyone is afraid. Even our *pujari*! Everyone is staying in their homes.'

In a village, misfortune striking a family is taken to be as a sign warning the whole community. The people of Harauni saw this tragedy as being precursory to an even greater disaster and thus hid in their homes.

Ananda Baba went to the *panchayat** to announce that he would perform a *yagna*, a purification and propitiation ritual. 'Tonight on the square,' he decided. 'For the good of everyone. Spread the word. Everyone should come with a handful of seeds.' Ananda Baba also had a few accessories brought in: a coconut, some flowers, a bunch of *kusha* grass, *ghee* and a large bowl.

I delimited a *dhooni* with a few stones in the centre of the square, and lit a fire. Connor swept around it and laid down his guru's *asan.* A red cotton cloth was given the authority of an altar. The solar disk slid dependably behind the horizon. Rice, barley and wheat grain, dry beans and mustard seeds filled the bowl as the villagers arrived. Men, women and children came together as a group standing in front of the fire.

Nothing made them different from the thousands of farmers we had seen elsewhere except that their heads were hung low, and were thus faceless and devoid of individuality. They seemed to be playing a mandatory, mimetic fright so that omniscient divine forces would not look into their own individual case soon. As if they were all guilty. Each tackling some inadmissible shame that was making them lose face.

To believe oneself, even for a moment, as being seen through by Omniscience is to remember what one is trying to conceal.

My guru gave them a sermon: 'Kumari is angry because Shiv Pal and his wife take their dreams for godly promises. If *Ishta devata** (the god you prefer, whatever his name) asks you to break the laws of the *rishis* and the ancients, it is not *Ishta* speaking, but *Kali*, the demon of your greed, your fears and your madness.' He concluded: 'Any life is God itself.'

A rainbow formed around the moon. I pointed it to the crowd as a sign, and each regained a face.

Ananda Baba mixed the grains and the seeds, rekindled the fire by pouring *ghee* over it and called: *O Agni! elected among Gods and by men, we choose you for our messenger. Come! Songs of praise have been prepared for you... O Agni, shining in darkness, access to the world of Gods...*Then he wished: *May Agni bring this offering to Kumari.* And finally, he threw the seeds in the flames, in handfuls, with an elegant detachment, while I repeated with Connor, "*May the curse of ignorance and selfishness disappear in this offering. May the seeds of pain perish in this fire.*" The fire was crackling, busting, popping. *Agni* led the homage to the goddess singing a hymn, and she calmed down.

Ananda Baba struck the coconut on a stone, spread its milk on the embers;

then he ordered Connor to share the pulp out and for everybody to take a piece of this collective ego. Finally, everybody had to go to take a bath in the river. The goddess was pleased.

They gave him the authority to assert it. He used it.

A sadhu at work!

The next day, the *panchayat* offered that he settle down in the village:

'If *Maharaj-ji* decides to live amongst us, we would consider ourselves fortunate.'

'Anand moves. Anand does not stay,' Ananda Baba defended himself with a laugh.

The village chief persevered. There was a small *mandir* at the end of the main street, he promised to build a *kutir* and expand gradually... 'Anand walks!' repeated my guru. The *panchayat* offered him money, but yet again he refused: 'You will engrave the story of Alopa on a stele with this *mantra*: *The life of any being is God itself.*'

We went from an *akhara* to a temple, from a village to a city, aimlessly, above all aimlessly! To abandon everything. The carefree life of being without desires! *Dhire-dhire...* Slowly. 'We are in no hurry,' Ananda Baba often said. 'Haste robs things of their taste. Enjoy!'

We stayed a few days in a beautiful ruin which was well equipped with terrace, *dhooni*, half-collapsed walls, stairs leading nowhere and the sky for a roof. Some kitchen utensils, a broom, a stack of firewood had been left there. It offered, in addition to peace, and except for a few snakes, a feeling of being at home.

Ananda Baba often found unusual, isolated and comfortable places where we could retire for a few days. He was our guide and he guided us... He prescribed me to meditate on Yogiraj: Shiva, motionless, absorbed in devotion to himself.

Motionless, absorbed in searching for self-devotion, there is no narcissistic megalomania of an imperial ego. In the failures of stillness that the restless mind demonstrates, ego is revealed as vulnerable. It has very little command; it cannot even command itself! But this powerlessness, considered through the perspective of devotion, that is to say an indulgent deference or a friendly bias, is an almost unconditional state of being which gets close to serenity. And sometimes even bliss...

When we had no more food supplies, we fasted.

The feeling of hunger changes into thoughts. Then the stomach gives up. I felt a little weak; then much lighter. Will calmed down and gave way to a pleasant hollowness: the sweet inebriation of surrender. Fasting is a victory over gravity. The earth rises to the sky and resembles it.

We set out on the road again.

A village. An old woman was exposing her wet hair to the sun's heat in her courtyard.

'Mother, they haven't eaten any food for three days,' said Ananda Baba simply.

'Sit down here Babajis,' immediately ordered this absolutely divine mother, 'I'll prepare something.'

She disappeared into her small brick house with a rusty corrugated iron roof and came out half an hour later with three large plates full of rice and *daal*, with milk and *chapati*. *Om Namah Shivayah*.

'Tell me more about bliss, Babaji.'

'There are many kinds of bliss. Bliss produced by contact with outer objects. Bliss from filling your stomach. Bliss produced by a modification of the intellect (*vritti*). Bliss as feeling to have accomplished whatever there was to accomplish. Bliss resulting from an appeased mind. Bliss which flows from forgetting oneself. Bliss resulting from knowledge. Bliss known in deep sleep. Bliss which happens through worshipping. The natural bliss of the Self... A yogi knows bliss in *samadhi* (gathering of subject and object), a *jnani** experiences bliss in consciousness, being One.'

'Here!' announced our guru, looking at a mineral clearing in a forest, alongside a river. And one by one I noticed half a dozen U-shaped stone walls a meter high spread on the shingle shore. Under the pebbles... the ground of these half, roofless houses consisted of fine sand. Two of them were inhabited by two sadhus, assiduous to silence and *tapasya*, chest raised, eyes fixed, in meditative attention.

'*Bhagwan* will bring us food,' Ananda Baba promised in a low voice. He cleaned out one of these *kutirs* of the debris that had accumulated, repaired it a little and laid down his *asan*. We did so too. Some twenty minutes later, a group of girls approached from the river bank with pots and jars. A nearby ashram had meals sent to those who practised asceticism in its surroundings.

'Prassad and Connor will live here without pronouncing words and with no unnecessary movements,' said Ananda Baba after we had eaten. 'Sitting in *kutir* and meditation. You will perform your ablutions, collect firewood and bring some to the two brothers, maintain a *dhooni*. *Bass*! Explore stillness.' He blessed and dismissed us.

A long time, the morning meditation seemed very long to me. I sat in the depth of my U-shaped home, in the tunnel view of a shingle beach, the shimmering river and a front of large trees on the opposite shore.

Several weeks passed this way. When a desire to move or speak would rise, I would chase it away with my Varanasi *mantra*: *Nothing has to be done*. I repeated it here, stretching it infinitely. And it took a new dimension. It was no longer an abstract deliberation as *nothing to become, to want, to win or lose, etc.* It was no more a decision to take, a truth to follow, as it had been five years earlier. It was now the core of the meditation work: immobility. The immediate as eternal.

When I wanted to get up, that is to say when I projected myself in time and action, trying to escape… No. Escape what? Nothing to do… to avoid or to be… Nothing not to be… I gave up setting apart "me" and "non-me", I gave up giving up thoughts and things, straddled consciousness and followed the harmonious undulation of moments following each other and occurring to themselves. And mind vanished in the contemplation of itself.

We slept like mummies, wrapped in our blankets half-buried in sun-baked sand.

'Waking up is like being born from Mother Earth,' said Connor when we had given up silence.

Talking created a similar effect of rebirth.

At the first hint of dawn, a din of screams and crackles heralded the arrival of the first ray of sun, before a great silence. A tribe of organized and discreet rhesus came to drink at the water's edge. The dominant male placed his lieutenants at strategic points and made sure of their alertness; mothers appeared next, a baby hanging from their belly.

We went a little upstream to take the *darshan* of a naked sadhu who lived on an island in the middle of Ganges. He meditated and slept on the sand. The shelter of a tree seemed superfluous to him, the use of words unnecessary. He was a *muni*. When he was sitting, his dreadlocks fell in front of his face like a curtain of creepers in an impenetrable forest. He looked like a strange plant. He looked like his gaze was half hidden in a cave. And he laughed at times, without reasons known to others, timidly, as if he had a secret relationship with an invisible and malicious friend.

'Four kinds of human beings are naked, that is to say true,' Ananda Baba later explained, 'a newborn, who has not yet acquired a mind; the dying man who concentrates on what is happening to him; the man who found the child in himself, and finally, renunciants and sadhus because they ignore desires.'

Miracle Babas, Sorcerers and Other Mysteries...

One woollen thread around the Andreswar ghat's wish-fulfilling tree in Pushkar, and prayers are granted! The trunk was wearing a colourful pullover of hopes. Bathing in the Luni guarantees that one will not die from a snake bite. Whoever takes refuge at the feet of Guruvayuruppa will be cured of leprosy or will not catch it; this is well known! Listening to a reading of the *Bhagavatha Purana* brings about enlightenment. If one wants a baby boy, reading the story of Prajapati Sutapa is enough. The newly weds who fail to present their respects and their offerings to the temple of Khobra Behroon (the mischievous) end up doomed to encountering unexpected conjugal complications. Tirupathi Balaji, who is none other than the Lord and God Venkateshwara (the main idol of the large and very rich Tirupati temple) likes helping his devotees in business matters... provided he is paid his share. To die or be cremated in Varanasi guarantees a place in Shiva's paradise. The sight of the Narmada delivers from rebirth... Bathing in the Shukla Pakshi during the month of Karitha, plus the *darshan* of Varah, ensures that one is not reborn on this Earth and also eternal bliss. Bathing three times in the Ganges erases past actions... Polytheism is generous in terms of absolution.

'Why should I worry about karma since bathing in the Ganges has completely washed it away?' I asked a sadhu, one day, in Varanasi.

'By bathing in the Ganges, did you lose your attachment to yourself? Immediately after your bath, did it not come back?' he answered. 'You surely cannot spend days and nights in the water!'

This is how the sublime oaths of mythology disappear.

Pilgrimages are haunted with promises and the sadhus are also pursued by a whole procession of highly colourful stories of psychic powers and miraculous events.

How many anguished students have passed their exams after receiving a baba's blessing! Gopta Swami had granted a woman's wish to fall pregnant after years of barrenness, and another to finally have a boy after four girls. Vyasah Baba had the power to stop his pulse; doctors had certified the phenomenon. Following a dispute with Poorandas, Mahantji Baba died in the night for no apparent reason, giving victory to Poorandas who had left him, the day before, with these premonitory words: 'Things are not eternal; tomorrow the problem will be solved.' Swapna yogi was buried alive six feet deep for three weeks. It was reputed that Atmayogi meditated sitting on top of flowers. He could fly in the air at the speed of light and become invisible. While he was teaching, Swami Satyajit's staff hung in mid-air. Ishata Baba walked on water repeating the name of Vishnu. It also worked with the name of Shiva... One could write a gospel everyday on the daily life of these supermen. The terminally ill who were healed after receiving their blessings were innumerable. But, like the evangelists, sadhus never remembered the blind man who had not recovered sight, nor all those who died because they had not seen a doctor in time.

Discussions about the supernatural are not a debate, they are a jousting match. One outbids the other. Locomotives were blown up in front of the Juna akhara in Lucknow. Pinaka Baba could dim the light without moving from his seat, just uttering *Om*. Shri Bhanuprassad had been bitten by a cobra. He called it back and ordered it to suck up the poison. The reptile complied. Satyendra Guru had brought a young cowherd back to life after he had been bitten by a snake, and had died and was already cold and stiff. He coated the boy's back with clay and put a bronze plate over it. Gradually the plate changed colour and the boy returned to life. Gods disguised as snakes visited Tapaswiji Baba and bowed before him. He was more than one hundred and fifty years old, said a sadhu who had known him. Satthya Sai Baba* was able to walk on water, be at two places at once and create gold *ex nihilo*! In *akharas* and circles, this miracle culture was perpetuated orally, renewing its heroes.

At times we came across one of these sadhus who had fasted, healed or flown... But the staff remained on the ground and no one was levitating. At Bang Handi temple, Mahobat Baba assured me that six months earlier he had seen Rujula Baba meditating on the branch of the banyan. But the author of the exploit remained quietly seated on his *asan*. I had not seen Ballaknath Baba from Kawali return to his room without having left it. I did not believe it. My path was different. I deemed the philosophy of Brahman and the *Advaita Vedanta* intelligent enough to have no need of legitimacy from such disguises.

And yet, I did encounter miracles. One day, the world became strangely orange in my eyes. *What are you looking for?* I was asked by the first baba I met in Varanasi. *Peace!* I had answered without thinking much about it and it turned out that I did finally find peace on the banks of Ganges… *I live where you live, even if you don't know where it is*, this absurd sentence had been pronounced twice in a matter of a few days by two different people, one of whom knew things about me that he could not have known. In Varanasi, two sadhus had called me Prassad, and five years later, Ananda Baba also gave me that very name. I have experienced strange states of consciousness being with several babas… I took these inexplicable phenomena to be some sort of kind attention of fate, or winks from the Whole to a part, to put it cautiously. Perhaps they were signs of a fantastical meta-communication to which I refused to grant the legitimacy of fact. I could only think of them as trivial details, entertaining enigmas. The temptation of mystery.

One day, shortly after my wandering life began, I lost Ananda Baba in a bazaar in Faizabad, a vast town and a place of pilgrimage where many sadhus spent some time. I inspected the market and its surroundings, the lanes, the alleys and the dead-ends, in the temples… Ananda Baba was nowhere. I explored the shops, retraced my steps at least ten times till I was unable to find the spot where this nightmare had begun. *'Lambi jataoun wala sadhu dekha kya?'* (Have you seen a sadhu with a high bun?) I asked everywhere. Everyone had seen sadhus. Many fitted the description of my guru. *He probably isn't even looking for me with his "greeting whatever turns up!"* I suspected. The eventuality that we would not find each other titillated me. And I felt very small in a world which had suddenly become much bigger without him.

At nightfall, the streets were no less crowded and there was still no sight of Ananda Baba. I looked for him a little longer then, exhausted, I resigned myself to finding a place to sleep. *He will be by the river tomorrow… But there will be one thousand sadhus by the river tomorrow…* The courtyard of a temple was just what I needed. A few sadhus were settling down under an open gallery along the outer wall. My downcast face must have moved an old baba who was unrolling his blankets next to me, for he kindly asked me:

'What is the matter? Why are you looking so unhappy?'

I told him.

'Call your guru as you call upon *Bhagwan*!' exclaimed the old man in a tone of urgency, 'and he will appear in front of us.'

The naivety of his faith made me smile. Ananda Baba did not walk on water or evaporate suddenly. But I hesitated, and then out of despair allowed myself to succumb to a desire to believe in it.

I called upon Ananda Baba, repeating his name non-stop, as if it were a *mantra*. Ten minutes later, I came back to my senses as my perplexity on the efficiency of such practices triumphed over the irrational hope that it could work.

'*Herrrle lyou arrre!*' said Ananda Baba, arriving in front of me.

'I told you!' exclaimed the old sadhu.

A tiny doubt, no thicker than a single thought, shook my confidence in a rational construction of the world.

I decided to get rid of it quickly, 'From now on let's agree if we lose each other, to meet in front of the closest railway station.'

I helped my guru spread out his blankets.

'Did you know that I was calling you?'

'You called me?'

'At the closest station,' I insisted, trying to take the expression of a determined Westerner, resolute in imposing something reasonable and prudent to a native brimming with a prodigious, instinctive and insane confidence.

'I told you!' repeated the old sadhu.

Ananda Baba was laughing.

Another time, when a sadhu had just said he needed one hundred rupees to buy medicine, Ananda Baba got up determinedly, walked about fifty paces, then bent down to pick up a bill, returned to his place and handed a one hundred rupee bill to the sadhu.

I could accept these *coincidental miracles*, they happened to us all the time. Vishnu, Krishna, Shiva and all the Gods embodied in our benefactors took good care of us, it was undeniable, but I could not consider with indifference that "natural" and "supernatural" were only mental distinctions. Or that anything is possible in *Bhagwan's leela*, that there is no rule to his game, as Ananda Baba said. There is certainly more to the world than the meanings that I can grasp, but people do not fly in the air! I had no less admiration for my masters and peers, but rather for their detachment and as models of temperance, than as wizards, miracle workers, fakirs or demigods. What is the use of acquiring the power to create anything you want, if one has renounced all desires to acquire this power? It was a typical Hindu issue, and was perhaps the meaning behind these myths.

Nothing seemed improbable to Connor. He believed anything was possible – flying, hovering, appearing, disappearing, healing or killing, dying and being reborn since for him even resurrection was possible! Whatever I could communicate to him of my disbelief left him speechless but was still in vain. It seemed his brains did not possess the propensity for scepticism when it came to psychic powers. In addition, he played his part towards the victory of irrationality, stating that he knew someone who knew someone who had witnessed the fact that Rinchen Rinpoche had visited one of his disciples in Arizona when, at the same time, he was giving a lecture in Melbourne. And I translated that into Hindi.

'The yeti is a resistant chimera and levitation an obstinate fantasy. Nobody levitates. Nobody walks on water,' I reminded him. 'Nobody is in two places at once.'

He liked the world to be mysterious. He was gathering its charm. He hoarded up India's magic as if he hoped to take it with him one day, later, when he returned to Australia. But when we were told about a yogi who did not drink or eat or move or speak for 40 years, Connor exclaimed honestly: 'That's fucked-up. Should the fact of existing be opposed to this extent?'

I could also reach the limit of my ability to hear without reacting to improbable stories. When I pronounced my vows, I had not thrown my critical mind into the fire. I participated in the joust, but in my own way – incredulously. 'The placebo effect works for half of all cases!' And I explained *placebo* to a baba even though it was hopeless as he preferred to believe in miracles rather than in the rigorous observations and probability calculi of scientific methods: 'Half is already quite good!' he considered. I gave voice to doubts. I played at educated remarks: 'Snakes cannot suck their venom back.' Ironic: 'When he levitates, does his *asan* follow him up?' Nit picking: 'As he is in two places at once, which one of him is wearing his clothes?' Suspicious: 'Who really saw the yogi levitating, coming back from the dead, flying?' But what can you say when the story-teller certifies having been there? I tried to point out inconsistencies: 'In maya, everything is possible. Even not being healed. Which of course happens very often.' Reasoned: 'This student. Had he actually studied at least a little?' Ethnologist: 'At what time does he come down again? And then, what does he do?' Debonair: 'Can he sometimes forget he is in mid-air and fall?' Off beat: 'The last ones will be the first, it's well known.' I also knew how to be wise: 'Birds can also fly in the air! How is your guru so great?' My outspokenness and my humour could be tinged with arrogance. It was my game. My way of being faithful to myself. 'But you, *Maharaj*, what can you do?' I would test the limits and persisting, go beyond, in provocation.

Once, in front of a fire, in a forest of the Narmada valley, I quipped to a circle of sadhus:

'*Bhagwan mar gaye!* God is dead, Nietzsche Baba has said. Can it be that the forest yogis have not yet heard about it? Nietzsche Baba is a guru in my tradition from Europe, Germany.'

This piece of news caused a short silence. Ananda Baba exploded laughing. Three sadhus stared at me with disbelief. A Shiva baba said:

'*Nahi! Bhagwan* is not dead. Look, you're still here.'

There was often a philosopher in the circle who would play with me: 'If he is a great guru this Nietzsche Baba, which way does he take to think that the uncreated can die?' answered a sadhu with thick glasses.

It was a nice objection.

'Can the uncreated exist before not dying?'

'It's me who does not exist!' burst out the sadhu, laughing.

'How can you be sure, Guruji?'

'Whatever the uncreated does, he does nothing,' he said seriously.

'Can he create himself then?' I asked.

'He manifests himself as Gods, in the realm of ideas and through the mouths of men,' he chanted, surprising me.

After all, I livened up the evening. They liked me all the same. And I made Ananda Baba laugh. I loved making him laugh.

But one evening...

Chillums had turned around and the conversation had got bogged down in tales of prowess. A sadhu of the circle turned to me and told me that his guru, *who never died but became invisible, had the power to create whatever he wanted*.

His voice was high-pitched and sounded metallic, childish and artificial but was also big and strong. His long hair, his full beard and his moustache combed like a curtain hid his neck and the lower part of his face. The upper part was coated with a thick layer of dried ashes which formed a grey mask that removed all expressiveness and quite a bit of depth. A thin red line rose up between his eyebrows. His eyes were laughing in a way. He was wearing several orange and yellow vests, one on top of the other, three rings on each hand, and bracelets on the wrists. He had well-kept nails. A rosary squeezed his biceps, another one his forehead. Numerous necklaces and amulets hung around his neck. His right hand was telling a rosary of large *rudrakshas**.

'Can you create a bottle of Champagne or didn't you learn that one, *Maharaj-ji?*' I suggested far too mockingly.

The whole circle turned to us in an immediate silence. I had defied him more seriously than I wanted to.

It was a circle of about ten sedentary Shiva babas gathered around a *dhooni* in front of a small temple at the end of a village in Uttar Pradesh. A black trident had been painted with broad gestures on the wall of their house. A bare bulb hanging from its wire threw a dim light at the entrance of the sanctuary and at this sadhu's face, static, indecipherable, sinister. Inhuman with this mask of ash and hair. His eyes were still laughing but lit by fire all of a sudden, in a dreadful way like Kali.

In spite of myself, my eyes settled on the sadhu's eyes, lit by the bulb. Two eyes behind a mask, as if belonging to no one, hanging from nowhere. But lively. And fascinating. And blinding suddenly, burning hot as if two incandescent fingers were directly pressing on my eyeballs. I tried to grab this invisible hand but there was nothing to catch hold of. And I managed to tear myself away from this hostile force of attraction only with a surge of my entire body.

'He did not ask what this atman (Self) can do,' said the mask, with no more laughter in his extraterrestrial voice.

I kept staring at the ground as my heart was pounding wildly. I have ensnared myself, I thought, stunned.

'What can he do, Maharaj Baba?' I asked to please him.

'He can destroy you with his gaze. *Tum dekhnaa tchaahoge?* (Want to try?)' he added.

The informal use of *tum*, the second person singular, was contemptuous. Aggressive. But the tone was still affable for a maximum threat.

'Won't *Maharaj-ji* ask me what I can do?' I retorted, trying to gain time and confidence, but still avoiding raising my head.

'What can you do?' he asked.

'I can swim. And him, can he?'

He did not answer.

'But I cannot walk on water,' I carried on. 'Visvam Guru can he?'

I was calling him grand sounding titles in hope of getting away with it.

'Who is talking about walking on water?' answered the mask.

'Too bad!'

'*Tum dekhnaa tchaahoge?* (Want to try?)' he said looking for my eyes.

'I know how to solve a biquadratic equation, dance flamenco, surf on the Internet, drive a car, calculate the optimal dimensions of a volume,' I listed speaking to him sideways on. 'I can give artificial respiration and have brought a drowned boy back to life.'

This time, I was the one on the defensive. This man was enjoining me to decide whether or not I believed he could do what he said, and accept the risks. But there was supposed to be none if I did not believe it. But my eyes were still hurting from having ignored something. And I was scared... I am rarely scared. This fear confirmed that I was not so sure. I did not know whether he could destroy me or not, but I understood that he would try to hurt me. Therefore I believed in the magic of this man. I was not sure, but I knew now that I was not sure of the opposite either. And in this perplexity slipped an impression of letting go of the inflexible but reliable reason. Of changing sides. Of betraying myself. Being reborn into an unknown world. Often eccentric. Unpredictable...

'Wouldn't Visvan Yogavartah[1] Guru prefer to propose a less aggressive and more pleasant experience?' I negotiated, not so brave after all and much less conceited.

'So you don't want to risk anything?' insisted the sadhu, staring at me.

The decision to back down was already made. I silently called Ananda Baba for help. He was not looking at me. He remained in his usual air of casual curiosity tinted with radiant bliss. I felt Connor was ready for anything to back me up, but against what? The whole circle was listening attentively, even those who were casting glances elsewhere. It was suddenly a sorcerers' gambling joint. Magic poker. Place your bets.

'Have you only learned to destroy?' I finally countered.

'Since when do monkeys wear the colour of fire?' the sadhu howled back.

The question challenged my guru. As I was his disciple, it was insulting his judgment. Ananda Baba slowly straightened up and then stared at him:

'*Bala Baba* has suckled tigress milk,' he stated with detachment, by way of explanation.

A compromise and a threat, smoothly delivered. Calling me *Little Baba*, he placed me in a position of inferiority which protected me. But in another sense, it meant he could measure up to tigers and tame them. The magician bore his gaze.

---

1 Visvan: Everything; Yogavartah: The one who creates time.

'Comparing this self to an exhilarating experience is like measuring the light of a firefly to the glare of the sun,' Ananda Baba added, laughing.

The ambiguity of the universal third person singular – me, him, you, maya, and even the Supreme-Power-who-rules-over everything – reduced tensions. Because everyone heard what they wanted to hear. By the time you figure it out, you have calmed down.

'He makes him laugh,' he still went on…

'Just as a craftsman reveals his secrets only to his apprentice, *Bhagwan* discloses his to his most faithful devotees only,' stated a sadhu of the circle who liked proverbs.

'Some Westerners are different,' explained Ananda Baba addressing everyone. 'They only know the world through the evidence they detect according to their own criteria. Little Baba is like that. Today, he met the guru who made him doubt doubts. And he has touched the limits of his temerity. His challenge. Devesah[2] Guru gave him the appropriate lesson,' he concluded, turning to the magician who showed his appreciation.

'Wolves keep silent when a lion roars,' seemed to be his confirmation of this.

Apparently we were among big cats…

'The one who is sought after recognises the one who is seeking him,' Ananda Baba approved mysteriously.

And that was the end of the matter.

To such questions about psychic powers and made-to-order miracles, Ananda Baba's answer was that nature is not only determined by nature and that the laws of the world do not limit those who are liberated from the world…
'*Existing* and *non-existing* are dualistic categories like any other. Everything is true and real in one sense; and illusory in another. Truth is beyond what one can formulate. Absolute certainty is also part of the transient. Without maya (magic), there is nothing.'

The method of massive doubt suddenly seemed unfit to struggle with the appeal of the strange beauty which could occur. To engender a lasting peace. Henceforth, I believed impossible less impossible. But I have never seen a flying baba, and nobody ever served us Champagne in Himalayas.

However, I have often admired the less mysterious and more heroic feat which consists of performing a pilgrimage prostrating one hundred and eight

2 Devesah: A God of the Gods.

times in front of a portable altar before moving on a distance equal to the length of the body and outstretched arms. Under a merciless sun and on the burning asphalt, or soaked with rain, bare-back, in rags. One hundred and eight pebbles, beside them, help these heroes count their mortifications and demonstrate again and again that this body is nothing, or that God is everything. Or to explore slowness... At the speed of three hundred thousand prostrations a year, they cover a distance of 7 kilometres. A snail moves faster.

Also heroes are those who travel endlessly rolling on the ground from one shoulder to the other. This sort of exploit terrified me, but the willpower at work to achieve it fascinated me.

The following day, we stayed in an ashram, as large as a village and as luxurious as a palace. A wide esplanade, high up, led to three vast marble halls surmounted with domes whose spires bore orange and yellow triangular banners. The laymen's quarters were organised into long, modern, two-storey buildings opening onto balconies. Three alleys of brick *kutirs* with thatched roofs were reserved for the sadhus. In the centre, in a high and wide temple were two carved and exuberantly gilded, royally kitsch thrones supporting the wooden effigies of Shri 1008 Jagatguru Shri Kripaluji Maharaj and his wife, in their absence.

Their praises were sung twenty-four hours a day. 'There is no difference between Krishna and Kripaluji,' we were told. An angular face lined with long curly hair and fleshy lips, Shri Kripalu was an *avatar*, God descended into living form, a *jagatguru*, guide of the universe, an *acharya* equal to Sankaracharya, teacher of Gods, philosopher and recognized master of non-duality. He was known to have reconciled the five schools of philosophy in three discourses. He attracted thousands of disciples and millions of devotees; several clinics, many schools and a university bore his name. He taught the path to happiness through love, and devotion to Krishna.

Thanks to large, back-lit, translucent posters, we could see him on a huge float pulled by a tractor, taking ecstatic poses, dressed in silk, with garlands, and cheered by the crowd. His most recent portraits indicated that he was very old. We were informed by the ashram's office that he was staying in his other, much larger ashram, near Lucknow.

'Prassadji,' my guru called me after a long silence, 'would you like to own a lot of gold?'

We were spending the afternoon at his feet in the veranda of our *kutir*. From the temple through loud speakers, a female voice rode on the hot air and waved a heavenly song: *Ramaaa aaa aaa....*

What would I do with a lot of gold? I asked myself searching for a desire in myself to discover that I had none. I was living the life I had chosen and felt happy in it.

'No, Babaji,' I replied. 'I want neither gold nor money. I am fine.'

'I accept gold and currency, Babaji,' said Connor, pretending to be unscrupulous.

'But to Connorji, Babaji did not ask,' Ananda Baba retorted.

'Too bad!' he grumbled.

'And would Prassadji want to walk on water, or fly in the air?'

Walking on water is a skill that once had the value of a boatman's pittance and today has none because bridges have been built. Devoting twenty years acquiring this ability is stupid, is the conclusion that Buddha had come up with some twenty-five centuries ago. Jesus, it seems, could do it, but he was the only begotten son of the *One-and-only* God. Yet, it would be wonderful to be freed from gravity. I imagined I was weightless… Like in a dream…

Liberation? This is not what I was hoping for from life. Or it would come, as the wise say, unexpectedly, since it is expectation that one is liberated from. I felt privileged to be a disciple of Ananda Baba and to enjoy the peace, patience and bliss emanating from him. I appreciated his fatherly friendship, his complicity with the right reserve, his sense of humour, his way of solving problems. I admired the plasticity of his intelligence. I fed on his *darshan*: his way of being and his wisdom. And thanks to him I marvelled at the little events that took place throughout the days… the adrenaline fuelled gaze of a baboon who crossed our road, or a mysterious and charming fragrance carried by the breeze. The kindness, the vitality, the enthusiasm of the people whose lives we passed through, their immediate friendship and spontaneous sincerity. Often very small things, but they gave the effect of a sudden lightening of gravity, a dazzling effect on the mind. A jubilation which transmutes everything into sparks of light. An exhilarating thought that I read… *Many wonder has the world, and yet it is nothing. Being aware of it, is to be nothing more than light without birth and becoming.* The answers my guru gave me… 'We owe modesty to the simplicity of Oneness.' 'Impatience is the leaven of suffering.' The friendship of the moon and the stars in the gentle night. The silence of a valley at noon, under a blazing sun. The breath of a landscape, feeling the vibration of the elements, this elusive twinkling, an instant that one hopes to convert into fate… I imagined weightlessness as such moments of inspiration rather than being in levitation or stupidly walking on water.

'And does Babaji know Father Christmas too?' I finally answered him.

He laughed.

'I would really like to walk on water, Babaji,' Connor cut in.

'There is too much you in you for you to float,' said Ananda Baba to provoke him.

'Since I'm too heavy, I'll trade weightlessness for ubiquity,' he tried to bargain. 'I want teleportation: Have you seen the sunrise in the Australian desert, Babaji? It's worth beaming up for,' he pleaded. 'The sky is on fire… I would spend an evening with my friends in Sydney. Then I'd hop over to Paris to buy a magnum of Champagne for Prassad and… Babaji, can you be teleported with a bottle of vodka without arriving dead drunk?'

What a joy this brother wandering gave me! Connor had finally adjusted to this philosophy which placed consciousness so high that holiness can only be seen as entertainment and the philosopher crazy enough to see himself in it as a figment of imagination.

'The light of this moment is your only future,' answered his guru.

We were sharing a *dhooni* and the stars with eight other saffron tunics in a village of Haryana. A young sadhu came to tell us that his guru would leave his body in front of his fire at ten o'clock the next morning. He smoked a *chillum* with us and then went on to inform other babas of the neighbourhood.

'The vision of the final *samadhi* of a baba is a blessing. They will go take this ultimate *darshan*,' Ananda Baba decided.

This extreme renunciant was an old man who lived in a palm hut outside the village. We found him seated in front of his his *dhooni*, on a blanket folded in four, in a circle of about twenty sadhus and three villagers. We smoked *chillums*, drank chai and kept watch almost silently around him. He was neither ill nor crippled, skinny but alive, yet already absent from the world in his stillness. Fixed eyes, firm chin. A wrinkle of will on his forehead.

'Your last teaching, Guruji,' pressed his disciple encouraged by several sadhus. He consented and said, but as if everyone already knew this: 'The poor man counts in tens, the less poor in thousands, the rich in millions, but in the last of their days, they will beg for one more day because they are still counting.

When the pot is broken, the air it contained mixes with the air of heavens. Expiring means to become everything. The One reality is everywhere equal.'

At dawn he got up, performed his ablutions carefully, took his last bath and then returned to the *dhooni* and practiced *pranayama*, increasingly spacing out inhalations. A gentle breeze made the foliage quiver; birds were singing; day labourers with spades on shoulders went to the fields joking; cowherds led their buffaloes to graze; the sun shone kindly on the good and the wicked, in a cloudless sky… Three hours later, he had stopped breathing. It was the sudden silence of nature that let us know.

We waited until his body stiffened; then put him on an improvised stretcher in his sitting posture. His eyes remained open, and he seemed to contemplate an eternal moment. A final *darshan*. Then, death is a body without life. A question of gravity and temperature. It is heavy and cold. It can no longer support itself. It becomes a thing. Life no longer inhabits it, but in a way it is still someone. Someone from the past.

Ram Naam Satthya Hai! Only the name of Ram is true! Everything else is transient. Thus we carried him. And gave him to the river's care. *Jay Shiva! Jay Ram! Hari Narayan! Om Namah Shivayah!* shouted the sadhus. It was a victory. We celebrated a sage who had completely undone his earthly ties. Someone going directly to the highest promises.

Connor did not find a cause for celebration and it showed on his face.

'What did you see?' Ananda Baba asked him.

'Do you agree with this suicide?'

'It's not a suicide. By this death occurring in a moment of perfect concentration, it is the death itself that dies. He killed death.'

'Then, it's a murder,' grumbled Connor.

'Give up your prejudices! He is now in *maha-samadhi*,' his guru explained.

'What is *samadhi* actually?' asked Connor.

'The eternal transcendence of subject and object. Indifference. The realm of bliss.'

'Yet, why die, Babaji?' I cut in. 'Without life, is there still wisdom?'

'There has never been any wisdom. What dies is an error.'

What did the *Avadhut* say that day?

> Whether the manifested world is real or unreal,
> Is not for me even a thought.
> My nature is bliss, I am free.

The disciple of the sadhu prepared a delicious *prassad* made with *ghee*, wheat flour and sugar. A *Ramanandrin* who passed by sang a few verses of Kabir:

> Where the movement? Where the rest?
> Towards which shore will you cross, O my heart?
> There is no road on that shore,
> Neither a raft nor any ferryman,
> Neither earth nor heavens, nor time.
> You will find nothing in this emptiness.

At Buria, another renunciant had also decided to leave his body. He was in meditation on the banks of Ganges where the river is narrow and deep, and her flow tumultuous. *To be or not be?* He had chosen. He was going to jump.

Sadhus and pilgrims came to honour this ultimate *darshan* with incense sticks, garlands and *pranam*, and we joined them in bowing to the man who had resolved to die. He was about fifty years old, lean, slightly worn out, eyes opened. Determined, serene, focused. Liberated.

He suddenly got up, ran up to the bank and jumped into the roaring torrent where he disappeared instantly.

For him the next episode takes place in the cataract where, in a suffocating environment, his body is shaken, bashed, broken, dislocated and crushed. He takes in ice-cold water; then loses consciousness in an ultimate whirlpool. The end. On the screen of consciousness: light without images or pitch-black? He knows.

'What have you seen, Connorji?'

'Nothing special. A man who looked at me looking at him. He was indifferent.'

'He has sacrificed the world by sacrificing his body. This death free of fear guarantees that he won't be reborn,' Ananda Baba assured .

'Babaji you said that we are not this body, that we are not even born!' I cut in. 'Whatever happens he cannot be reborn!'

'You make Babaji laugh. That, you have not seen.'

'Prassad makes Prassad laugh, Babaji,' I admitted.

'What did you really see?'

'I saw a man who preferred *not to exist* look at me in the eyes calmly. The *darshan* of a farewell. By his choice, he told me "You are only an illusion."

But is it not taking philosophy too seriously to lead it to this extreme contempt for life?'

'Is it not taking life too seriously not to lead it there?' Ananda Baba answered laughing.

In the *Astavakra Samhita*:

> He who considers himself free is free indeed
> And he who considers himself bound is bound indeed.
> As one thinks, so one becomes. (I, 11)

What should I think about that?

We left Buria.

The road climbed the mountain alongside a river. 'Here!' said Ananda Baba to indicate the place where we would spend the rest of the day and night. A field-keeper's empty hut, with a plunging view over emerald and ochre patches, hazy in the hot air.

'Are they wise or are they crazy?' Connor asked me seeking agreement between right minded Westerners, while we were looking for firewood.

'Life can be so light,' I replied.

That night, Ananda Baba talked to Connor:

'"Me" is mind. The mind projects the thought, "this is me" about this body and this memory, and "this is mine" about objects.'

'No, Babaji, it observes,' argued Connor. 'The body comes before the mind. It was after birth towards the age of two that a child discovers that he is this body. Before he was in a universal fusion.'

'And when he was crying of hunger or from being cold or too hot, in which fusion was he? It is fair to say that he was in the illusion of a universal fusion,' corrected Ananda Baba. 'When the mind has developed, it has identified with the body and entered the illusion of differentiation.'

Connor was about to answer, he added:

'Imagine for a moment that you could be freed from the idea "I am this body", what would you be then?'

'I'm not sure I want to be freed from it, Babaji,' Connor replied.

'And yet, you are freed from it every night with pleasure! When you sleep, you do not observe anything any more. You are without a body in deep sleep, and without thought, and nevertheless when waking up, you believe you have existed without interruption while you slept. There is an existence outside of a "me" identified with the body. And it is pleasant. This is what the Self is.'

'This Self is a black hole!' exclaimed Connor.

'In the morning, you remember your body. You find it. Who had forgotten it? Who finds it? Who goes back to it? Who is re-embodied? The same Self that existed in the black hole of deep sleep. That consciousness in which there is no experience of duality and which is not deep sleep is Brahman's consciousness.'

Babaji Baba and Balayogi...

A few hundred thousand steps farther, we stopped in a small ashram, above Uttarkashi. A single large room, white-washed walls, a cone shaped *mandir* dedicated to the first seven *rishis* and a *dhooni*, along a rocky bank of the Ganges, in the Himalayas.

Om Namoh Narayan! Hari Om! Namah Shivayah!

One of the incarnations of Babaji Baba or the legendary immortal Mahavathar Babaji was living here.

He was a little over twenty, had large black eyes and a benevolent and serene gaze. His thick red lips opened to reveal white teeth like *a row of swans on a clear lake*, as can be read in the *Puranas*. His sun-burnt, almost ginger dreadlocks hung down over his manly shoulders. A thin frizzy beard enrobed the contours of his square-jaw. A slight powdering of ashes covered his face and torso. He invited Ananda Baba to take a seat on his right as he was presiding over a circle of a dozen of his *shishyas* on a large flat rock overhanging the young and effervescent Ganges, where the banks formed a catchment.

Ananda Baba bowed before him:

'This mind is as blind as an owl in broad daylight, and as dark as night's darkness,' he said in a fit of modesty.

'*Atman Ekam*,' replied Babaji Baba helping him up, 'Self is One.'

Ananda Baba and Babaji Baba examined each other smiling. Two dazzling smiles. Babaji Baba set his eyes on Connor, then on me. And in turn the same smile appeared on our faces. One Self.

He was wearing a saffron *lungi* tied up to his stomach and a long tiger-skin waistcoat opened on his beardless, brown, matt, sculpted chest. This Apollo of the Ganges shores was sitting upright and spoke little. His presence was beaming with grace, joy, serenity and authority.

In this circle of sadhus was a *Ramanandrin*, who was accompanied by an *ektar*, a one cord instrument, and he sung a song repeating one word only: *Narayan*. And a digambara baba (clothed by the wind), with shaved head and pubis, who whistled with birds and rustled with the breeze, like Francis of Assisi, in a kind of ecstasy. From time to time, a Muni Baba would point a finger to the sky and then spin it before his eyes. Gurudas Baba was massaging Babaji Baba's feet... And five other *mahatmas*. All of them older than their guru.

A rich *grihastha* arrived as the sun was declining. He pulled two beautiful rings mounted with precious stones from his pocket and set them down at Babaji Baba's feet, before taking his place in the circle. He was on the look out for a reaction from his guru with an avid anticipation that swelled his chest; this eager expectation of happiness shone forth from his face.

'What would you want me to do with that?' Babaji Baba questioned with evident disdain, but without looking at him, as if speaking to God or to himself.

The radiant face became overshadowed.

'Wear them for beauty, Babaji,' suggested the householder. 'Enlarge the ashram... Use them to become financially independent...' he added in English, still clinging to a hope of gratitude.

Babaji Baba looked elsewhere and forgot about the rings. We forgot them too. We enjoyed the soft whispers of the river, the breathing of the trees, the bright bursts of light on the rock, the turbaned ecstatic faces of Onesness... while the Ektar Baba endlessly sang *Narayan Narayan Narayan...*

A little later, as Babaji Baba got up to go take his bath; his foot hit one of the rings which fell into the stream. The devotee rushed over, but it was too late. The jewel had sunk. He went and probed the soft and muddy sand here and there and was still searching well after Babaji Baba had taken his bath and returned to his place. The night was falling. The circle began to move to the *dhooni*.

'Babaji! If only you would show me where it is!' shouted the devotee bending over the stream.

Babaji Baba picked up the second ring and threw into the Ganges, saying:

'There it is!'

Whatever is incorruptible is eternal.

Ananda Baba agreed to stay a few days in this circle. Everyone would go to perform his *tapasya* or quietly do nothing and then just sit on the banks of Ganges or around the *dhooni*.

One of the babas would eat only once every two or three days. Gurudas

Baba was Babaji Baba's servant disciple: he washed his clothes, brought him chai, prepared the *chillum*, cleaned around the *dhooni*, massaged his feet endlessly… overflowing with love; delight accompanying each of his services. The digambara baba did not cover himself up under the sun, nor at night, which could be cold. He was a Jain and took the principle of non-violence very seriously, carrying it to its extreme conclusion: not to kill anything, even inadvertently, including every minute being that teemed invisibly in the air, on the ground and in water. He swept and he filtered. 'May I be filled with an overflowing love for all creatures; may I be allowed to share all sentient being's sufferings; may generosity bind me to all those who wander; *Bhagwan, O Bhagwan*, grant that I may be so!' This was his constant prayer. His asceticism. His ideal. He inhabited what he saw. He sang with the birds and rustled with the trees.

One could easily take these *mahatmas* for lunatics if one were to confuse *tapasya* with whims. Pointing to the sky, and then simulating a spinning top, the Muni Baba reminded himself to discriminate between oneness and multiplicity, the stable and the changing, eternal and transient. And reminded others and heavens as well. The Ektar Baba designated Vishnu in everything and incarnated sweetness from this evident truth by singing the name of *Narayan*. Gurudas Baba had lost himself in love, personified by his guru, idol and doll all at the same time. *Atman Ekam*, only Oneness… Each of them embodied a spiritual path. Dissolution in worship, union through love or awareness, alchemy of fire…

Prakash Baba was in charge of the *dhooni*. Making his fire was a meditation and a different work of art every evening. Red or blue or golden, slender or flat, dancing, crackling or thrifty, fire of flames, aerial and noisy, or heavy and intense glowing logs… White smoke rising up like a woollen thread linking earth to the heavens, here and nothingness, matter and its absence; or dark and dense smoke which coagulates into clouds and the clouds into images, which turn into something else in the very moment of their appearance, and disappearing in a motion which produces a new one… Just like thoughts. An epic passage from appearance to dust, from illusion to emptiness, from movement to ashes, from a moment to timelessness. One evening, the artist placed a large upright log at the edge of the *dhooni*. Flames licked and ate away at this *lingam* for several days, digging glowing cavities into it, transforming it into a model of Mount Kailash where we could see the caves of legendary *rishis* and the *rishis* themselves sitting at their fire.

The holy hearth manifests *Agni*, the God whom all the Gods claim to be represented by. He drives away darkness and demons and designates the third eye, oblation and ascent. As Guru of the Gods and God for the babas, *Agni is the fire and that which is consumed, the poison and the cure, the beginning and the end, the beginning without an end, the end without a beginning. He is immortality and death*. He reduces everything to ashes, a condition which cannot be reduced further and has thus reached eternity. He will be the one to set our pyre alight and swallow our body. He served the purposes of making chai, cooking rice, keeping mosquitoes away and consuming the ego.

A *sadhak** came in the evenings and sang love poems to Ram, in a dull, flat voice, in tones which married naivety with sorrow, with the textures of longing for a beloved.

> Adorable Lord of my heart
> Come, materialize in front of me
> Ram, O Ram, my friend...
> The thirst of my heart alone
> Knows the taste of my tears.
> I repeat your name, Ram O Ram
> In each of my breaths
> Ram, at all time
> Ram, in each of my hopes
> And you hear it, Lord of my heart.
> Such is the power of the truth
> Which beats in the temple of my heart
> And in all that is.

This is how Gods live. We formed an ideal Olympus. *Atman Ekam*.

One morning, Babaji Baba told the circle that, in a dream, he had seen one of his *sadhaks*, bedridden, ill, and afflicted. He gave the digambara baba the mission to go to Dehradun to comfort this devotee. Ananda Baba decided to accompany him there; such was the extent of his fondness for him. He called him Darshan Baba, a divine sight.

He was a beautiful boy in all respects. An Amazon's small of the back on a brown, slim and slender twenty-five year old body. He was shaved from head to toe. His black penis, immature without hair, swayed to the rhythm of his steps. Clothed by wind and ashes alone, he carried nothing except for his *komandalu* and, under his armpit, a small bag which contained a razor and the cloth he used as a filter. The universe was his clothing.

Whilst walking, Darshan Baba observed, enjoyed, marvelled at everything and pointed out the landscapes, the shape of clouds, somebody's face, flowers, pebbles, an insect crawling too close to our feet… He also impersonated animals. He would mimic the buffaloes' massive jaw and relaxed gaze, he accentuated a shy goats' side-hopping, or growled with dogs, looking worried. He answered birds in their chirping tongue, buzzed with flies, aped the monkeys, and that could provoke tense encounters with these ancestors who see a threat in a smile and cannot abide being mimicked. But that's how he learnt to understand and sometimes to talk with all living beings. He answered each of their gazes.

'Look at the sky!' Darshan exclaimed pointing to a word, written by a cloud skimming over the crest of the hill, just in front of us: *Roko*, "stop" in Hindi. Clear. Undeniable.

'*Atcha!* The sky is writing to you!' Ananda Baba proclaimed.

'*Atcha!* What does he want?' Darshan wondered, looking around.

A buffalo was there. An open and purulent wound gashed her rump; she had probably been injured by a barbed wire fence. He approached her, mooing long deep sounds in buffalo tongue, swung his chin several times, called her *Mata*, mother, and then began to wash the wound with water from his *komandalu*. At times, the buffalo would raise her leg to kick but would not complete the attempt. Darshan then mooed grave sounds. The animal pissed. He collected the precious liquid in his *komandalu;* then poured a little on the opened cut pressing with his palm, uttering reassuring, short, grave sounds to hearten his patient, and she remained docile. He then examined the surroundings, collected a handful of clay that he mixed with fresh dung, watered with the remains of urine and he applied several layers of this antiseptic paste on the wound. Once this treatment had been made, Darshan Baba led her to the sun and gave her his instructions: probably something like, not to rub her rump for a few days. I am sure she had perfectly understood. He bowed. She returned his salutation.

'*Om Namah Shivayah,*' praised and blessed Ananda Baba.

'A Walt Disney production!' admired Connor using his terms.

Darshan did not carry any blanket and slept anywhere he would find, but after having carefully swept the place with grass or straw. Mosquitoes seemed to spare him, as if they acknowledged his universal pact of non-aggression. In towns, as soon as they saw him remorselessly naked, passers-by looked away and deviated; crowds parted like the sea before Moses.

'Why don't you cover yourself?'

To Connor's questions, he answered with smiles. He could not theorize his life. He was simply open, available. In the flesh of the moment. He had overcome neither sensuality nor modesty and the self image which imposes it. He lived in a sexless, egoless reality. He had no self-image. Such was his freedom. His liberation. An innocence prior to original sin if there ever was one. The whole world as Eden.

In a small town, a shopkeeper offered him two meters of the finest cotton cloth, beseeching: '*Maharaj*, be so kind as to cover your waist so that girls do not think immodest thoughts.' Darshan accepted to drape his hips without reluctance. But this *lungi* quickly became a turban.

While we were walking through a market, a very angry vegetable seller started beating a cow.

'Hit me instead, Babuji, hit me and soothe your anger!' Darshan said, rushing between the stick and the divine ruminant.

The retailer had immediately stopped the beating. He was a kind man, exasperated for a moment by this greedy Goddess who taxed his stock too often. He even offered us carrots. Darshan shared his with his new friend, and mooed in front of her right eye a sermon on good manners for wandering cows.

When we reached a river, near Rampur, Ananda Baba decided that we would rest on its banks for a couple of days. I laid my *asan* under a large wild-cherry tree. Darshan Baba joined me. A large colony of black ants had their nest near-by. They came and went, touching antennas, carrying vegetable debris and prospecting our bare feet, without fear or aggression. We observed them at length. It was the image of a quiet and industrious village. The first ten minutes of a western, when the arrival of the bad guys is still improbable.

The next day, looking for my ant friends, I discovered with horror hundreds of their little corpses, strewn over the area around the cherry tree. Small, stiffened, twisted bodies, turned over on their back, scattered or in heaps. I also saw much smaller black ants patrolling in groups of three to ten. I showed this disaster to Darshan Baba.

The battlefield revealed the violence of the attack and the futility of resistance. A war from the world's beginning – invasion and ethnic cleansing had taken place during the night. The small venomous ants had gained total victory over the big ants who were devoid of ways of defending themselves. They were now tracking the survivors, *cleaning-up* the area.

'Terminator!' exclaimed Connor.

Maybe the Gods are watching men like we were considering ants that day. With dismay.

'Maya creates a cruel nature. Love is not the most powerful instinct in Shiva's *leela*,' I thought aloud around the improvised *dhooni* we had built.

'The logical ultimate consequence of the theory of evolution is that the world will end up belonging to the gene of genocide,' Connor expatiated. 'It is the most cunning, the best armed, the utmost ruthless who will be the winners in the game of natural selection. Not the most loving.'

'Cro-magnon, the belligerent, has supplanted Neanderthal, the peaceful,' I added to the pathetic facts.

'What should we see Babaji?' asked Connor.

'You imagine, you project, you dramatize... Everything is innocent. No one is guilty. You cannot ask for mercy. But if the other's misfortune is your own misfortune, your peace is their peace as well.'

We carry the gene of love too...

I went with Connor to greet the sadhus who haunted the riverbanks and questioned them.

'Neither nice ants nor killer ants,' summed up a man of few words, definitively, self-confident and insensitive. Beyond it all. Had I even spoken to him? But as we stayed longer, he added: 'Neither birth nor death, neither pain nor pleasure; no question, no answer.' We left.

'Gods could not bear silence and stillness. That's why they created sound and passion,' explained a wise, old somewhat Shakespearian man, smiling helplessly. Fatalistic even concerning illusions.

'The sun is necessary to the world's activities, but can we say it acts? Similarly, although there is a world, *Bhagwan* does not do anything,' said a yogi who was motionless for twenty-three hours a day.

'So, what good is he then?'

'He's good for remembering oneself,' the yogi replied, laughing.

Darshan Baba spent the day observing the ants and he saved a few. Ananda Baba joined him and said: 'Cats play with mice, tigers eat calves, and mosquitoes feed on your blood before they are gulped by swallows. It's not your concern. Everyone accomplishes his own *dharma*.' Darshan accepted that.

'The worst thing in this outlook,' Connor remarked, 'is that the gene of genocide goes back a long way and we're still carrying it. As far as that is concerned, evolution has not evolved much.'

'You get freed from your genes when you stop identifying with your body. For sadhus, that's the ultimate evolution of life,' I remarked.

'But the gene of the renunciant reproduces little. Whereas the gene of genocide proliferates,' calculated Connor.

'The genes of genocide will genocide one another,' I prophesied in an extravagantly risky way.

'But we, we will be dead by then, brother,' Connor sang, pretending to be completely despairing.

'For someone who has renounced his existence, how would he be affected?' I carried on, feigning wisdom.

'Hmmm,' Connor uttered in doubt.

'There have never been so many words around this head as there have been since two such garrulous disciples arrived,' interrupted Ananda Baba. 'Everything born must die – this is certain – exhausted by old age or illness, eaten up or injured. And yet death does not exist because "me" is only a tiny part of existence. One being manifests in all forms of existence and non-existence. *Sarvam khalvidam Brahman*, all this is Brahman,' he concluded. 'And you are him. See that.'

It was dark when we arrived at the *dharamsala* in Saharanpur. We were served the last ladles of rice and what was left of vegetable *daal*, on a banana leaf, in the courtyard. Other sadhus, having finished their meal, had thrown their remains in a corner. A dog was feasting on it. Two buffaloes were waiting for their turn. A sadhu arrived and as there was nothing left to eat he squatted next to the dog, put his arm around his neck as to a friend, and asked him: 'We share, *Gurubhai*?' And they searched and licked together.

I took what was left of my meal and put it down at the latecomer's feet.

'Will this self accept an offering from himself?' I asked him bowing respectfully.

The sadhu turned, examined me with satisfaction, and declared grandiloquently:

'When the dog's food will be for him the same as his food, and water from the tank will be for him as pure as the holy Ganga; when his fast will be his fast, and when he will see no difference between me, you, him, the dog and the dog-eaters, he will be a free soul.'

And he blessed me saying: 'He will be free from hunger.'

But he returned to the remains.

In turn, Darshan Baba put down his banana leaf full of rice before the sadhu. He growled, frowned and grimaced the terrible smile of Kali, waving his hands in the air. The sadhu resigned himself to accept the offering and shared it with the dog. United in misery, partners in wealth. 'Blessed are the poor,' confirmed Connor who made us feel obliged to share his rice. A few sadhus were giggling. Ananda Baba was smiling. The buffaloes were getting impatient.

We resumed walking; then stopped in a temple whose ablutions tank was the size of a swimming pool. It also was home to carp; devotees offered them the best: puffed rice, sold in cornets at the gate.

Puffed rice is light; it cannot be thrown very far away and it floats. The fish draw near the first immersed steps of the tank. There are families. It's fun. Children are delighted to see the big pink and grey fish coming to the surface and gulping down the white spots. The eagle is too, hovering over the temple.

The fish are as hypnotized by the manna as much as they are blinded by the brightness of the light. The eagle slowly slides down facing the sun, skims over the tank, stoops and swoops down on its prey, seizes it, takes off, and flies away swiftly. Its claws grip the twisting catch as they disappear behind the walls.

May its meal be blessed.

Sitting on the stone steps, feet in water, I was meditating on the blessing: 'All this is Brahman, offered by Brahman and taken by Brahman.' It depends a bit on your place in the food chain – carnivore or herbivore, eater or eaten, and in the scale of conscience – guilty or victim. Everything is innocent. No one is guilty. My peace is Peace. I'm a vegetarian.

The devotees elevate carps to the status of sacred creatures and feed them. The eagles have a good laugh about it. They are also sacred creatures anyway. And why not small ants! When I would no longer see a difference between me, you, him, venomous ants, laughing eagles and dog-eaters... – forgetting everything just to be here, I will be free.

In the reliable *Astavakra Samhita*:

> Neither joy nor sorrow for he who has transcended everything,
> Not even the desire to renounce anything
> Neither joy nor sorrow.
> [18, 22-23]

When we reached Dehradun, our naked angel flew away to comfort the *sadhak* Babaji Baba had seen in a dream.

Goodbye Darshanji! May the love I am filled with when I think of you, be in me forever.

It had to be said with laughter.

Ochre and green chequered plains under a uniformly blue sky. Mud houses enclosed by thorn hedges. A crystal clear silence. Two buffaloes pull the plough in a flooded paddy field. A cell phone rings a song; the farmer answers, feet in water. On the front page of *The Deccan*: INDIA, SECOND LARGEST SOFTWARE EXPORTER.

'You will find Balayogi – a *Mahatma!* – at Mummidivaram, East Godavari District, Andhra Pradesh,' said an enthusiastic and precise shopkeeper, in Bihar. 'His *darshan* alone can accomplish the purpose of your life,' he promised.

A few days later, a police officer spoke to us about this yogi:

'He does not live in an ashram or a *kutir* but in a temple, in a padlocked room, on the second floor of the tower, above the *garbha griha* (the room for emptiness, behind the idol).'

'Why is the door padlocked?' asked Connor.

'Because he does not want to be disturbed. His room is opened only for one hour every day.'

In circles and *akharas*, a few sadhus had spoken about this hero of asceticism who was a cowherd and, at fifteen, had sat down under a tree and stopped moving, absorbed in deep and continuous *samadhi*. He had not left his *asan* and neither eaten nor drunk anything for more than thirty-five years. Connor had distinguished him with a *"That's fucked-up!"*

'To protect him from sun and rain, his parents built a hut around him,' a rich widow told us who offered us hospitality in her garden. 'The villagers from the surrounding areas came to take his *darshan*. His reputation slowly expanded. They came from further and further afield to see him. Thanks to donations, which became ever more numerous, his parents built a temple in which, one morning, they found him sitting. A few months later, over a few minutes, he dictated his teaching and never spoke afterwards.'

'What does this teaching say?' I asked her.

'I don't really know. He says he unites his soul with the supreme soul.'

'He says he has reached perfect concentration and *samadhi* in less than twelve hours,' her son cut in. '*Samadhi* in twelve hours is a record in this discipline,' the twenty-four year old medical student emphasised.

'They will take this *darshan* if it happens that way,' said Ananda Baba. But we were slowly going in that direction, walking through a horizon of paddy fields bristling with coconut palms.

At dawn, wild peacocks courted each other, screaming desperately. In the mornings, the amplified Christian school's jarring songs overlapped the temple *puja*. The muezzin had gone back to bed. Puffy eyed, cheerful, buffaloes had their ears cleaned by crows. But rhesus monkeys sometimes attacked villages, in gangs. These wild hunting animals were not playing around. Adults had to throw firecrackers banging as loud as dynamite to frighten them away and children practised their slingshot.

I found a book on Balayogi, in Vishakhapatnam, but the seller would not part with it. However, I was able to read the beginning. The author, a retired judge, made every effort to remove doubts about the authenticity of the yogi's *tapasya*. He informed the reader that the Government of Andhra Pradesh has ordered an investigation. The police had carefully examined his room and for several years two officers had watched over his door, closed with two padlocks whose keys were kept in two police stations several kilometres apart in opposite directions. In vain. Balayogi did not leave this bare room and never ate.

Along a very minor road stood a modest two-storey limed white concrete temple topped with a conical tower. Next to it was a courtyard bordered by five small houses with verandas, white walls and blue doors. A few clumps of pretty flowers, a well… we had arrived.

The next day at dawn, on the first floor of the tower, the director unlocked a big padlock and opened a door on a small room painted white. A man in his fifties, eyes closed, was sitting on a tiger's skin spread on a platform. He was wearing a loincloth. Flabby chest, big round stomach, thick thighs… One wouldn't have guessed this flaccid body belonged to the greatest ascetic. Fair skinned, scant beard, face slightly tilted, totally relaxed features, the tip of his fingers crossed on his thighs, fingernails several centimetres long. He was breathing. His long black hair fell in a heap behind him. A tiny window near the ceiling, and a light bulb hanging on its wire, brought light into the room.

Balayogi slowly straightened up and raised his head, but did not open his eyes. This body was not an abandoned object with consciousness carried away somewhere else. His face did not express torpor. There was somebody, though very much withdrawn within himself, behind his eyelids when I took his *darshan*. In an extreme deep tranquillity. Very near the centre of things perhaps, wherever that is.

I had already watched men in *samadhi*. I was sure this one had not moved for a very long time. I was contemplating what I had not believed. The living legend of the hermit in a one thousand year long *samadhi*.

What does a still man do? Nothing. Minutes, hours, days, weeks, years, decades, almost forty years, fourteen thousand days, three hundred and fifty thousand hours, in a radical passivity. Without need, without exchange, without another. *Advaita*, not-two. Before the creation of nothingness.

The tranquillity of Balayogi could be contagious. I admired it, praised it, envied it, hoped for it, calmed down, and bowed to this absolutely autonomous life. Fully one. I dreamt of immobility. But other pilgrims were waiting.

This was no miracle show, exhibitionism, or lucrative business. This open-door hour set out the boundaries of friendship this yogi granted his fellow men. A little later, the director closed the door and padlocked it.

There were thirty-eight framed black and white photographs hung on the temple walls showing Balayogi first as a teenager, then year after year, ageing, seated in his hut and then in the small white room. The yogi had not stopped time. His asceticism did not prevent his body from ageing. From one picture to the next, his hair and nails lengthened, his body thickened, his legs deformed, his face filled out, his cheeks fell, his features became flabby. Portraits of a still man.

The feat was not a miracle; we could see a human achievement happening in thirty-eight poses.

The only constant factor was his closed eyes. They shut his face on itself, withholding the question the young cowherd had asked himself, as well as the answer he had discovered. But each photograph was a call to wonder about the interiority of Man through the perseverance of this one in observing it exclusively. Thirty-eight hidden gazes. And for the viewer, thirty-eight silent answers. And the mystery of this perfect control of life and consciousness.

On the first photograph, a three-quarter length portrait, Balayogi was 17, sitting on his heels, straight back, lean, fine lines, hairless and gaunt face, his hair in a coil on his delicate, stretched neck and his head leaning slightly forward. Already crossed fingertips resting on his thighs; eyes closed. With a very slight frown, one could imagine him to be resolute. Then, very quickly in the following photographs, his face was relaxed as if there was no more effort, nor anything to seek probably. He enjoyed bliss. One could venture that he must be absorbed in a deep silence.

He was a *jivan-mukta* (liberated alive); he was the embodiment of the

Atman – Brahman state of consciousness (the identity of the part to the whole), of *advaita* (not-two), the metaphysical summit of the Self philosophy. He was *the great-soul whose mind is freed from desire and from desiring to be free from desire, having found satisfaction in self-knowledge*, sung by the *Astavakra*.

Connor joined other pilgrims in the courtyard and sang *bhajan* in an ambiguous mood between joy and reverence. *Sankara Shiva Sankara Shiva Shambu Mahadeva... Oh Lord, I worship the one who always remains unique in his own form, without attributes and without desire.* I examined with Ananda Baba, one by one and at length, the thirty-eight portraits of the ideal yogi.

We were offered a meal, and the book that I wanted: *Message of Bhagwan Balayogi*. We left on foot that morning and we stopped early, under a banyan, in a village.

'What did you see Babaji?'

'Yogiraj! Shiva when he is appointed *Lord of the yoke*, meditating on himself for one hundred thousand years on Mount Kailash, absorbed in himself, controlling mind and breath,' our guru said.

The conversation continued on a hospitable villager's veranda.

'What does he do all that time?' asked Connor.

'*Beyond he who enjoys and that which is enjoyed*, as an Upanishad says,' Babaji replied.

'So it exists!' I marvelled.

How was it possible? I found the answer in the book. The author had translated into English the only message Balayogi had dictated, in Telugu, two and a half years after he started his *tapasya*, thirty-six years earlier. Three pages. The practical and spiritual testament of a child and a sage. He was then just seventeen.[1]

He recounted that one day he had sat under a coconut palm, worshipped an image of Krishna and... *My tapasya has borne fruit*, he said. He then outlined his efforts and progress in fasting and radical non-action. He took only milk at first. After a month, he gave up taking a bath. *Absorption of milk stopped then. Excretion as well. The fresh water placed beside me sometimes reduced in volume.* Thus he expressed himself. Through his *tapasya,* he reached what he called *maha-swarga*, beyond heavens.

---

1 *Message of Bhagwan Balayogi, by* Polamuri Sampatha Rao.

He recalled that he had not been understood by the villagers and his parents who believed him to be lazy. Then followed a list of rules and regulations regarding the *darshans'* procedure. *One should not speak, nor touch him, and not be fidgety...* for he found the temple too noisy and wanted to continue his meditation in a state of calmness. He recommended not to beat an animal or cut a flower around the temple... *If everyday life goes on without problems, that is in itself great wealth.* At the request of his devotees, he consented to be celebrated the day following *Mahashivaratri*. That day no alms will be requested*, ordered this foresighted and meticulous young man. *If a devotee wishes to build something, let him do it. But it is for himself that he does it. I need nothing.*

He then described the transformation he had produced upon himself, the exit door he had found, the secret of immobility: *The Self (*the Atman*) is in God's image. The five senses take one into maya. Senses draw their strength from food. If one wants to control his senses, he must reduce the quantity of food he takes. Then stop eating. Then the senses are under control. Then in the soul, the five elements are quiet, subdued, and remain unconscious. If the senses are unconscious, food is not necessary. The individual soul merges in Oneness. He who knows himself and controls his wandering thoughts does not need a guru. The Self becomes his guru. If the Self is pure, the Self reveals everything.*

During my meditation, before sunrise, I remembered the story of Prahlada told by Kaushal Giri in Bang Handi Temple. The one thousand years *samadhi* this demon had accomplished appeased the whole creation. But Vishnu had woken Prahlada up and the world had returned to normal... This demon represents the five senses and the mind, Partib Giri Baba had explained. When they are controlled, there is no more movement. Or feelings, or perceptions. Balayogi also embodied that myth. And he was resisting Vishnu.

> Anything you know is unstable reality. It is from renouncing
> everything you know that renouncing unstable reality is possible.
> Then only Being as an energy is left.

'Babaji, in the *Trimurti* (God in three images), Brahma is the creator, Shiva destroys and, between them, Vishnu preserves. If Vishnu is the God whose function is to maintain Creation, it means keeping the waking and dreaming states of consciousness active. In them, consciousness is absorbed in maya, the world.'

'But they disappear in *samadhi*. Shiva destroys maya in the fire of his third eye.'

'But Vishnu plays with it. He holds on to the possibility of a dream and a world. In the *Purana*, Vishnu wakes Prahlada up from his *samadhi*, he awakens him from his awakening.'

'Prahlada and Balayogi are also part of the dream.'

'So what does it mean to annihilate maya?

'Annihilation, is to see it as it is.'

'So, awakening is also part of the dream?'

'There is no outside of consciousness.'

Shanti Guha

In Roorkee, a strange young woman wearing a tattered sari spent most of the day sitting on the steps of the banks of the Ganges, her gaze absorbed by the waves, hair undone.

The *pujari* of the nearby temple told us that five years earlier her young husband had drowned there while he was fishing. Ashalata, this young widow, was waiting for the river to give him back. 'Once, according to a legend,' the *pujari* explained, 'a young man who had drowned in the river while he was fishing, walked out of it twelve years later. His wife had made a vow not leave the bank, constantly begging Shiva to give her back her beloved.'

'She's waiting for God to look into her case,' I uttered with sadness.

'She believes in legends,' thought Connor.

We left. But at around noon, Connor decided to return to Roorkee.

'I will look into her case; I'll make a legend,' he announced to Ananda Baba. 'After all, I am God too!'

He asked me to translate three sentences he learned by heart. Back in Roorkee, Connor was going to walk out of the river and stand before Ashalata saying: 'Your husband has drowned while fishing; he has become a fish. But you'll be a *sadhvi* because you have abandoned the world to wait for him.'

'You will find Babaji in Rampur,' Ananda Baba said, blessing him.

At the end of a long ascending track which crossed a sparse forest, we arrived at a cave opening onto a wide flat rock which made a terrace in front of the narrow and deep valley. *Shanti Guha!* the cave of tranquillity: two cavities of the height of a man followed one another, connected by a funnel-shaped passageway. A few stones gathered at the entrance formed a threshold.

Ananda Baba beat the floor with a stick for a long time to warn snakes, tarantulas, rats, cockroaches, bugs and other inhabitants that we were coming in. We entered. In one place, a stalactite, like an upside down *lingam*, hung from the belly of the mountain. 'There is either mindfulness training, or sudden awakening here!' my guru cautioned striking his forehead with his hand in a roar of laughter. A low and narrow slit in the second cavity opened out onto the valley and far away, the tiny village we had crossed, with its few stone houses with schist slab roofing could be seen. A few yaks looked as if they were motionless; yellow, brown and green terrace fields, held by low walls rose up the slope in wide undulating steps. Higher up was the dark forest and in the sky, seven snow-capped peaks.

At the terrace, a stone *dhooni* and a *lingam* on the precipice's edge were waiting to be honoured once again. A brook ran alongside the track for about twenty meters before reaching a natural basin below. A wooden chest contained a few aluminium bowls, a dented pot, a tin bucket and three plastic bags containing rice, lentils and some tea that a previous guest had left.

'Fill the bucket and fetch some wood. And also make a broom from some branches. Don't disturb much and beware of snakes.'

I also gathered together a small log pile.

Om Namah Shivayah! Ananda Baba put down a fresh flower on the *lingam*, then turned the ashes of the *dhooni* and swept and splashed water around it. He built a campfire and then lit it saying: 'O *Agni*, may ignorance and the habits of ignorance be consumed in the fire of discrimination.'

We drank our tea, breathing in the beautiful valley at length.

Ananda Baba set down his *asan* in the second cavity. I settled down in the first one.

I gathered wood, swept, took a bath and washed my clothes and sat in the cave or on the terrace. Visits were rare. Three farmers came to take our *darshan* and offered us provisions. Shanti Guha was at the end of a track leading nowhere else.

To reach it we had climbed up and down steep roads, tracks and trails, some of them winding around hills. We had crossed small stone bridges, followed torrents, made our way through a jungle of high trees encumbered with creepers and ferns where we saw deer, stags and a grey fox.

We had stayed in hamlets which turned golden when the setting sun splashed their schist roofs. A few single room stone-houses built over wooden barns, gathering four generations of mountain folk with slightly slanting eyes, poor yet welcoming, simple and joyful, and much less noisy than the people from the plains.

We had also walked through a small mineral desert spread with golden rocks. Life was not visible. Silence was absolute. Immobility produced vertiginous effects there. But the earth continued to revolve: struck by the sun, the caps of the peaks covered by everlasting snow were transformed into a rosary of diamonds during the day and ruby at dusk.

One morning, Ananda Baba called me in front of the *dhooni* and said:

'Prassad will stay here. Anand will come back to find him.'

'What will I do here on my own, Guruji?'

'Contemplate, the same being in all forms; see *That*,' he said casually.

'What being, Babaji?' I asked to stop him.

'Look beyond appearance and disappearance, behind the changing world, like an absolutely pure intuition, without images, without expectations, without conditions: Being.'

He folded his blanket, picked up his bag and his *komandalu* and he went down the track. I prostrated to his absence.

But until when? I thought, a little panicked. '*Until there is no more* when *and* until, where *and* why,' Ananda Baba answered, laughing, as if he were there.

I sat in front of the *dhooni*, and the valley. *If there is no goal, there is no concern about attaining anything*, I remembered. *There is nothing to do.*

I contemplated a moment.

A wood fire is a companion. And I had visits from a hedgehog, and an otter that lived next to the reservoir. A crow attempted the *look here* trick whilst I was having dinner, but I had spotted the other one, waiting on a branch, and he knew that I knew the scam. They came back regularly to say hello. The blackbird's song makes a conversation if you reply to it. The crackles and rustles under dead leaves betrayed shyer neighbours. But soon the squirrel dared to come close and make friends. And sometimes, in the valley, a goat-antelope crossed a clearing.

Over the course of the days, I remembered the first sadhus I had met in Varanasi. And again, I heard their words. The whispering of Ram Tilak Baba through the window of his room – *Maya should not be hated, she must be loved*. And Maya Baba, an allegory of Virtue defended himself, drawing back before Jane, a manifestation of Temptation: *We must relinquish the benefits of illusion to escape illusion... The world and the mind appear and disappear together*, I had read in a book. *There is no exit. The exit is also part of the dream. All you need to realize is the dream as being a dream....* That's how it had all begun... *There is nothing to do*, the sparkling Ganges had whispered. And everything became light. *We see a circle, there is only one flame, and motion*, Laurie explained imitating *Nataraja*. It's a dance! A flow of appearances. *You project a world and then you enter it. All this is Brahman*. A single cause. *And you are him*, my guru had said. Purity in anonymity. Perfection in stillness. The modesty of eternity...

The teachings of my masters came back in no particular order. Sometimes contradictory, often questionable, these words had been working on me from within. At times, they plunged me into the vacuum they hinted at.

One plus one equals one.

Neither real nor unreal, or both.

What you think of as real is always a mental construction, whether in a dream or not.

I am not what I think, I had discovered meditating.

The water in the jar and space in the sky are both contained in the space limited by the jar. Everything is nothing but the play of illusions.

When name and form disappear, consciousness knowing the destruction of name and form remains. There is no outside of consciousness. When the duality of the knower and the known is dissolved, that which remains is Self.

The feeling of belonging to the forest.

When it is quiet, the mind returns to its cause.

A tiny unshakeable joy.

Oh bliss of nothingness.

On the wall, in front of me, two lizards remain in a yogi's immobility. The patience of hunters. Almost a mineral stillness, but with acute attention. Gurus.

Om Namah Shivayah.

And days went by as a single day, and time as a single moment.

I am That.

The desire or fear of becoming someone else... disappeared. But who was it that knew this?

I fed on rice and *daal*, milk and vegetables if someone brought them. But less and less… Before dawn, I moved my *asan* onto the terrace in front of the valley. All around, in the woods, there were soft hisses, scratches and gnaws: a symphony for claws, dead leaves and small fleeting steps. When the birds began the second movement, the sky turned from starry back to uniformly dark blue and all those who feared daylight ran underground. The concert became aerial. The snowy peaks turned pink and orange, like a circle of sadhus in front of a heavenly *dhooni*. And then our star pierced between two mountains, red, round, incandescent. The *darshan* of illumination. The forest, the fields, the yaks, the valley and far away the golden roofs of the village appeared, one by one. From this height, everything seemed slow. And the eagles looked as if they were taking a nap on the wind.

I bowed to heaven and earth.

A brown fox crossed through a distant orchard every morning, and stopped for a few seconds to face me. He gave me his *darshan*, taking mine. I greeted him, tilting my head slightly. He always replied courteously.

At around noon, a blue beetle walked all over the terrace at its modest pace of a minute pachyderm. The imperative cawing of my two crow friends called me back to mindfulness and the whole forest as well. In the evening, the sun hit the high peaks and everything became red. In the clear night, crickets endlessly chirped the stars' *mantras*. And the sky listened, winking from time to time. The faint, tenuous, suctions of the lizards' fingers on the rocks as they move. In the middle of the night, the crystalline crackles of the vault.

One evening, a cobra slithered over the still warm stone of the terrace. When I noticed, it was too late to react. Nagaraj hauled himself into my lap and coiled up there. Immobility or the end of the story.

An almost full moon flooded the valley with a bluish glow which did not dispel darkness but made it diaphanous, caressing. A goat-antelope slowly crossed the clearing swaying its hips, breathing in and nibbling here and there. Just as it turned to the darkness of the undergrowth, a white leopard sprang out and, in one jump, held it by the throat. The prey collapsed on the spot. A cloud plunged the valley into gloom. Crickets stayed quiet for a moment. When the clearing appeared again in the moonlight, everything was serene.

The immutable has freedom as its form.

Dawn… The Lord of snakes had gone.

At mid-afternoon, about two hours before sunset, suddenly, all the forest's denizen remained still and quiet at the same time. Even leaves stopped rustling. A hush held time. An almost religious daily ritualistic pulse; the forest was meditating. Absorbed in its one self for a moment. As a single being.

It is during one of these hushes that the intuition of reality as an expression of Being appeared, was there.

A bird flew off. The forest came alive.

I am That.

The following days, I stopped going out of the cave. The outside world gradually disappeared. The inner world settled.

Behind my closed eyelids, everything became vibrating light particles, energy, bright waves. This radiance gathered in a column of fire which ran across my body.

Then even that disappeared.

He will be free from hunger! a sadhu had promised me for a handful of rice.

I remembered Balayogi. This master of immobility had starved his senses in order to stop their activities. *If the senses are unconscious, food is not necessary*, this *Mahatma* had explained. *The individual soul then merges in Oneness...*

Non-being as being a possibility.

I resolved not to move at all.

Bringing senses to a standstill.

I closed my eyes.

And days passed.

Motionlessly.

Life contemplating the minute sparkling of its source.

My body wanted nothing, and nobody knew.

Immobility is a state in which being and non-being join. Waves of joy rose from myself in myself, but who could know it? And who would testify? I saw myself sitting in front of myself, taking my own *darshan*.

It's a dream! The dream of a universe which is dreamt in the dream of a dream which has no author and ends in no dawn.

I saw the leopard walking along the terrace and progressing towards the opening of the cave. I saw the outside as if my eyelids and the rocky walls had become transparent. I saw the starry sky and the crescent moon, the forest's line of foliage and the cold *dhooni*.

The beast sniffed the threshold and then lay outside.

The world disappeared.

Later, I saw four hairy sadhus arriving from the ascending path and soon I heard them yelp *Namah Shivayahs!* announcing themselves. They appeared at the entrance, lit a lighter, then a candle and came in...

Four strange ageless human beings wearing long ancestor's beards and *jatta-mukutas** like crowns of fire, and their giant shadows. One was dressed in ashes and held a trident. Another wore a turban and a saffron tunic and was twirling around in front of him, like a sling, a rosary of large *rudrakshas*. The third was bent and frail as if dwelling in a cocoon of rags, but he had mischievous eyes and a shrewd little smile. And the fourth, dressed in white, seemed not to touch the ground.

A dream, a hallucination, an apparition? I opened my eyes. They were there. Sitting in front of me, they were whispering among themselves.

The naked ascetic turned to me and asked:

'What is the sign of right action?'

'Not to act,' I answered from a remote corner of consciousness.

'What can you find beyond forms?' inquired the levitating one.

Neither something nor nothing.

'What is the greatest happiness?' the Ragged Baba questioned.

Having Oneself as abode.

'When consciousness is everything, what is there?' asked Sling Baba.

Silence.

Four pairs of black eyes that reflected the candle flame examined the moment without one more word.

I closed my eyes.

The world disappeared.

The crickets became quiet. The birds announced the arrival of dawn...

Where am I? murmured a remote corner of consciousness. This question vanished without a trace. I brushed past a woman who was collecting eggs in a farmyard, stroked a child's head, sat down on a buffalo's back lying in an enclosure.

I'm weightless... I am a dream...

Ananda Baba sitting in front of me. I prostrated.

From a remote corner of consciousness, the telling of a story: *Prahlada had managed to calm the devils and all of creation due to a one thousand year long samadhi.*

One thousand years... I considered from a less remote corner.

And then Vishnu awoke Prahlada and the universe was back to normal... I remembered.

It was of no use, I reasoned.

Vishnu is waking me up, I thought opening my eyes.

How did Vishnu wake Prahlada up? I found in my head waking up.

My cell-phone was singing The Walkyrie.

I rushed to the bathroom and vomited in the toilet.

Yes!

It's eleven o'clock, Ludo!

The ugly voice of my boss.

I am sick. I won't be coming in today.

I threw my phone down on the bed...

Heavens! I had dreamt I was in India... I remembered.

I opened my eyes and saw the two lizards looking at me. No, I had dreamt I was in Paris...

'You have a fever,' said Ananda Baba bending over me.

'Where am I?'

'Atchaa!' Swami Ananda Baba exclaimed slapping his hand down on this page. 'This is how the book ends...'

'Not quite,' I answered.

'The readers will think Ananda Baba is not a real person,' Prassad Baba said worriedly.

'No. They will ask themselves: since when has this been a dream?' I explained.

'Forever. Since the beginning of time. They know that by now!' said Swami Ananda Baba.

'Prahlada is a *jivan-mukta*, a victorious one. For the *Purana* philosophers, he reached the ultimate state of consciousness. It has always intrigued me that Vishnu pulls him out of his *samadhi* and somehow destroys the ideal. 'Guruji, how did Vishnu wake up Prahlada?' asked Prassad Baba.

'The *Purana* doesn't say,' Swami Ananda Baba answered laughing. 'But maybe the writer knows?'

'A long time ago, Swamiji, at Bang Handi Temple, you said: "Vishnu dreams he creates worlds, and in a world he creates Prahlada, but in this dream Prahlada puts the worlds to a halt. So Vishnu awakens Prahlada to awake himself and keep on dreaming." Vishnu awakens Prahlada out of his *samadhi*, he awakens him from Awakening, by telling him a story, and that's how he goes on dreaming.

'Men have created a state of consciousness which is neither the waking state, nor a dream, but which is somewhere between both of them and is both at the same time: legends, myths, tales, fables, novels, *Puranas*, another way of living in the world, and of sharing a dream, which is told by someone else, and in which one enters and exits like in a dream too, and where everything is true in an illusory sense, just like in real life.

'I am writing a novel in which the main character, who is also the narrator, recounts his exploration of a philosophy which argues that consciousness is in an illusion when it believes whatever happens to it, but also pledges that consciousness can tear away from the attraction of illusion. Its weight. The character is going to succeed... The moment when nothing happens is happening. He is disappearing from the narrative. But if there is no narrator, who told the story?'

'A sadhu has no past! They have told me this over and again,' Connor intervened.

'You come out of your *samadhi* remembering the *Prahlada Purana*, which is like your tale since it tells the story of a character who frees himself from his own story through a *samadhi*, so that you'll tell the story I'm telling, just as in the dream of the dream of a dream...'

'A dreamer who knows he is dreaming, what does he see?' Connor asked.

'He tells himself the story of a dream.'

'And so, he awakens,' Swami Ananda Baba cut in. 'Because to tell a story of a dream, he must be awake and somehow awakened from it.'

'Is there any follow-up to Prahlada's story? What happened after Vishnu pulled him out of his one thousand year *samadhi*?' Prassad Baba asked his guru.

Swami Ananda Baba burst out laughing and said:

'The *Purana* tells this. Vishnu granted him the state of *jivan-mukta* and eternal life. He became the king of three worlds and *acharya*, guru of the Gods.

And the worlds continued on their natural course.'

'He was already a liberated *soul*. That was not the issue,' Prassad Baba clarified. 'Someone who stays still for one thousand years does not need anything.'

'That is true. And as for eternal life, it is the *Purana* which grants it. Vishnu makes him a king, an *acharya*... He tells him a story, which *rishis* tell us too, and we tell it in turn; he gives him a life. And Vishnu goes on with his dream. Just as you, Prassad Baba, are a part in my dream, or I, at times, participate in yours as well.'

'We are all awakened if we know we are dreaming.'

'The name of Ram is more powerful than Ram.'

'Because only the name of Ram is true.'

'Who says?'

'It doesn't matter anymore.'

Anyone who has read this *Sadhu Purana* will be freed from the affliction of bad dreams. Those who hear a reading of it will be redeemed of their unworthy acts. Poverty will avoid those who translate it into a foreign language. Those who remember a baba from this book will consider the world and all its creatures with a heart filled with kindness. They will reap the fruits of wisdom and become a model for all creatures...

Since those who praise living sadhus and the legendary *rishis* obtain all blessings.

Shri Ram Jay Ram Jay Jay Ram!

Hari Krishna!

Om Narayana!

Om Namah Shivayah!

Acknowledgements

First of all, I want to express my love for India, and my gratitude to this land and its people. And to all the sadhus I have met. I cannot name all of them and cannot express my admiration enough. This book itself is a tribute to them. Their mere existence is for me the everlasting hope of a better world, for they tackle selfishness in a world dominated by egocentricity and greed.

My thanks to Ms. Shikha Sabharwal – the Publishing Director, for her extreme patience, to the Editor – Ms. Sonalini Chaudhry, and the Assistant Editor – Ms. Taniya Sachdeva, for reviewing this translation. And a special thanks to Andy Paice for his hard work, his keen understanding of the Hindu philosophy and his writing style and talent.

Glossary

A

Acharya: Great scholar also called guru of the Gods.

Advaita: *Not-two.* Non-duality or transcendent unity of Brahman (the absolute and unique Being) and the universe.

Agni: God of fire. He is the common denominator of all the Gods. The messenger. He symbolizes divine power and will in consciousness.

Akarma: Non-action, actionlessness, action leaving no trace.

Akhara: From the Xth century, a training camp for ascetic warriors. Today, the institutions they have initiated. Also, monasteries of sedentary sadhus that host wandering *samnyasins* and, at different times of the day, *grihastha*, householders and benefactors.

Allak: "Not-perceptible", "formless". Interjection inviting consciousness to be present to what is.

Ananda: Bliss, supreme causeless happiness, delight, joy without cause, one of three attributes of Brahman. "If I am supreme bliss, the ultimate reality is equal everywhere, and just like space." *Avadhuta Gita* I 27.

Arati: Dawn and dusk.

Asan: The place where a sadhu sits, meditates and sleeps. The personal, private and taboo space for someone who has renounced having a home. Demarcated by a blanket, or four pebbles.

Asana: To firmly take up the posture of Oneness. A physical or mental yoga posture.

Ashram: *To endeavour*; a place where one makes efforts. A type of Indian monastery open to laymen.

Atcha: Generic exclamation which includes approval, consent, astonishment, wonder, expectation, or is used to temporise.

Avadhut: *One who has gone beyond*, ascetic, follower of the school of Avadhuta.

Avadhuta Gita: *Song of the unbound*, poem attributed to Dattatreya (twelfth century).

Avatar: *Descent* of a God. Incarnation of a God in a living being, human or animal. Gandhi has recently been added to the list of Vishnu's *avatars*, which also includes a fish, a turtle, Rama, Krishna and Buddha.

Avidhya: Non-knowledge, ignorance or non-understanding of the spiritual path, non-experience of the ultimate reality. The mind bound in the dualistic vision of the world and phenomenon. Appearances taken to be the sole reality.

Ayurveda: *Veda of Long Life*; Indian traditional medicine.

B

Baba, Babaji: *Dad, father*; honorary name used to address a sadhu. Synonym with sadhu. The suffix -*ji* is honorary and affectionate.

Babu, Babuji: *Sir*. Used for a lay man. The suffix -*ji* is honorary and affectionate.

Bass: Enough!

Bhagwan: *God, Lord*. A generic term to refer to God or a God, whatever his name.

Bhajan: Chants, devotional songs.

Bhakta: Devotee, faithful, one who follows the *bhakti marga*, the path of love through devotion, or of devotion through love.

Bhandara: Dinner hosted by a benefactor, a wealthy baba or a temple and in which sadhus are the guests.

Bhang: Chopped fresh cannabis leaves.

Bhang lassi: Drink made with fermented milk and fresh chopped cannabis leaves.

Bharatnatyam: One of the four major classical dance schools.

Bidi (or Biri): Traditional Indian cigarette made of a rolled up kendu leaf wrapping a few strands of tobacco, and held together by a small cotton yarn.

Brahma: A major God; creator of the world, creator of mankind, and also the inventor of theatre.

Brahman: The *oldest*; the ultimate Self, the supreme being, One, indefinable, unlimited, unchanging, without qualities, the Whole, the universal, the One in diversity. Brahman is the central topic of the philosophy of non-dualism: the impersonal absolute, unchanging, non-born, eternal; also synonymous with impersonal consciousness (not bound by identity or identifications). Should not be confused with Brahmin (caste), and Brahma, the creator of humanity. Brahman and atman are different levels of the self. *Jiva*, designates the impersonal consciousness taken in the illusion of being a separate being, distinct from the universal.

Brahmin: *The One who has charge of the Brahman.* First of the four castes. Caste of priests or individuals belonging to this caste. Some Brahmins are *pujaris*, officiating priests, servants of rites dedicated to a God. Most have occupations unrelated to religion. They wear a *janehyu*, nine threads making cords of three strings, worn from the right shoulder to left hip.

Brahmachari: One who lives in Brahman. Has reached, or searches, the ultimate bliss. Student of the path.

Brahmacharya: A set of rules of life, including chastity, followed by the student and by the *brahmachari*, whatever his age.

Burkha: Clothing covering the person from head to toe, used by Muslim women.

C

Catogi (katori): A stainless steel container – a cross between bowl and cup.

Chai: Tea boiled with sugar and milk, and sometimes spices.

Chaiwalla: Chai shopkeeper.

Chapati: Thin bread made with flour, salt and water, without yeast, cooked on a plate or baked in a Tandoor.

Chappals: Sandals.

Charas: Hashish.

Charpoy: Bed made of a rope net tightened on a frame.

Chidambaram: A city of Tamil Nadu, India's southernmost state.

Chillum: Cone shaped hashish pipe made of baked earth or carved stone.

Chowk: Bazaar, market and commerce area.

Cit: Consciousness, awareness, intelligence and knowledge, in a single word.

D

Daal: Lentils.

Dakshina (Guru-Dakshina): The offering for a teaching.

Dalit: "Oppressed," Untouchable; individuals belonging to the caste of untouchables.

Damaru: Small hourglass shaped drum in the middle of which a string is attached with a bead at its end. The tip where the two cones meet represents the beginning of… or the contact point between fire and water.

Darshan: This Sanskrit word has no English equivalent. We could translate it with *gaze*, as suggested by its Sanskrit root, *Drik*, to see, but it is to see *differently*, to see and meet at the same time, having seen and known, having seen and feeling blessed to have been there, sensing a positive and beneficial inspiration from it. One is said to "take" a *darshan* as this gaze is then deeply rooted in oneself.

One takes the *darshan* of a saint or a sage, if one sees him as a realised man, the one who is the epitome of all wisdom, the goalless goal of the path of liberation. One also takes the *darshan* of an idol, a sacred object, a striking view, a mountain, a tree, a light, the sweetness of a moment, a knowledge, if these sights transport and show one something else, something pertaining to interiority; having experienced a particular kind of exaltation.

A *darshan* is an opportunity to somehow face the Real. To be present. Free from the influence of the past (which no longer exists) and of future (which is not there). Something approaching freedom.

A *darshan* is also a point of view, a demonstration, a way of saying the unutterable or indicate it; an intellectual construction leading the mind to its limit, to the admission of its ineptitude...

A *darshana* is a school of philosophy, a metaphysical construction.

The ultimate *darshan:* when the veil of duality disappears in the non-dual transcendent state.

Dharamsala: A lodge, often next to a temple or an ashram, which offers food and shelter for sadhus and pilgrims.

Dharma: The Law, the basic laws. This word has three meanings: set of rules governing the natural order of things towards universal harmony; the personal duty and ethical rules determined by birth and more or less attached to one's caste; and finally, one's personal destiny.

Dhobi: A person who washes clothes for a living.

Dhooni: The hearth and the sacred fire of a sadhu. *Agni's* dwelling place.

Dhoti: A piece of clothing for men, made of a cotton strip, five meters long and one and a half meters wide, worn around the hips, and of which the end is passed between the legs, and fastened to the belt.

Digambara: Clothed by the wind, space clad. Naked ascetic.

Domra: Caste, and members of the caste of those who approach cadavers and tend the funeral pyres.

G

Ganga: Daughter of Himalaya and Mena, a feminine aspect that Indra took. The

Ganges, a sacred river, especially sacred in Varanasi. In mythology, she falls down from heavens, on Shiva's coil, somewhere around Mount Kailash, in the Himalayas. It carries mica particles which gives it glittering waves.

Ganja: Female flower of Indian hemp or cannabis.

Ghat: Broad steps built on a river bank, or at the edge of the ablution tank in a temple, for easy access. The *ghats* are visited daily by pilgrims coming for ritual purifying ablutions, but also, more prosaically, by women who do their laundry. A sidewalk, halfway up, allows one to walk along the river, or sit on the bank. The *ghats* are also the mountain ranges which ascend in stages from the Deccan plateau to the coastal plains of Tamil Nadu to the southeast, and Kerala and Maharashtra to the south-west.

Ghee: Clarified butter.

Gomcha: Short loincloth.

Grihastha: Householder disciple and benefactor. Lay man.

Guru: Teacher, guide.

Gurubhai: Brother, used by men who have the same guru.

Guru-dakshina: The disbursement for the teaching.

H

Haan: Yes.

Hare: Greeting, invocation of Shiva.

Hari Om: Greeting, invocation of Vishnu.

I

Ishta Devata: Generic term referring to the personal god of a Hindu.

Ishwar: Generic term to designate a personal, chosen, preferred God. The devotee chooses the God and not vice-versa. This changes the perspective and the relationship.

J

Jain, Jainism: A Hindu religion founded in the sixth century AD by Mahavira, the twenty-fourth Tirthakhara (prophet) of his lineage. The doctrine of Buddha would be a "middle path" between Brahmanism and Jainism.

Janehyu: Caste cord; nine threads making cords of three strings, worn from the right shoulder to left hip.

Jatta, Jatti: Dreadlocks, tangled locks of hair, plait-like.

Jatta-mukuta: Coil made of *jatti*.

-Ji: Honorific and affectionate suffix.

Jiva: Vitality, life, individual, human being absorbed in the idea of being an "I"; the subjective world; the individual in the subject-object relation.

Jivan-mukta: Alive-free, liberated. Said of a sage who has reached ultimate knowledge.

Jnana: Knowledge of ultimate reality, wisdom, enlightenment, intuitive experience of the ultimate non-dual reality. The mind and its resources, logic, discrimination between Brahman and maya, are used to reach knowledge and experience that knowledge.

Jnani: A person who has reached *jnana*.

Jnaneshvari: *Treaty of knowledge*, long metaphysical poem written by Jnadev in 1290.

K

Kabir: Fifteenth century weaver and mystic poet who lived in Varanasi, a recognized saint by both Hindus and Muslims.

Kali: Demon of greed. One of the many Shiva's consorts. Image of the destructive power of Time (Mahakala). She is depicted grimacing a fierce, frightening and satisfied smile, revealing her sharp blood dripping fangs. Screaming and uncontrollable fury, she wears a necklace of human heads and, sticking out her red blooded tongue, seems to scoff at us mortals bowing before her. At the same time a Goddess, monster and mother, who gives birth to the world and all sentient beings, and kills them. She dances on Shiva's body who, in this role, symbolizes eternity, because she will devour all that appears to exist.

Kali-yuga: Dark age. A *yuga* is a cosmic cycle. A cycle of four *yuga* (appearance, evolution and extinction of a universe) lasts 4 320 000 Earth years. The *kali-yuga*, the fourth cycle of the present cosmic era, began in 3102 BC.

Karma: Law of causality; the act, the action and its consequence; this life's given qualities; destiny, the cause of oneself. Also, code of ethics governing ethical conduct. It is a key concept in the belief in reincarnation: every thought and action produces an effect on a never ending Self, determining its future rebirths.

Karma Yoga: Yoga of action. Unselfish and voluntary work.

Kashi: Ancient name of Varanasi.

Komandalu: A container made of copper or stainless steel used by sadhus to carry water.

Kumbh Mela: Major annual Hindu pilgrimage held every three years in one of the four sacred cities.

Kurta-pyjama: Long shirt and cotton trousers tied by a cord.

Kutir: A hut or a small house inhabited by a hermit.

L

Lakshmi: Goddess of fortune or wealth in her quality of enchantment. Kamala, the "red lotus", i.e. the heart, is one name of Lakshmi.

**Langur (Hanuman langur)*:* The name applied in India to certain species of monkeys of the genus *Semnopithecus*; also called entellus. Monkey with a black face.

Leela: God or Gods's play. Creation.

Lingam: *Sign*. Erected stone, more or less cylindrical shaped, having a phallic appearance, which represents the universe and the virile member. Symbol of Shiva. Associated with the **yoni**, the vulva, they represent the male and female energies.

Lungi: A two meter long by one meter wide cotton cloth, tied around the hips making a sort of skirt, worn by men. They keep one's legs ventilated and protected from the sun.

M

Mahabharata: The Great History of the world, Great Indian epic composed between the IVth to the VIth century. Contains the Bhagavad Gita.

Mahant: Title, third rank in the bureaucratic hierarchy of the sadhu orders, a sort of bishop.

Maharaj: "Great king". Manner of addressing someone to show respect.

Mahashivaratri: Religious festival in honour of Shiva, the day of the new moon in February-March.

Mahatma: Great Soul.

Manas: The mind function of the brain; the sixth sense, which collects the information given by the five senses. Function from which arises the concept of "I".

Mandir: Temple or chapel; can be very small.

Mantra: From the Sanskrit root *man*, to think, and the suffix *tra*, the instrument:

an instrument of thought. Sacred formula of varying lengths condensing divinity and which allows the mind to concentrate on one activity.

Masjid: Mosque.

Math: Religious institution run by a guru. Set of institutions connected to the same guru. Mission. Ramakrishna Math.

Maya: The creative power of God, personified by his consort (Shakti). The world of appearances created by the divine *leela* (play). The power of illusion which hides the ultimate reality, God and ultimate knowledge. In philosophy, maya is often translated as *illusion* or *delusion*: whatever exists does not exist independently of perception and the interpretation made of it. The projection power of the intellectual faculty which transforms that which is perceived into the belief that that which is perceived is real. Thus, a fundamental and parallel mistake is created: the belief that we exist as a separate entity.

Mlecha: In the caste classification, a *barbarian*, under, below, worse than a *pariah* or an untouchable, a foreigner! Someone who does not believe in caste classifications!

Moksha: *Untied.* Liberation; continuous and definitive knowledge of the ultimate reality. The final liberation of the individual soul (*jiva*) from the idea of being an individual soul or a person. Union of consciousness with God for God believers, or with the formless for philosophers. State of liberation resulting from having the intuition of Brahman.

Mudra: Hand-and-finger gestures and positions depicted in iconography and used during worship and in dance, rituals and yoga. Often symbolic of spiritual and philosophical postures.

Muni: Silent. Renunciant who gives up talking.

N

Naga (Naga Baba): (litt: *snake*), Order of warrior ascetics, naked or clothed, often castrated.

Namah Shivayah! I salute Shiva (through you).

Namaste, Namashkaar: Usual greeting. "I revere holiness through you."

Narayan, Narayana: *Dwelling of men*; important Sanskrit name for Vishnu. All living beings are *Narayan*. It is also the name of Brahma as creator of mankind, in the *trimurti* (the three figures of God), with Vishnu, the God responsible for maintaining and animating Creation, and Shiva who symbolizes Time, the destructive forces, and therefore renewal.

Nataraja: Lord of dance. Shiva dancing cosmic activities: creation, preservation, destruction, incarnation and liberation.

Nath: Order of Vishnuit renunciants founded by Jnanadeva in the twelfth century.

Nirakhara: "Without form", God without form image, totally abstract.

O

OM: Original sound. First cosmic vibration which put movement in motion. Essence of all sounds in the three times. The vibratory cause of the universe, source of speech and words. *Om* creates the world.

Omkar: Very deep bow, prostration.

P

Paan: A quid (chewable tobacco or betel nut).

Paanwalla: Quid vendor.

Paisa: One hundredth of a rupee, aluminium coins whose value does not exceed one tenth of a rupee.

Palla: Caste of farmers, quite low in the scale of innate purity of caste classifications.

Pallu: The loose end of a sari is called the *pallu* or *pallav*. It is draped diagonally in front of the torso.

Pancadasi: A treatise of fifteen chapters, written in the fourteenth century by Swami Vidyaranya.

Panchalas: Caste of craftsmen.

Panchayat: Village chief or assembly of five prominent villagers who make a council. Elected municipal council.

Pandit: A scholar, a teacher, particularly one skilled in Sanskrit and Hindu law, religion, music or philosophy.

Pariah: Untouchables, lower castes and castes of outcasts which include many sub and sub-sub-castes in a precise hierarchy.

Pipal: Ficus *religiosa*, fig pagodas, or Bodhi tree; tree dedicated to Shiva. *Pipals* can grow up to 30 meters high.

Prakriti: Female nature, complement of *Purush*; matter and nature. Synonym of Shakti, the feminine active energy; creative power.

Prahlada: Son of a demon, who became an ascetic, meditated one thousand years and brought the entire creation to a standstill, before Vishnu woke him from his meditation.

Pranam: Salutation; little bow with joined hands.

Pranayama: Yoga *sadhana* (posture) focused on the breathing.

Prassad: Religious offering. That which Gods have touched the substance or quintessence of.

Puja: Prayer and ritual, public or private.

Pujari: Officiating priest, hired by a temple.

Purana: *Old.* Group of Sanskrit texts which are part of the Hindu sacred literature, consisting of narratives of the history of the Universe from creation to destruction, genealogies of the kings, heroes, sages, and demigods, and descriptions of Hindu cosmology and philosophy. The major *Puranas* are dedicated to Brahma, Vishnu and Shiva. They were written from the 4th century AD to transmit the teaching of the Vedas, the Brahmanas and the Upanishads.

Purush: The latent male power, motionless. Pure consciousness. Complement of *Prakriti* in the beginning of duality.

R

Raga: (colour, mood, atmosphere) Indian classical music.

Raj: King, kingdom.

Ramakrishna: Nineteenth century Bengali saint. *The gospel of Ramakrishna.*

Ramanandrin: Order of wandering troubadours; Kabir's spiritual descendants.

Ram Naam Satthya Hai: The name of Ram is truth. Only the name of Ram is true. The Name of Ram is the only truth. Ram is an *avatar*, a "descent" of Vishnu. Words shouted while carrying a corpse to the cremation ground.

Rickshaw: Tricycle or scooter cab.

Rickshaw walla: The driver.

Rig Veda: "Praise verses" and "knowledge"; an ancient collection of Hindu Sanskrit speculative hymns. The Rig Veda is one among the four canonical sacred texts (*sruti*) of Hinduism known as the Vedas (1000 BC).

Rishi: *Seer*; poets and sages of Vedic times, authors of the Rig Veda, and in a larger sense all the sages of ancient times. The first men who started inquiring about their own nature, the ancestors of the Greek philosophers.

Rudraksha: Stone of the Eleocarpus ganitras' fruit. It looks like a human skull. One to three centimetres in diameter, they are used to make *malas*, rosaries.

Rupee: Indian currency. One Euro is worth sixty five Indian rupees. One US dollars, 47 rupees; one Pound, 80 rupees. *(At the time of publication)*

S

Sadhak: A person who has a strong desire to achieve realization or liberation (*moksha*). Someone who follows a particular practice (*sadhana*), or a way of life designed to realize the goal, reach one's ultimate ideal, whether it is merging with Brahman or the *realization* of one's personal deity. The word is related to the Sanskrit *sadhu*, which is derived from the root verb *sadh*, to accomplish. Often applied as a generic term for any religious practitioner.

Sadhana: From root *sadh*, success, to accomplish. The path to success (which leads consciousness or soul to liberation). Spiritual practice; discipline a disciple (*sadhak*) follows to reach the aim: the absorption of the essence of man into the essence of reality.

Sadhu: From *sadh,* to lead to the goal. One who has reached the goal. Good person or saint. Mendicant monks, wandering renunciants. Synonym of Baba.

Sadhvi: Female sadhu.

Sakhara: "With form"; God in a form, an image or a figure.

Samadhi: *Gathering*; state of perfect concentration. Consciousness aware of itself without object. Fusion, non-differentiation. State in which subject and object are dissolved. Also, a monument sheltering the body or the ashes of a great yogi.

Samsara: Life, the cycle of lives, the cycles of life. The desire to be. The realm of becoming.

Samnyasin: Renunciant, hermit or wandering ascetic. Also fourth age of life, when a person withdraws from worldly concerns to devote himself to the realization of Brahman.

Sanatana Dharma: The eternal laws which govern things and their interactions, keeping them harmonious. It would be translated as *religion*. The Law of balance; a code which, if complied with, makes one's actions free of consequences.

Sankaracharya: (Adi Shankaracharya, 788 – to 820, date disputed) One of the greatest philosophers and spiritual masters of Hinduism, reformer, and commentator of the Vedas and Upanishads. Founder of four *maths*, monasteries established in the four regions of India.

Sarvam khalvidam Brahman: All this is Brahman.

Sat: Being, existence and reality in a single word.

SatCitAnanda: The three attributes of Brahman when one uses qualities to describe it. Sat: being, existence and reality; Cit: intelligence–consciousness